W9-CBV-153

BIGGEST BOOK OF HISTORY

Text by
Vanessa Giancamilli Birch
& Tony Tallarico

Illustrated by Tony and Tony Tallarico

Kidsbooks®

Visit us at **www.kidsbooks.com**

GET READY TO LEARN EVERYTHING YOU'VE EVER WANTED TO KNOW ABOUT WORLD HISTORY!

Find out

- How long dinosaurs roamed the earth
- What people ate during the Middle Ages
- How colonists made money
- All about Sir Isaac Newton
- How cellophane was invented
- What the Y2K bug was

And much, much more!

Includes Search & Find® puzzles, mazes, word searches, and other fun activities!

Impress family and friends with your knowledge of history!

Kids**books**®

How Old is Earth?

I'M FEELING OLD!

Earth was formed between 4.5 and 4.6 billion years ago, when the solar system took shape around the sun. It was formed of rubble from exploding stars called supernovas.

HOW LONG DID DINOSAURS ROAM THE EARTH?

Dinosaurs roamed the earth for about 180 million years, from the Triassic period (245 million years ago) through the Jurassic period to the Cretaceous period (66 million years ago). Scientists think the event leading to their extinction might have been a massive asteroid impact or a huge surge of volcanic activity—something that might have blocked out sunlight, changing the earth's ecology and eventually causing the dinosaurs to die off.

What were the earliest living organisms?

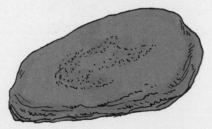

The earliest living organisms were microscopic bacteria, which appear in fossils from as long ago as 3.4 billion years.

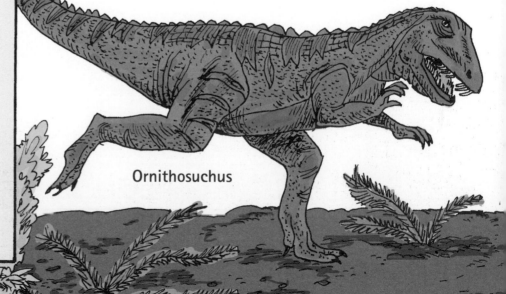

Ornithosuchus

TEST YOUR KNOWLEDGE!

What do you know about dinosaurs and prehistoric times?
Test your knowledge with this True or False quiz and
then read more about it in the following pages.

1. Earth was formed two million years ago. TRUE or FALSE?

2. Insects were the first living organisms. TRUE or FALSE?

3. The Mesozoic era was divided into three periods: the Triassic, the Jurassic, and the Cretaceous. TRUE or FALSE?

4. It is believed that most dinosaurs roamed the earth during the Cretaceous period. TRUE or FALSE?

5. Dinosaurs and people lived on Earth together at the same time. TRUE or FALSE?

6. All dinosaurs were carnivores. TRUE or FALSE?

7. The Iguanodon was among the first dinosaurs identified by scientists. TRUE or FALSE?

8. A Stegosaurus would use its spiked tail as a weapon. TRUE or FALSE?

9. The Tyrannosaurus rex was an herbivore, meaning it did not eat meat. TRUE or FALSE?

10. The smallest dinosaurs were only as big as today's birds. TRUE or FALSE?

11. The largest dinosaur known stood as tall as a four-story building! TRUE or FALSE?

12. The largest dinosaur was also an herbivore! TRUE or FALSE?

Answers on page 302

What was Compsognathus?

Compsognathus, which until recently was the
smallest dinosaur known, was about the size of
a chicken. It walked on two long, thin legs and
had three-toed feet, a small, pointed head, and
a flexible neck.

WHAT WAS THE MESOZOIC ERA?

The Mesozoic era was the time from 252.2 million to 66 million years ago. Earth was very
different during the Mesozoic era. Many old life forms had just gone extinct, allowing a burst
of new life forms—including dinosaurs, mammals, birds, and flowering plants—to flourish
during the Mesozoic era.

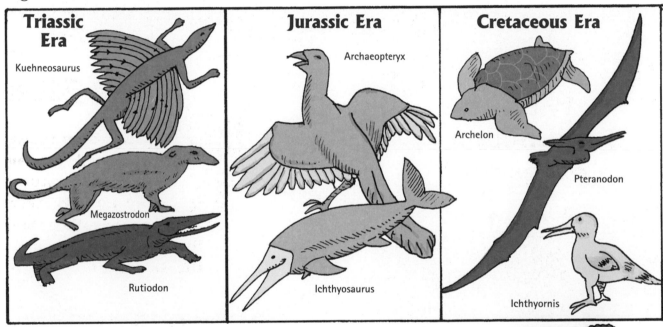

Triassic Era

Kuehneosaurus

Megazostrodon

Rutiodon

Jurassic Era

Archaeopteryx

Ichthyosaurus

Cretaceous Era

Archelon

Pteranodon

Ichthyornis

WHEN DID MOST OF THE DINOSAURS EXIST?

Many dinosaurs roamed the earth during the
Cretaceous period. In fact, 40 percent of the
dinosaur fossils that have been found date
from the period's last 15 million years.
Unfortunately, the Cretaceous period
ended with the extinction of the
dinosaurs and many
other prehistoric
animals.

Triceratops

Tyrannosaurus

Diplodocus

Which dinosaur is known as the giant dinosaur?

Brachiosaurus, the giant dinosaur, is the tallest and heaviest plant-eating animal for which complete skeletons have been found. It had a long neck that helped it reach high into tall trees, and it swallowed stones to help aid in digestion. It lived 150 to 130 million years ago and weighed up to eighty tons!

It lived 150 million years ago and weighed **80 TONS!**

Was a Pteranodon a dinosaur?

No! Even though Pteranodons may look like dinosaurs, they actually were flying reptiles that lived during the age of the dinosaurs.

HAVE YOU SEEN MY PALS ALLEY OOP...

...OR FRED FLINTSTONE?

What was the Paleolithic Age?

The Paleolithic, or Old Stone Age, was the earliest and longest period of the Stone Age, which was a time of human history marked by the use of stone tools. It began approximately 2.5 million years ago and lasted until about 10,000 years ago. Our first human ancestors made their appearance on Earth at the beginning of the Old Stone Age.

When did the first humans evolve?

The first ancestors of human beings may have lived around 4.4 million years ago in caves along the coast of Africa. Humanlike creatures that walked upright are known as hominins.

Where did the earliest hominins live?

Scientists think early hominins lived in caves, though some may have lived in huts constructed from the bones of the mammoth, an early ancestor of the elephant. The huts were covered with hides and carpeted with mammoth fur. Hominins probably gathered and ate seeds, fruits, vegetables, nuts, and other edible parts of plants. Meat increased in the diet as our ancestors developed hunting and trapping techniques.

Who were Neanderthals?

Neanderthals were relatives of humans who lived in Europe and Asia from perhaps about 100,000 to 30,000 years ago (they are named for the Neander Valley of Germany, where the first fossils were found). They had large noses, stocky builds, heavy jaws, and thick eyebrow ridges. They made tools, and some wore heavy clothing made of animal skins. Most Neanderthals lived in groups, possibly of up to fifty people, in open-air camps, often along the shores of lakes and rivers.

WHAT WAS THE GREAT ICE AGE?

While several different ice ages have occurred since the earth formed, the most recent one is called the Great Ice Age. It peaked about 20,000 years ago, when a third of the earth was covered in ice.

What animals existed during the Great Ice Age?

Some of the animals that existed during the height of the Great Ice Age were the woolly mammoth, the woolly rhinoceros, cave bears, horses, wolves, bison, and reindeer. While some of these animals are now extinct, scientists have found pictures people painted of them on the walls of their caves. Scientists also have found the skeletons of these animals.

How did people survive during the Great Ice Age?

It is thought that the men hunted while the women and children made food, clothing, and shelters. Every part of the animal that was hunted was used in some way—the meat was used for food, the skins were cut and sewn into clothing, the bones were used for weapons and tools, and even the stomach was used to carry water!

WELCOME HOME!

I STILL WANT A HOT DOG!

IT'S BRUTAL OUTSIDE

HOW IS THE COLOSSEUM STILL STANDING?

The ancient Romans began making concrete more than 2,000 years ago, and used it to build structures like the Pantheon and the Colosseum. Even though this material was weaker than today's concrete, it proved to be very durable against the elements, perhaps due to one of its key ingredients—volcanic ash. The volcanic ash was mixed with a paste made of limestone, chunks of brick, and volcanic rock, and then packed into place to form structures like columns and walls.

HERE'S SOME FRESH ASH

A·A·C·H·O·O!

Why was purple considered the color of royalty in ancient Rome?

Purple was the color of royalty in ancient Rome mainly because it was very expensive to produce. "Tyrian purple," as it was called, was harvested from the glands of certain species of marine snails, which were boiled for days in large lead tubs. This produced more than a bright purple dye: heating the snails also caused a horrible odor.

When were the first Olympic Games held?

Started in southwestern Greece more than 2,700 years ago, the Olympic Games began as part of a religious festival. The games honored Zeus, the king of the Greek gods. They were held every four years in Olympia, and attracted competitors and spectators from throughout Greece. These ancient contests were thought to have inspired the modern Olympics.

WE WON!

Who ruled Ancient Greece?

Ancient Greece was not one country—it was made up of many small city-states, each with its own government. However, one man—Alexander the Great—ruled all of ancient Greece. In the fourth century B.C. he led an army that conquered a territory spanning from Greece to present-day Afghanistan and India.

What are The *Iliad* and The *Odyssey*?

The *Iliad* and *The Odyssey* are long poems thought to have been written in the 700s B.C. by a Greek storyteller named Homer. *The Iliad* describes the Trojan War, while **The Odyssey** tells the story of Odysseus, a Greek soldier, after the war.

WHAT WAS THE TROJAN WAR?

IT WAS A FAMOUS WAR FOUGHT ABOUT 3,000 YEARS AGO BETWEEN THE GREEKS AND THE PEOPLE OF THE CITY OF TROY. PARIS, PRINCE OF TROY, RAN AWAY WITH HELEN, THE WIFE OF KING MENELAUS OF SPARTA, WHICH WAS GREEK. THE GREEKS SENT AN ARMY TO GET HER BACK, STARTING THE TROJAN WAR, WHICH LASTED TEN YEARS. EVENTUALLY THE GREEKS WON BY USING A WOODEN HORSE TO TRICK THE TROJAN ARMY.

WE GOT HER NOW!

WHAT DID THE GREEKS DO WITH THE TROJAN HORSE?

They used it to capture the city of Troy. The Greeks left the giant wooden horse behind and appeared to sail away from Troy in their ships. The Trojans didn't realize Greek soldiers were hiding inside, and they dragged the horse into Troy. While the Trojans slept, the Greek soldiers hidden inside the horse emerged and opened the gates of the city, allowing the Greek army to enter and destroy Troy, ending the Trojan War.

What did houses look like in ancient Greece?

Houses in ancient Greece were small and had a garden or yard in the middle. Houses were constructed of bricks made of sun-dried mud, and the roof was made of clay tiles. Wooden shutters kept out the sun. These mud structures lasted only a few years, so there are few ruins of ancient Greek homes—archaeologists know about these buildings mainly from drawings and writings.

What were "wall diggers" in ancient Greece?

Ancient Greeks called house thieves wall diggers. The homes of ancient Greece were constructed of bricks made of mud, which were easy to dig into.

What was the Praetorian Guard?

Each Roman emperor was protected by a troop of special soldiers called the Praetorian Guard. Some of the more unpopular emperors, however, had to watch their guards closely—a few emperors were so disliked that their Praetorian Guards killed them.

What was the most valuable tree in ancient Greece?

The olive tree was highly prized. Greeks ate the olives produced by the trees, but they also crushed them to make olive oil. They used the oil for many purposes, such as cooking, fuel for oil lamps, and in cosmetics.

How did Rome get its name?

The legend of how Rome began is one of the most famous in history. Romulus and Remus were twin sons of Mars, the Roman god of war. Their uncle took them from their mother when they were babies and threw them into the River Tiber. The babies floated to land, where a wolf found and cared for them. When the twins were grown, Mars told them to build a city where they had been found. The twins argued over the site, and when Remus made fun of the wall Romulus began building around the city, Romulus killed his brother. Romulus then named the city of Rome after himself.

What did gladiators do?

Gladiators were fighters of the ancient Roman Empire. They usually fought each other in pairs, but they also fought animals, such as lions and bears. Different types of gladiators used different weapons, such as spears or swords. When a gladiator lost a fight but was still alive, the members of the audience would get to decide whether he would live. They would indicate their preference with hand signals—if they wanted the gladiator to live, they would close their thumbs against their fingers. If they wanted him killed, they would put out their thumbs.

What was a chariot race?

Chariots were small, two-wheeled carts pulled by two, four, or six fast horses. In ancient Rome, chariots competed in seven-lap races in a large stadium called the Circus Maximus. While exciting, chariot races were very dangerous.

STOP

?

What are aqueducts?

Aqueducts were used in ancient Rome to transport water. Some of the Roman aqueducts were built on arches, similar to a bridge, and had a stone channel on the top along which the water flowed. They were used to supply cities with water from springs, lakes, and rivers. Aqueducts were sloped because water will only flow downhill.

ONE WAY

What was the first building to have a dome?

The Pantheon in Rome, built around 118 to 128 A.D., was the first big building to be topped with a dome, a round-topped roof. The dome was developed from the arch, and while the Romans didn't invent the arch, they were the first people to use arches in the construction of big buildings and aqueducts. Unlike the Greek temples, the Roman buildings topped with arches didn't need pillars or columns to hold their roofs up.

Did the Romans use machines to build buildings?

No, the Romans used people to build buildings! They used slaves to do the heavy lifting in building, road, and bridge construction. The Romans used cranes to lift heavy stones, but these cranes didn't have an engine; slaves or animals powered them.

19

How was ancient Rome ruled?

Early Rome was a republic, ruled by two elected officials called consuls, and a senate. Senators, who were wealthy men, ran the government. Poor men, called plebeians, had very little power, although a plebeian could be a Roman citizen. Women and slaves, however, could not be citizens, so they could not vote in elections.

I OBJECT!

What were catapults?

Catapults were machines used for war that fired rocks and other objects, such as balls of burning tar. Catapults worked by a system of twisted ropes and springs. Giant catapults handled by soldiers were called onagers. The Romans also used big wind-up crossbows called ballistas.

CRASH!

I WANT TO TAKE THAT RIDE!

Who was Julius Caesar?

Julius Caesar was Rome's best and most famous general. He lived in the first century B.C. He invaded Britain twice and came to be dictator of Rome, but he was murdered in 44 B.C. By that time, Rome had become an empire that stretched far beyond the city—the Romans eventually ruled lands from Britain and France to North Africa.

HAIL, CAESAR!

WHO WERE ROMAN EMPERORS?

Roman emperors were men who ruled over the Roman Empire. The first Roman emperor was named Octavian. After years of fighting among rival leaders, he became emperor in 27 B.C. and took a new name, Augustus. As emperor, Augustus worked to bring peace to the Roman Empire.

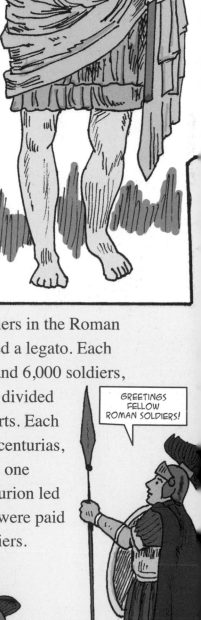

Why did Julius Caesar wear a wreath on his head?

The wreath, made of laurel leaves, was a symbol of honor.

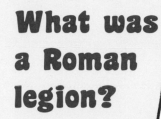

OOPS!

WHO SERVED IN THE ROMAN ARMY?

Only men could be in the Roman army. The soldiers belonged to various formations, some of which were composed only of Roman citizens, while others included men from places outside of Italy, including Africa, France, Germany, and Spain. (Later, all men born within the boundaries of the empire were considered citizens.) Soldiers of a certain type had to stay in the army for at least 25 years before they could retire and be made Roman citizens. Soldiers could retire with a pension—a gift of land to farm. Older soldiers often retired to a colonia, or a military town, where they helped the empire maintain its defenses.

WE'VE NOTHING TO DO.

What was a Roman legion?

A legion was a unit of soldiers in the Roman army led by an officer called a legato. Each legion had between 4,000 and 6,000 soldiers, called legionaries, and was divided into ten groups called cohorts. Each cohort was made up of six centurias, which were troops of about one hundred legionaries; a centurion led each centuria. Legionaries were paid the most of all Roman soldiers.

GREETINGS FELLOW ROMAN SOLDIERS!

What did Roman soldiers wear?

A Roman soldier, if he could afford it, wore a tunic of body armor made from strips of iron, steel, and leather; sandals with iron studs on the leather soles; and a metal helmet. He used a curved shield made of metal or wood and leather to protect his body. Roman soldiers carried various kinds of weapons, including swords for stabbing and long spears, or javelins, for throwing.

What did Romans like to eat?

Poor Romans ate bread, vegetable soup, and porridge. Meat was a luxury for most, unless they lived in the countryside and could hunt or fish. The wealthiest Romans sometimes ate exotic foods, such as stork, roast parrot, and flamingo tongues. Romans ate lettuce at the end of the evening meal because they believed it helped them sleep. They often ate their food while lying down on a couch, and they ate with their hands or sometimes used a spoon, but they didn't use forks.

Yum!

WHAT KIND OF CLOTHING DID ROMANS WEAR?

Most Romans wore tunics made of two pieces of linen or woolen fabric sewn together at the sides and shoulders, with openings for the arms and head. Wealthy Roman men wore togas—a kind of woolen shawl wrapped around them—to show their status.

22

What were the Twelve Tables?

The first Roman set of laws was written on twelve bronze tablets, known as the Twelve Tables, and displayed to the Roman public. These laws, written in 450 B.C., included issues of legal procedure, civil rights, and property rights, and they provided the basis for all future Roman civil law.

What was a SCRIBE in ANCIENT EGYPT?

Scribes were ancient Egyptians who were trained to write. Scribes started training to write in hieroglyphics at about five years old. Because writing in hieroglyphics was so complicated, it often took years of education and practice to become a scribe. Scribes didn't have to pay taxes or enter the army and were very respected members of ancient Egyptian society. Mainly boys of the middle and upper classes got the opportunity to train as scribes; most of the rest of the population of ancient Egypt could neither read nor write.

WHAT WERE HIEROGLYPHICS?

Hieroglyphics were picture words the ancient Egyptians used to write. Hieroglyphics were used as early as 3000 B.C. in a very complicated writing form made up of hundreds of symbols. Some of the symbols represented sounds and some represented entire words. When a single picture symbol stood for a whole word it was called an ideogram; when it stood for a sound it was called a phonogram. Hieroglyphics were usually read left to right, but could be written in any direction. The reader would figure out which way to read them by the direction of the symbols. The writing usually left out vowels, and there was no punctuation. In addition to communication, one of the purposes of writing in hieroglyphics was to produce writing that would look like beautiful artwork.

What was papyrus?

While ancient Egyptians often wrote on clay tablets or walls, they also wrote on a type of paper called papyrus. This paper was made from the tall, reedlike papyrus plant. The inner stem of the plant was used to make the paper. Ancient Egyptians would layer these stems in strips in two layers—one horizontal and the other vertical. They then would dampen the sheet, cover it in a linen cloth, and apply weight with stones, causing the strips to bind together and form a single flat sheet.

WHAT ARE MUMMIES?

I APPEARED IN MOVIES, TOO!

Mummies are the result of an elaborate embalming ritual ancient Egyptians performed when someone died. Egyptians preserved the body because they believed the soul of a dead person reunited with the body in the afterlife. The afterlife was very important to the ancient Egyptians. A process called embalming, which took more than 70 days to complete, would be done to prepare for the afterlife and preserve the body for as long as possible. Egyptians then covered the entire body in linen wrapping, covered it in a sheet called a shroud, and placed the body in a stone coffin called a sarcophagus or a coffin made of wood, papyrus, or even precious metal.

What did ancient Egyptians wear?

Ancient Egyptians paid a lot of attention to how they looked, and both men and women wore jewelry. The wealthy wore jewelry of gold, silver, beads, and gemstones, while poorer Egyptians wore copper or pottery jewelry. Both men and women also wore eye paint and other makeup. Because of the heat in ancient Egypt, most people wore lightweight clothing made of white linen. Men wore skirts similar to kilts, women wore dresses, and slaves and servants wore very little at all.

Who were the pharaohs?

Pharaohs ruled ancient Egypt. However, a pharaoh didn't govern by himself—he had a team of leaders below him who ran different aspects of the government. Not only was the pharaoh the leader of the government, he was the religious ruler of ancient Egypt as well. The ancient Egyptians considered the pharaoh to be a high priest and the main intermediary to the gods.

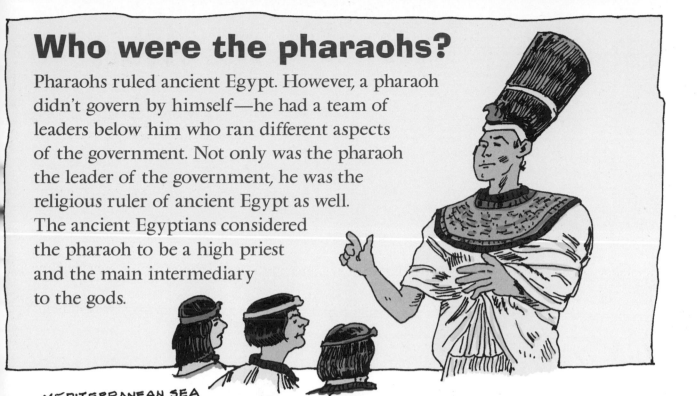

What is the Nile River?

The Nile River is the longest river in the world. It is more than 4,100 miles long and is located in northeastern Africa, where it flows through many countries, including Egypt, Sudan, Ethiopia, Uganda, and Burundi. The Nile River was important to the life and society of ancient Egypt—it provided the ancient Egyptians with food and transportation, and also provided them with very fertile land. Even though most of Egypt is desert, the land along the Nile River is good for growing crops. The Nile also divided ancient Egypt into two regions—Upper Egypt, where the river flowed through highlands, and Lower Egypt, where the river met the Mediterranean Sea at the Nile Delta.

What were some of the most important crops in ancient Egypt?

Important crops to ancient Egyptians included wheat, flax, and papyrus. Wheat was the main food of the Egyptians; not only did they use it to make bread, they sold a lot of their wheat to other countries. Flax was used to make linen cloth, and papyrus was used to make paper, baskets, rope, and sandals.

WHY DID THE ANCIENT EGYPTIANS BUILD PYRAMIDS?

Pyramids were built as burial places and monuments to the pharaohs. The Egyptians believed the pharaoh needed certain things for the afterlife, so the pharaoh would be buried inside the pyramid with those items.

FOR RENT

IS ANYONE THIRSTY?

I DON'T KNOW WHICH PYRAMID TO SELECT?

?

WHERE SHOULD I PLACE THIS ONE?

I CAN'T WAIT TO PUT THIS DOWN.

What did the pyramids look like?

WHERE'S MY MUMMY?

I'M THE GREAT PYRAMID OF GIZA.

Egypt's earliest pyramids were step pyramids. These pyramids had large ledges that looked like giant steps and were believed to serve as stairways for the pharaoh to climb to the sun god. Pyramids built later have flat, sloping sides. These pyramids are said to represent a mound that emerged from floodwaters at the beginning of time, where the sun god had risen. The largest pyramid is the pyramid of the pharaoh Khufu, called the Great Pyramid of Giza, which stands more than 450 feet tall. It is estimated that the Great Pyramid was built from 2.3 million blocks of limestone rock and weighs 5.75 million tons.

What is a Sphinx?

A sphinx is a mythological creature with the body of a lion and the head of a human. Ancient Egyptians often depicted a sphinx with the head of a pharaoh or a god. The Egyptians built sphinx statues to guard tombs and temples.

THIS IS PRETTY HEAVY.

How were the pyramids built?

It is not really known exactly how the pyramids were built, but it is believed that the pyramids were built one block at a time. Thousands of slaves cut large blocks of limestone and moved them up the pyramid on ramps, rollers, and sleds. It is estimated it took at least 20,000 workers more than 23 years to build the Great Pyramid of Giza. Pharaohs typically started the construction of their pyramids as soon as they became ruler.

FASTER! FASTER!

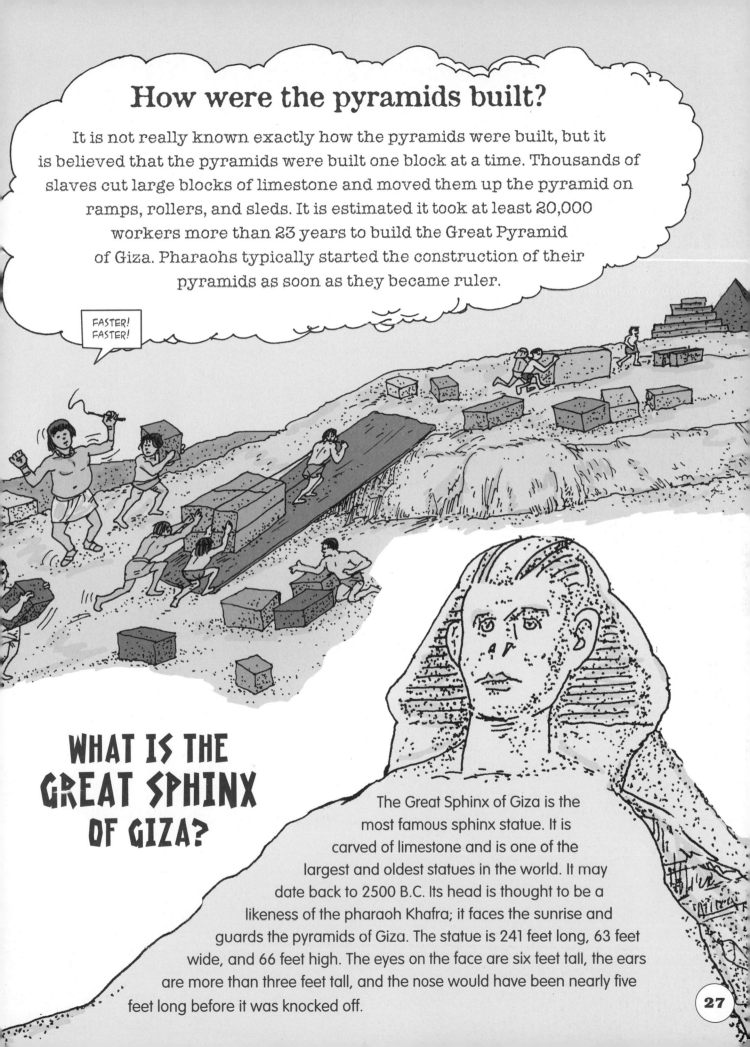

WHAT IS THE GREAT SPHINX OF GIZA?

The Great Sphinx of Giza is the most famous sphinx statue. It is carved of limestone and is one of the largest and oldest statues in the world. It may date back to 2500 B.C. Its head is thought to be a likeness of the pharaoh Khafra; it faces the sunrise and guards the pyramids of Giza. The statue is 241 feet long, 63 feet wide, and 66 feet high. The eyes on the face are six feet tall, the ears are more than three feet tall, and the nose would have been nearly five feet long before it was knocked off.

THE PYRAMIDS AND THE GREAT SPHINX

LEARN ABOUT THE PYRAMIDS AND THE GREAT SPHINX AS YOU LOOK FOR THESE FUN ITEMS:

- ❏ Arrow
- ❏ Bone
- ❏ Camels (2)
- ❏ Cup
- ❏ Elephant
- ❏ Fire hydrant
- ❏ Fish
- ❏ Flying carpet
- ❏ Ghost
- ❏ Golfer
- ❏ Hammer
- ❏ Heart
- ❏ Helmet
- ❏ Horseshoe
- ❏ Jack-o'-lantern
- ❏ Key
- ❏ Mouse
- ❏ Mummy
- ❏ Photographers (3)
- ❏ Sand castle
- ❏ Shovels (2)
- ❏ Sled
- ❏ Snake
- ❏ Star
- ❏ Telescope
- ❏ Tent
- ❏ Trumpet
- ❏ Umbrella

WHAT IS THE VALLEY OF THE KINGS?

Around 1500 B.C., the pharaohs of Egypt no longer built great pyramids and instead were buried in tombs in the Valley of the Kings. There are more than 60 tombs in the Valley of the Kings, some of which are small and some of which are large enough to hold dozens of underground chambers.

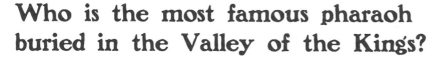

Who is the most famous pharaoh buried in the Valley of the Kings?

The most famous tomb in the Valley of the Kings is the tomb of the pharaoh Tutankhamen, sometimes called King Tut. It was discovered in 1922 by Howard Carter, an English archaeologist, and unlike nearly all the other tombs in the Valley of the Kings, had been largely untouched by thieves. When found by Carter, the tomb was full of artifacts and treasures, including King Tut's mummy.

What does the word "pharaoh" mean?

Pharaoh means "great house" and can describe a palace or a kingdom, as well as an Egyptian ruler. Pharaohs wore a crown that had an image of the cobra goddess. Only pharaohs could wear the cobra goddess; she would protect them by spitting flames at their enemies.

HOW WAS THE ANCIENT EGYPTIAN ARMY ORGANIZED?

The pharaoh served as the head of the Egyptian army and two generals led the army: one led Upper Egypt and the other led Lower Egypt. Each army had an infantry, chariotry, and navy.

Infantry   Chariotry   Navy

What was the Silk Road?

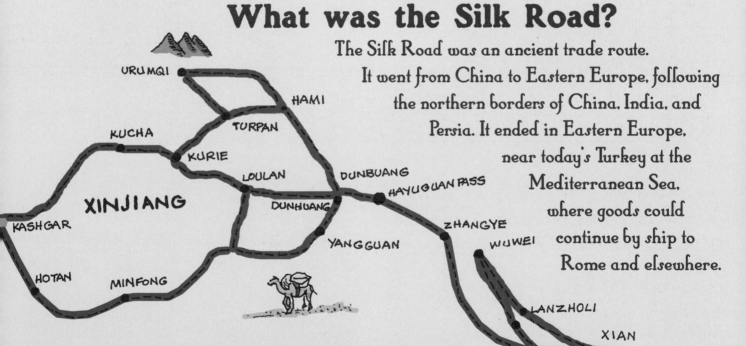

The Silk Road was an ancient trade route. It went from China to Eastern Europe, following the northern borders of China, India, and Persia. It ended in Eastern Europe, near today's Turkey at the Mediterranean Sea, where goods could continue by ship to Rome and elsewhere.

URUMQI

HAMI

KUCHA

TURPAN

KURIE

LOULAN

DUNBUANG

HAYUGUAN PASS

XINJIANG

DUNHUANG

KASHGAR

ZHANGYE

YANGGUAN

WUWEI

HOTAN

MINFONG

LANZHOLI

XIAN

Why was it called the Silk Road?

This important trade route was called the Silk Road because one of the main products traded was silk cloth from China, which was valued for its exquisite softness. In addition to silk, the Chinese also sold other luxury goods, such as tea, salt, sugar, spices, and porcelain.

Silk   Tea   Salt   Sugar   Porcelain

Why did Chinese girls want small feet?

Chinese women had tiny feet because in ancient China small feet were considered attractive. Young girls had their feet painfully bound in cloth to prevent their feet from growing. This caused their feet to become deformed and often made it difficult for the girls to walk.

WHAT COLORS WERE MOST IMPORTANT IN ANCIENT CHINA?

There are five primary Chinese colors—red, black, green, white, and yellow. Colors (and numbers) had important meanings in ancient China; some colors were considered lucky, and some were unlucky and were avoided. For example, red symbolized good luck, happiness, and success, and even today is often used at celebrations such as weddings and birthdays.

WHAT COLOR WAS RESERVED FOR CHINESE EMPERORS?

Yellow.
Yellow is the color of earth, the change of the seasons, and the world's center, and was reserved for the emperor and his family.

When was silk invented?

There is a legend about the invention of silk cloth. Leizu, the wife of the Yellow Emperor, discovered silk around the year 2696 B.C. She had the idea for silk cloth while she was drinking tea in her garden. A silkworm moth cocoon fell into her tea, and she noticed, as it unraveled, that the cocoon was made from a long fiber that was soft but also very strong. Leizu discovered how to combine the silk fibers into thread, and she invented the silk loom that fused the threads into cloth. Legend states that she taught the rest of China how to make silk cloth.

How did the Ancient Chinese make silk?

Moth

Eggs

Baby worms

Cocoon

The ancient Chinese bred special moths to produce high-quality silk. Each silk moth laid 300 to 500 eggs before dying. Caterpillars hatched from the eggs and ate mulberry leaves for one month until they became fat. Each silkworm then generated a long fiber and spun it into a cocoon. The cocoons were then steamed, rinsed in hot water, and unwound. The fibers were combined to make silk thread, which was woven into cloth. The cloth would then be pounded to make it soft.

What happened to anyone caught taking silkworms outside of China?

Silk cloth was considered extremely valuable in ancient China and was an important status symbol. Because of this, only members of the royal family, people of the noble class, and some scholars were allowed to wear silk. Silk became a prized export for the Chinese. Other kingdoms would pay high prices for silk, so the emperors of China wanted to keep the process of making silk a secret. Anyone caught sharing the secret of silk-making or taking silkworms out of China was put to death.

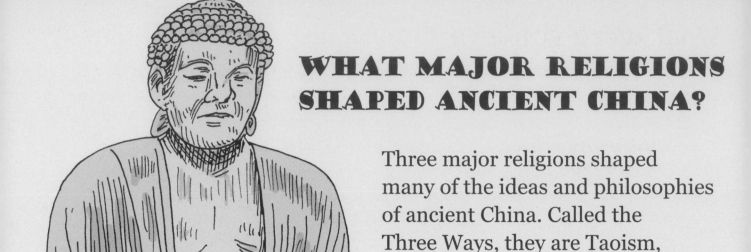

WHAT MAJOR RELIGIONS SHAPED ANCIENT CHINA?

Three major religions shaped many of the ideas and philosophies of ancient China. Called the Three Ways, they are Taoism, Confucianism, and Buddhism.

Who was Confucius?

Confucius was a philosopher of ancient China who believed people should be respectful, polite, and fair. He valued honor and morality and also felt that people should honor their families.

WHAT IS YIN AND YANG?

Yin and yang come from an ancient Chinese belief that everything in nature has two complementary forces—yin and yang—which are opposites, but always equal and balanced. One represents dark and one light; one the earth and one the heavens; one female and one male.

What were some of Confucius' famous sayings?

There are books of Confucius's teachings, but he didn't write them; his followers did. Confucius is famous for many of these teachings, including:

- Everything has its beauty but not everyone sees it.

- Forget injuries, never forget kindnesses.

- When anger rises, think of the consequences.

Who was Buddha?

Buddha was born in Nepal, between China and India, around 563 B.C. and founded the Buddhist religion. Buddhists believe beings go through a process of "rebirths" and in Karma, which is based on the concept that all actions have consequences.

What is the Chinese calendar?

Versions of the Chinese calendar, which is used to mark traditional Chinese holidays, have been around for thousands of years. Around 100 B.C., Emperor Wu of the Han dynasty created a calendar that was the basis for the calendar used today. The Chinese calendar arranges the years on a 12-year cycle. Each year is named for an animal, and every twelve years the cycle repeats. Some Chinese believe your personality reflects aspects of the animal that represents the year you were born.

HAPPY BIRTHDAY!

I WAS BORN IN THE YEAR OF THE DRAGON!

I WAS BORN IN THE YEAR OF THE RABBIT!

WHICH ANIMALS ARE USED IN THE CHINESE CALENDAR?

The 12 animals in the Chinese calendar are the rat, ox, tiger, rabbit, dragon, snake, horse, sheep, monkey, rooster, dog, and pig. According to ancient Chinese legend, the order of the animals was determined by a race across a river—how the animals finished determined their position in the cycle. The rat won because it rode on the back of the ox and jumped off at the last minute, winning the race.

What are the major Chinese holidays?

There are nine major Chinese holidays:
Chinese New Year
Spring Festival
Lantern Festival
Dragon Boat Festival
Night of Sevens
Mid-Autumn Festival
Double Ninth Festival
Qingming Festival
and the Winter Solstice Festival

WHY ISN'T THE CAT PART OF THE CHINESE CALENDAR?

According to ancient Chinese legend, a cat also tried to ride on the back of the ox, but the rat pushed him off and he fell into the water. This caused the cat to lose the race and fail to get a place on the Chinese calendar.

Did the ancient Chinese invent ice cream?

Yes!

The first version, made in 200 B.C., was a mixture of milk and rice put in the snow to freeze. The ancient Chinese also are credited with inventing paper, the compass, and the clock.

Did the Ancient Chinese play games?

The ancient Chinese played a game called *t'su chu*, which many historians think might have been a type of soccer. It was played with a stuffed leather ball. The feet and body were used to move the ball…but not the hands, just like in the game we know as soccer. Early drawings of *t'su chu* show the teams trying to kick the ball through a tiny hole in a net made of silk.

What is calligraphy?

Calligraphy is artistic handwriting. Since ancient times the Chinese have considered writing an important form of art. There are more than 40,000 symbols in traditional calligraphy, and each needed to be drawn precisely. In fact, each stroke in a character had to be drawn in a specific order. Calligraphers would practice for years to learn to write perfectly!

What were "paper birds"?

The ancient Chinese invented kites, or paper birds. They were used to send messages in times of war, and could be used to predict the success of a voyage by sea. It was considered bad luck to let a kite go.

What type of clothing did the ancient Chinese wear?

Poor people, or peasants, wore loose-fitting clothing made of hemp. Hemp was a rough material made from plant fiber, but it was good for working in the fields. Wealthier people wore long silk robes that were dyed specific colors or had intricate designs.

Where was ancient Phoenicia located?

It is believed that around 3000 B.C., people known as the Phoenicians settled an area that is now the coastline of Lebanon. It is thought they originally came from the Persian Gulf area. Their culture was one of the earliest to use the sea for transportation and trade. In fact, the name they called themselves—*Kena'ani* (or *Canaanites*)—means "merchants" in Hebrew.

What did the ancient Phoenicians trade?

They would trade cedar wood, cloth died royal purple, glass, colorful pottery, and other precious items for silver, iron, tin, lead, horses, ebony and ivory, linen, coral, honey, spices, oil, and precious stones. The ancient Phoenicians were known as the "merchants of all things."

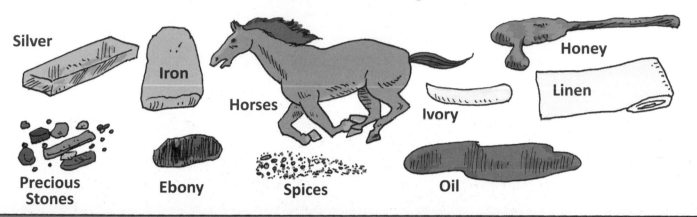

Silver

Iron

Horses

Ivory

Honey

Linen

Precious Stones

Ebony

Spices

Oil

Why was Mesopotamia called the "Cradle of Civilization"?

Humans first formed civilizations, gathered in large cities, learned to write, and created governments in ancient Mesopotamia, an area mostly within Iraq today. Because of this, Mesopotamia is often called the Cradle of Civilization.

What were some of the great cities of the Mesopotamian Empire?

There were quite a few great cities of the Mesopotamian empire—Uruk, which was one of the first major cities in the history of the world; Akkad, which was the center of the world's first empire; Ashur; Babylon, which had a population of more than 200,000 people; Calah (now Nimrud); Nineveh; and Persepolis, which was the capital of the Persian Empire.

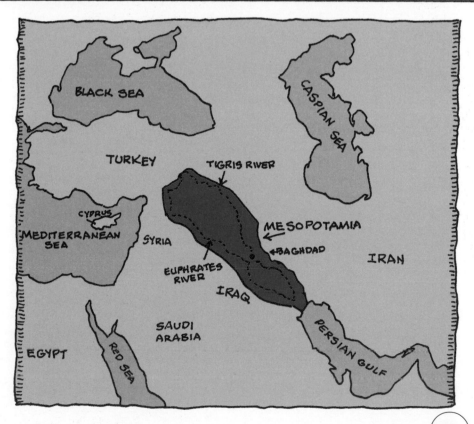

What was a ziggurat?

At the center of each major city in Mesopotamia was a ziggurat—a large structure built to honor the main god of the city. While the Sumerians started the tradition of building ziggurats, other civilizations of Mesopotamia built them as well. Ziggurats looked like step pyramids, the early Egyptian pyramids. They had from two to seven levels, or steps, and they were built to be tall, so they could reach toward the heavens. Some ziggurats were topped with a shrine or temple where priests would perform rituals.

Where was the largest ziggurat?

The largest ziggurat may have been one in the city of Babylon. It is believed to have been seven levels tall, reaching a height of nearly 300 feet, and to have covered a square area of 300 feet by 300 feet at the base.

WHAT WERE THE PERSIAN WARS?

The Persian Wars were a series of wars fought between the Persians and the Greeks from 492 to 449 B.C. The Persian Empire was the largest and most powerful empire in the world at the time of the Persian Wars, stretching from Egypt to India.

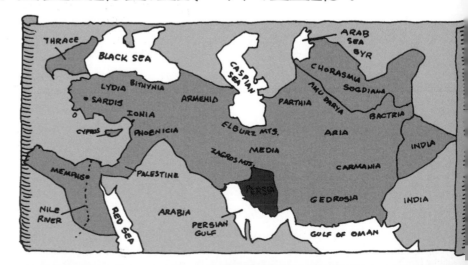

What was the Battle of Marathon?

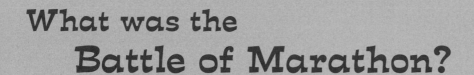

...PUFF!
...PUFF!
...PUFF!
...PUFF!

The Battle of Marathon was a battle fought during the Persian Wars. The Persian fleet landed at the Bay of Marathon, about 25 miles from the Greek city of Athens. While the Persians had more soldiers than the Greeks, they underestimated their enemy's fighting ability. The Persians killed 192 Greek soldiers but lost 6,400 of their own fighters. After the battle, legend tells us, a Greek soldier ran the 25 miles back to Athens to announce the Persian defeat. This tale inspired the running race we know as the marathon.

WHERE WERE THE HANGING GARDENS OF BABYLON?

Nobody really knows where the Hanging Gardens of Babylon were or whether they really existed, even though they are listed as one of the great wonders of the ancient world. They may have consisted of a series of large terraces covered in trees, plants, and flowers built by King Nebuchadnezzar II.

HELP!
I'M LOST!

Who was King Hammurabi?

King Hammurabi conquered all of Mesopotamia and established the first Babylonian Empire, becoming its first great king. He is best known for establishing a set of laws that is today called the Code of Hammurabi.

What was the Code of Hammurabi?

The Code of Hammurabi is one of the oldest recorded sets of laws in the world. It was written on clay tablets and etched into stone. One of the best surviving examples of the code is written on the "diorite stele," which is a large stone about seven feet tall and two feet wide. It contains around 4,000 lines of text describing 282 different laws. It is on display in the Louvre Museum in Paris, France.

OUCH!

Who was Gilgamesh?

Gilgamesh may have been a real king in Mesopotamia, but the legends about him make him sound like the first superhero! The ancient stories written about the warrior Gilgamesh, who was said to be part god and part human, tell of the adventures he had with his friend Enkidu.

What is Cuneiform?

Cuneiform is a system of writing first developed in ancient Mesopotamia. Scribes used a writing tool called a stylus to press wedge-shaped impressions into soft clay. "Cuneiform" comes from *cuneus*, the Latin word for "wedge."

Ancient History Word Search

Search for the ancient history words listed below. Circle horizontally, vertically, backwards, or diagonally as you find each word.

```
C S C U N E I F O R M N B W G Q Y G V J
O L V M B B M R K V N J T Y Y M D J T Y
M A E K R Y G P C S P Y X K G M Z A Q L
P H A M M D R L P O Y B J Y J L Q K D X
S T V B P D N H A G N B T S G U Y Z Z Z
O R O L K W I Z P D K F C A E Y Y N R D
G E N P P N Y T P L I I U D R D Z E Q L
N D R L X H J H J B H A U C N U M Y T Q
A N E C S Y A T P P G C T R I O G D D N
T A P O D U V R Y A T I R O H U Z G D N
H E U L N K M L A S R L L O R N S Z I P
U N S O H P G E B O D G M G M S Z P R Z
S D R S T O P Y R D H K I Q A U V D N B
J X G S R L Z Y L T J X X L T M L X N J
T M D E A J M V R Q L V V Y L M E U T D
W M I U E R V B M A N L D K L A X S S J
Y H N M L M L Y L Z M M T L Q T C X H J
W V D N Q J L W T Q N I L P Y L X D Y K
Y L Y N Z N T R G Z Q M D J L Q Z Y M Y
```

AQUEDUCTS	EARTH	PYRAMID
CALLIGRAPHY	GILGAMESH	REMUS
COLOSSEUM	GLADIATORS	ROMULUS
COMPSOGNATHUS	HIEROGLYPHICS	SPHINX
CONFUCIUS	HOMER	SUPERNOVAE
CUNEIFORM	NEANDERTHALS	ZIGGURAT
	PHARAOH	

43

Answers on page 304

WHEN WERE THE MIDDLE AGES?

The term "Middle Ages" refers to a period of history that occurred in Europe from 500 to 1500 A.D. This 1,000-year period started at the fall of the Roman Empire and ended at the rise of the Renaissance. The Middle Ages are also called the medieval times.

What were the Dark Ages?

The Dark Ages refers to the first half of the Middle Ages (500 to 1000 A.D.). When the Roman Empire fell, many of the traditions of culture and learning, in art, civics, invention, engineering, and history, came to a stop. The Romans had kept records during the empire, but after their fall, Europe lacked a central government to keep track of events and developments. Therefore, the period remains "dark" to historians.

WHAT WAS THE FEUDAL SYSTEM?

The feudal system was the basic structure for government and society in Europe in the Middle Ages. A local lord, who lived in a manor house, owned the land in a small community and everything in it. The lord ruled over the community's peasants and servants, and he kept them safe in exchange for their service. The lord provided the king with soldiers and taxes.

What was the manor?

The local lord lived in a large house or castle. A small village often formed around this large house or castle, which was called the manor and was under the lord's rule. People came to the manor for protection if they were attacked but also for celebrations. Included in this small village was the church, and surrounding it were farms that were worked by the peasants.

What was a baron?

Barons ruled large areas of land called fiefs, which were given to them by the king. Barons were loyal to the king and answered to him, but they were very powerful themselves. Barons divided their land up among lords, who ruled over manors. Barons paid the king by providing him with an army; if they couldn't raise an army, they would pay the king a tax called shield money.

King   Baron   Lord   Servants   Peasants

Who was the bishop?

The bishop was a leader of the medieval church, who ruled an area called a diocese. The Catholic Church was very powerful in medieval Europe, so the bishop was very powerful too. The church also collected a donation from every person in the diocese, and this made some of the bishops very wealthy as well.

Answers on page 305

Search & Find® for these fun items in the

Middle Ages

- Animal horns (2)
- Axe
- Baseball caps (2)
- Bird
- Candles (3)
- Clothespin
- Crutch
- Donkey
- Dragon
- Duck
- Fan
- Fish
- Flags (5)
- Hat feathers (4)
- Helmet with horns
- Lances (3)
- Mouse
- Propeller
- Queen
- Red bows (2)
- Sergeant's stripes
- Stars (2)
- Sunglasses (2)
- Tombstone
- UFO
- Weather vane

47

What was a guild?

In the Middle Ages, guilds were groups of craftsmen focused on a specific skill, such as the painters' guild or the bakers' guild. Members of a guild passed their skills down from generation to generation.

What were the different positions within a guild?

The craftsmen in guilds held three distinct positions: apprentice, journeyman, and master. Apprentices usually were boys in their teens, who trained with a master for about seven years. They would work for the master to learn his craft, and in exchange the master would provide food, a place to live, and clothing.

Once a young man finished his apprenticeship, he was known as a journeyman. He still worked for a master, but now he was paid for his work.

To become a master, the journeyman needed the guild's approval. He not only had to demonstrate his talent, he also had to make friends with the members of the guild so they would accept him as a master. Once he became a master, he could open his own shop and train apprentices.

OPEN FOR BUSINESS

Why were monks important during the Middle Ages?

The monks wrote books and recorded the events of the time, and if it weren't for these histories, we would know very little about what happened during the Middle Ages. Monks were among the few people in the Middle Ages who knew how to read and write. They also provided schooling for boys of their communities.

What was a monastery?

A monastery was a building (or buildings) that housed monks, men who devoted their lives to religious service. Monasteries were self-contained communities that provided everything the monks needed. Monks living in monasteries spent much of their time in prayer and meditation, but they also made their own clothes, grew their own food, and did other kinds of work.

What were sumptuary laws?

Sumptuary laws were passed as a way to separate the wealthy from the peasants by giving them different rights. For example, these laws stated who could wear what kind of clothing and what materials they could use. Peasants wore plain, woolen clothing, while nobles— or the wealthy class— wore nicer clothes made from finer fabrics, like velvet and silk.

What did people eat in the Middle Ages?

Peasants ate mostly bread and stew. The stew was made of beans, cabbage, and other vegetables, and the bread was so gritty from the stones used to grind the grain that it caused people's teeth to wear down! Peasants rarely ate meat. They were not allowed to hunt on the lord's land—in fact, the punishment for killing a deer was sometimes death! Wealthier people ate a wider variety of foods, including meat, and almost everyone drank wine or ale because the water was so bad it would make people sick.

Did people in the Middle Ages play games?

Yes! People in the Middle Ages liked to play games. Chess was very popular among the wealthy, but people also enjoyed playing checkers, cards, and watching horse races. There even was a version of soccer that had no rules—just two teams, two goals, and one ball!

What was **May Day?**

May Day is a celebration of the beginning of summer. It was a popular festival in the Middle Ages; people would dance around a maypole, light bonfires, and crown a young girl from the community the

"Queen of May."

WHO WAS IN A MEDIEVAL KING'S COURT?

Kings in the Middle Ages gathered a group of relatives, barons, lords, family members, and members of the church together; these made up his court. The court traveled with the king wherever he went and gave him counseling and advice. The word "court" refers to the fact that the king made judgments in courts. For example, a king and his court would listen to complaints between barons and lords and then make decisions about who was right and who was wrong.

WHY DID KINGS AND OTHER RULERS BUILD CASTLES?

Castles were built for defense, usually in the center of the land ruled by a king, prince, or lord. From the castles, the ruler could defend himself, his land, and his people, and he could prepare to launch attacks if needed. Castles typically were built of stone, because stone was stronger and more stable than wood, and oftentimes they were built on top of a hill or near water or some other natural land feature that also could serve in defense.

Arrowslits

Gate

Moat

Drawbridge

WHAT FEATURES WERE BUILT INTO A CASTLE TO KEEP IT SAFE?

There were many features designed to make a castle safer. A moat was a trench dug around the castle that could be filled with water. Oftentimes there was a drawbridge across the moat to get to the castle. Castles also had a curtain wall, which was a protective wall around the castle; soldiers could shoot arrows down onto attackers from the wall's top through arrow slits, which were holes cut into the walls. Battlements were built at the tops of castle walls. They had sections cut out from the castle walls so soldiers could attack and then duck back behind the wall for protection.

Tower of London

What were some famous medieval castles?

Two of the most famous medieval castles are Windsor Castle and the Tower of London, both originally built by William the Conqueror. Windsor Castle is still the countryside residence of the British royal family. William began fortifications at the Tower of London in 1066. He began the White Tower, which gave the complex its name, in 1078. The tower has been a prison, an armory, a palace, and even a zoo.

51

Why were cats and dogs allowed to live in medieval castles?

Cats and dogs were kept in castles to help kill rats that otherwise would eat the castle's storage of grain, which was used for food.

What was a siege?

A siege was a type of assault: enemy forces would surround a castle or town and, in addition to attacking the castle and its residents, hold their position and try to starve the castle-dwellers out. Many castles were built on a brook or a spring or some other small body of water so there would be water to drink during a siege. The pieces of artillery used to attack during a siege—the battering ram and ballista, for example— were called siege engines.

WHAT WAS A BUTTERY?

The room in a castle where ale was kept.

How did a man become a knight?

A man in the Middle Ages could be awarded knighthood by fighting unusually hard or well during a battle; or he could become an apprentice to a knight (often his father) and earn knighthood through training.

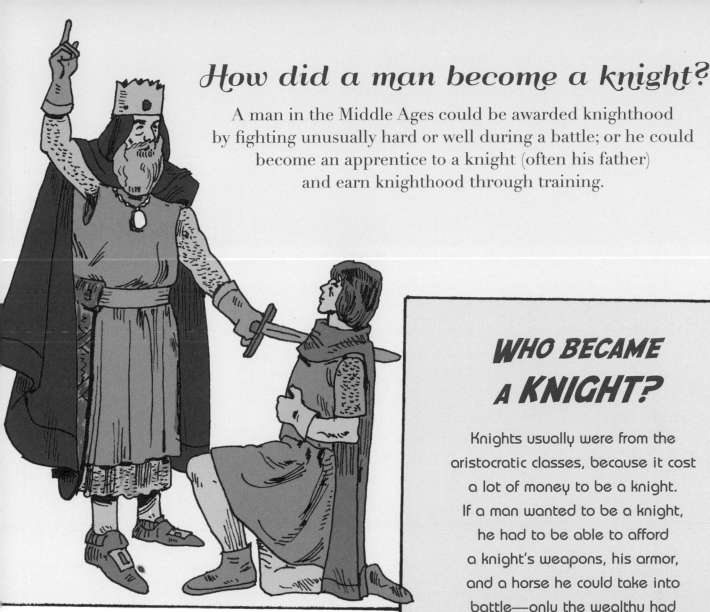

WHO BECAME A KNIGHT?

Knights usually were from the aristocratic classes, because it cost a lot of money to be a knight. If a man wanted to be a knight, he had to be able to afford a knight's weapons, his armor, and a horse he could take into battle—only the wealthy had the money to pay for such things.

What was a **page**?

If a boy wanted to become a knight (or his parents wanted him to), the boy would start serving a knight when he turned seven years old. He would live with the knight and serve as a page. As a servant for the knight, a page would have household chores and other duties. In return he would learn proper manners, how to ride a horse, and how to fight.

Lead the Knight to the Castle

Help the knight find his way back to the castle by following the maze from start to finish.

START

FINISH

Answers on page 306

WHAT WAS A SQUIRE?

Before a page became a knight, he would be a squire. Squires had additional chores, such as taking care of the knight's horses and cleaning his armor and weapons. Sometimes squires even got to go into battle with the knight, so squires had to be ready to fight. Unlike pages, who practiced fighting with wooden swords and shields, squires practiced with real weapons.

When did a page become a squire?

A boy became a page when he turned seven. He served as a page until he turned fifteen, when he became a squire. Most boys worked as a squire for five or six years.

Page   Squire   Knight

What was a dubbing ceremony?

A squire became a knight when he turned 21. The squire would undergo a dubbing ceremony: he would kneel before the king or another knight, who would tap the squire on the shoulder with a sword and officially name him a knight. The new knight took an oath, and vowed to protect his king and the church. The squire spent the night before the dubbing ceremony praying.

WHY DiD KNiGHTS FORM ORDERS?

Groups of knights pledged themselves to defending Christianity and formed military orders to do so. There were three famous military orders: the Knights Templar, the Knights Hospitaller, and the Teutonic Knights. These orders fought in the Crusades, which were a series of wars during the Middle Ages between Christians and Muslims.

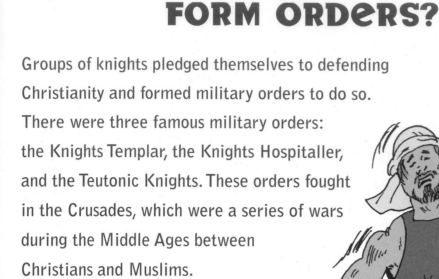

What was the Knights Templar?

The Knights Templar was an order established in the 1100s. Its members were known for wearing red crosses on their white robes. They fought during the Crusades, establishing their headquarters in Jerusalem. They were known for being the first into battle. They are famous for fighting in the Battle of Montgisard, where 475 Knights of the Templar joined forces that defeated 26,000 Muslim soldiers.

What was the Knights Hospitaller?

The Knights Hospitaller became an official military order in 1113 but grew from a group founded around 1023 to protect the poor and sick. While defending the Holy Land from Muslim forces during the Crusades, the Knights Hospitaller wore black clothing with a white cross.

What were the Teutonic Knights?

The Teutonic Knights were Germans. They started as a branch of the Hospitallers, so they too wore black clothing with a white cross. They fought in the Crusades, and later took over Prussia (Germany) and parts of Eastern Europe. They were very powerful but were defeated by Polish forces in 1410 at the Battle of Grunwald.

What was chain mail?

Knights wore two types of armor—chain mail and plate armor. Made from thousands of metal rings, chain mail was very flexible. While it offered good protection, it easily could be pierced by an arrow or a sword. To keep themselves safe, knights began wearing metal plates over the chain mail.

What was a hauberk?

A long coat of chain mail armor with long sleeves was called a hauberk. It could weigh as much as 30 pounds, so knights wore pads underneath the armor to help them carry the extra weight. Knights had to practice putting on, wearing, and riding a horse with armor on.

WHAT WAS PLATE ARMOR?

Plate armor gave knights more and better protection than chain mail armor. But it wasn't as flexible, and it was heavier—a full set of plate armor could weigh 60 pounds. The pieces of plate armor had special names, such as sabbaton (foot covering) and poleyn (knee covering). A plate and chain mail armor suit was sometimes called a "harness."

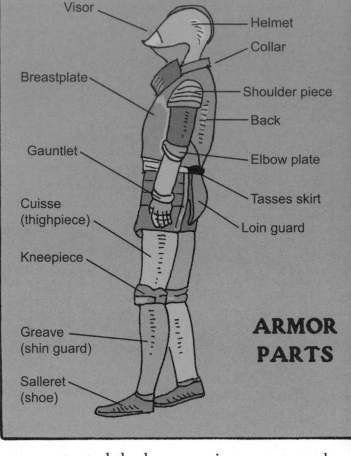

Visor
Helmet
Collar
Breastplate
Shoulder piece
Back
Gauntlet
Elbow plate
Cuisse (thighpiece)
Tasses skirt
Loin guard
Kneepiece
Greave (shin guard)
Salleret (shoe)

ARMOR PARTS

What were the pieces of plate armor called?

Plate armor pieces had unique names: greaves protected the lower legs from knee to ankle; sabbatons protected the feet; poleyns protected the knees; cuisses protected the thighs; gauntlets protected the hands; vambraces protected the lower arms; rerebraces protected the upper arms; pauldrons protected the shoulders; a breastplate protected the chest; and the helmet protected the head.

What types of weapons did knights use?

Knights used different kinds of weapons depending on how they were fighting—some weapons were better when fighting on horseback, and others were better when fighting hand-to-hand. A lance was a long wooden pole with a metal tip and a hand guard that was carried on horseback. The lance was used to knock an enemy off his horse. Once a knight got off his horse, he used a sword and shield. Occasionally a knight would use a longbow or a mace, which was a club with a large head made of metal that could crush an enemy.

Lance

Sword

Shield

Spear

Dagger

Mace

What was a destrier?

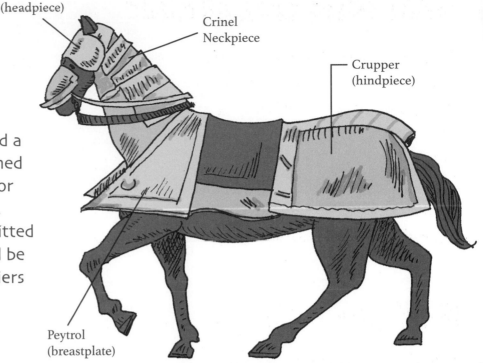

Chamfron (headpiece)

Crinel Neckpiece

Crupper (hindpiece)

Peytrol (breastplate)

A knight's warhorse was called a destrier. A warhorse was trained for battle, and also wore armor over its head, neck, and sides. Warhorses sometimes wore fitted shoes made of iron that could be used as weapons against soldiers fighting on foot.

What weapons were used to capture a castle?

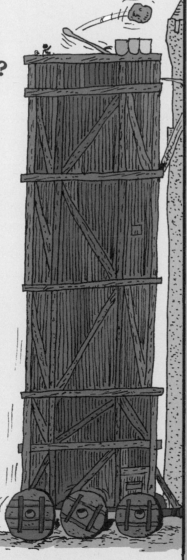

While knights carried individual weapons in battle, they also needed to know how to use siege weapons, or weapons used to capture a castle. A belfry or siege tower was a tall, wheeled tower that could be rolled toward a castle. Once the belfry reached the castle, the knights could climb from it onto the top of the castle walls. A catapult was designed to launch huge rocks, destroying castle walls and the buildings inside them. A battering ram was a log big enough to crush the castle gates.

What was a coat of arms?

A coat of arms was a symbol that represented a knight's identity. Originally, the coat of arms was used to tell one knight from another. When a knight had on his full set of armor, it was hard to recognize him, so knights painted symbols on their shields. It was called a "coat of arms" because the knights also painted their symbols on the coat they wore covering their armor.

What was a herald?

A herald was an officer who kept a record of each coat of arms and which knight it belonged to. A herald also made sure that each new coat of arms was unique.

What was the escutcheon?

An escutcheon was the shield shape that the coat of arms was drawn on. The exact shape of the shield varied. The designs on the shield were called charges and ordinaries.

What was the coat of arms' field?

A coat of arms' background color was called the field. Sometimes the field was a solid color, and sometimes it had a pattern. Different background colors had different meanings—red meant strength and was the color of a warrior, blue symbolized truth, black meant wisdom, and green meant joy.

WHY DID KNIGHTS PARTICIPATE IN TOURNAMENTS?

When not fighting, knights needed to keep in shape. One of the ways they kept up their skills was by taking part in tournaments, which were practice battles between groups of knights from different areas. These pretend battles took place in a large field. Each side would line up facing the other, waiting for a signal that it was time to charge. When a horn sounded, the knights would advance toward the opposing team. The knights that were still on their horses following the first charge would turn around and charge again until one side won.

What was jousting?

Jousting was another game played by knights. Two knights on horseback, each armed with a long lance, would charge at each other, trying to knock the other off his horse. The winner of a joust often was awarded money, as well as the admiration of the local townspeople.

WHAT WAS THE CODE OF CHIVALRY?

The code of chivalry was the set of rules and standards a knight lived by. Knights were expected to be loyal and fair, to follow and defend the church, to protect women and children, to serve the king, to be honest, and to live with honor.

WHAT WAS THE BLACK DEATH?

The Black Death was a disease that spread throughout Europe from 1347 to 1351. There was no cure and it was very contagious. The Black Death is also called the bubonic plague, which is spread by rodents and the fleas that live on them. It's believed that rats living on European merchant ships brought the plague from Asia to Europe.

How many people died from The Black Death?

The Black Death killed at least one third of the people in Europe. At its peak, it is said that 800 people died each day in Paris. The Black Death wiped out entire towns and villages. So many people died that they couldn't be individually buried—they were carried to massive pits and buried together. It is estimated that between 75 million and 200 million people died.

What were the Crusades?

The Crusades were a series of wars between Christians and Muslims. The Christians were from Europe, and they wanted to retake control of Jerusalem and the Holy Land from the Muslims. Jerusalem was important in Christianity, Judaism, and the Muslim religion of Islam during the Middle Ages—each religion believed sacred things happened in Jerusalem.

How did the Crusades start?

In the early Middle Ages when Arabic peoples occupied the Holy Land, they allowed Christians to visit the city of Jerusalem. In 1070, the Seljuk Turks took control of the Holy Land from the Arabs and refused to allow Christians in. Alexius I of the Byzantine Empire asked the Holy Roman Empire for help in defending the Holy Land from the Seljuks. The Roman pope helped to gather a European army, mostly with soldiers from the Holy Roman Empire, and thus began the Crusades.

Who fought in the Crusades?

European armies fought against the Islamic armies who controlled Jerusalem. More than 30,000 knights and peasants made up the European army who fought in the First Crusade. Some men chose to fight in the army as a way to make money, but others saw their participation in the war for the Holy Land as a way to Heaven.

WAS THERE MORE THAN ONE CRUSADE?

Yes, there were seven main Crusades—some historians count eight or nine, and there was also an attack largely considered a legend named the Children's Crusade. The Crusades took place over 200 years, starting in 1095. The symbol of the Crusaders was a red cross, which soldiers put on their clothing, their armor, on flags, and on banners.

WHAT WAS THE HUNDRED YEARS' WAR?

The Hundred Years' War was fought from 1337 to 1453 between England and France. The war was a series of battles with long periods of peace between them.

WHAT STARTED THE HUNDRED YEARS' WAR?

In 1337, King Edward III of England claimed he was the rightful king of France, which fueled the disputes that had been occurring between England and France for years. Once the battles started other disagreements occurred, such as who controlled certain areas of land, and kept the fighting going for 116 years.

WHAT WERE CHEVAUCHÉES?

King Edward III believed he should be the king of France through his mother, Isabella. Her brother, King Charles IV of France, died without a male heir when Edward was 15 years old. The French instead crowned King Philip VI of France, and Philip then took control of Aquitaine from the English. King Edward fought back, but instead of invading France in an attempt to conquer the land, he led a series of raids called *chevauchées*. Edward would stage attacks deep into French territory, burning crops and raiding cities.

Who was the Black Prince?

In the 1350s, the son of King Edward III, known as Edward the Black Prince, commanded his father's army. He led the English to many victories over the French and, at the battle of Poitiers, captured the king of France, John II. The Black Prince died before his father, so he never became king. When King Edward III died, the Black Prince's son became King Richard II—when he was 10 years old! Richard II started a period of peace between England and France.

Who was Joan of Arc?

The English invaded southern France in 1428, taking hold of a city called Orleans. A young peasant girl named Joan of Arc took leadership in the French army, saying she had seen a vision from God. In 1429, she led the French to several victories over the English before she was captured and burned at the stake.

WHAT ENDED THE HUNDRED YEARS' WAR?

The bravery and success of Joan of Arc inspired the French to go on fighting to push the English army out of France. They finally succeeded in 1453, ending the Hundred Years' War.

What was the Magna Carta?

Widely considered one of the most important historical documents, the Magna Carta stated the rights of the people of England. It was signed in 1215 by King John. The Magna Carta offered protective rights to the people and stated that the king was not above the law of the land.

How did the Magna Carta cause a Civil War?

Neither King John nor the barons intended to keep the agreements laid out in the Magna Carta. After he signed the document, King John attempted to have it nullified and had the pope declare the document illegal. The barons refused to surrender London, sending the country into a civil war (called the First Barons' War) until King John died in 1216.

Why did King John sign the Magna Carta?

King John was crowned after his brother, Richard the Lionheart, died. John wasn't a very popular king. He wasn't well-liked, and because he was constantly at war with France he levied high taxes on his people. Some of the feudal barons who lived under King John's rule decided to rebel. They marched to London and seized the city. King John agreed to sign a document, the Magna Carta, which guaranteed the barons, the church, and the people certain rights, limited the king's powers, and established a more fair government.

WHAT WAS INCLUDED IN THE MAGNA CARTA?

There were 63 clauses, including statements about the church's rights, guarantees of a person's access to justice, and protection from illegal imprisonment. A council of 25 barons was created to make sure King John followed the laws—this council eventually became the English Parliament. The ideas of the Magna Carta became the principles that formed the basis of liberty for the English people. They also influenced the constitutions of other countries, including the United States: Many of the Magna Carta's rights resemble those written into the Constitution and the Bill of Rights.

Who were the Catholic Monarchs?

King Ferdinand II and Queen Isabella I of Spain were called the Catholic Monarchs. They authorized Christopher Columbus's first exploration in 1492.

WHO WAS CHRISTOPHER COLUMBUS?

Christopher Columbus was an Italian explorer looking for a direct western water route from Europe to Asia. Columbus made four trips across the Atlantic, and he landed in the Americas in 1492. His voyages set the stage for further exploration of the New World.

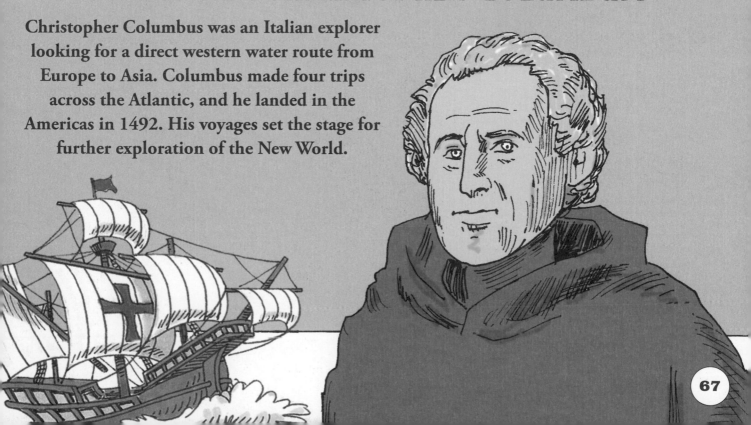

Who were the Moors?

The Moors were Muslims who lived in Morocco and Algeria in northern Africa and in Spain and Portugal.

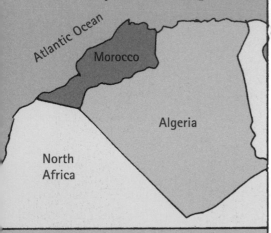

Atlantic Ocean

Morocco

Algeria

North Africa

WHAT WAS THE WARS OF THE ROSES?

The Wars of the Roses were a series of civil wars fought in England over 30 years, from 1455 to 1485.

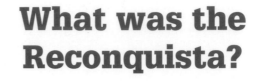

What was the Reconquista?

The Reconquista was a long series of wars between Christians and Muslim Moors from 718 to 1492. The wars were fought for control of the Iberian Peninsula—that is, Spain and Portugal. The Moors and Christians fought for nearly 700 years until the Christians took back the peninsula. The Reconquista ended in 1492 when King Ferdinand of Aragon and Queen Isabella of Castile, who were married in 1469, united Spain and took back Granada, the last area still ruled by the Moors.

Atlantic Ocean

Portugal

Spain

CLANG!

CLANG!

WHO FOUGHT IN THE WARS OF THE ROSES?

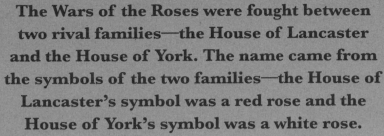

The Wars of the Roses were fought between two rival families—the House of Lancaster and the House of York. The name came from the symbols of the two families—the House of Lancaster's symbol was a red rose and the House of York's symbol was a white rose.

WHAT STARTED THE WARS OF THE ROSES?

Both the Lancaster and the York families felt they were the rightful heirs to the English throne, as they both were descendants of King Edward III.

Who was Elizabeth of York?

Elizabeth of York became queen consort of England when she married King Henry VII. (A consort is someone who is married to a king or a queen.) But she also was the daughter, sister, niece, and mother of English kings. She was well known for how beautiful she was. It is believed that her picture was used for the queen in a deck of playing cards!

Do you want to play?

How can you tell when a medieval painting was made?

One way to tell if a medieval painting or tapestry was made before or after the fourteenth century began is by looking at the men's shoes! Paintings done before the turn of the century will show men wearing shoes with square toes, but in the mid-1300s, shoes with long, pointy toes, sometimes even curling up, became fashionable. These shoes could be made of cloth, including silk or velvet, or leather.

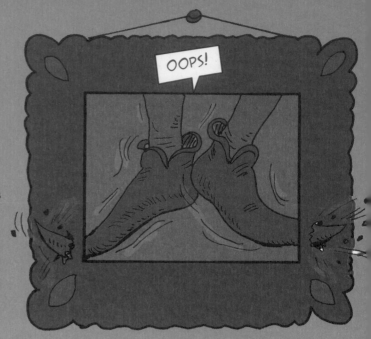

What was Romanesque style?

Romanesque was a style of architecture used between the eleventh and thirteenth centuries. Many European monasteries and churches built during that time were in the Romanesque style. Buildings created in this style were solid and substantial. They had rounded arches and barrel vaults (a type of arch), which supported the roof, stone walls, and only a few windows.

What was Gothic style?

Unlike Romanesque-style buildings, Gothic buildings, which started being built around 1200, had enormous stained-glass windows, pointed vaults and arches, tall spires, and support structures called flying buttresses.

What was an illuminated manuscript?

An illuminated manuscript is a handwritten book in which the words, or text, are enhanced by color illustrations, gold and silver lettering, and border designs. Before the invention of the printing press in the fifteenth century, craftsmen in monasteries and sometimes in universities created these books, which also were works of art. They were sold mostly to the wealthy.

Where did medieval peasants live?

Medieval peasants lived in huts with walls made of wattle and daub. The wattle was a wooden framework made of twigs that was daubed, or smeared, with a sticky substance made of soil, clay, sand, and other materials. A hut would have a thatched roof but no windows. An area of the hut would be penned off for animals that would live inside with the family.

What was a garderobe?

In medieval castles, the garderobe was the toilet. It usually was a chute opening straight into the castle's moat. While not pleasant, one way to capture the castle was to climb up this chute and into the castle's interior.

What were the stocks?

Medieval criminals were put in the stocks, which were wooden boards with holes for the feet, hands, and head. The stocks, like many medieval punishments, were cruel. Crimes like stealing could even be punished by hanging.

WHAT WAS THE DOMESDAY BOOK?

In 1086, William the Conqueror ordered the taking of a survey to record the number of people and their land holdings in England at that time. William wanted to find out how much his land in England was worth and how much he could earn by raising taxes. It took years to gather this information; the complete record of the survey was called the Domesday Book.

What was a dovecote?

A dovecote is a structure used to house and rear pigeons. In medieval times, these were often round-shaped buildings that could hold several hundred pigeons or doves. The birds were kept for their eggs, feathers, and meat—which was eaten as a delicacy.

HOME SWEET HOME!

Who were villeins?

Villeins were peasants who lived within a lord's manor. They did not own their own land but were given housing and often land so they could grow their own food. They worked the lord's land as well, plowing fields and taking the food produced to be sold at markets. The majority of medieval peasants were villeins.

What was a tithe barn?

In medieval times, 10 percent (a tithe) of everything a village produced was given to the church. The food produced by the farms of a village was stored in a barn called the tithe barn. The church would distribute some of this food to the poor or sick.

What was a DUNGEON?

Dungeons were rooms in the lowest levels of castles that were designed to hold prisoners. In order to prevent prisoners from escaping, very few dungeons had windows. The only way to access some dungeons was through small trapdoors.

What is a stained-glass window?

Stained-glass windows are found in many cathedrals from the Middle Ages and later. A stained-glass window is made up of different colored pieces of glass put together to make a picture, typically a scene from the Bible.

What is the Ars Minor?

The *Ars Minor* is a book that was written before the medieval period but was still read in the Middle Ages. It was written in Latin and was important for scholars studying grammar in medieval monasteries. Most medieval literature was written in Latin, which was the spoken and written language of educated people, many of whom were monks.

What is The Canterbury Tales?

The Canterbury Tales is a collection of more than 20 stories written by Geoffrey Chaucer between 1387 and 1400. Unlike most texts written in medieval times, *The Canterbury Tales* was written in Middle English, which was the language spoken in England in Chaucer's time, instead of in Latin.

MIDDLE AGES

Search for the Middle Ages words listed below. Circle horizontally, vertically, backwards, or diagonally as you find each word.

```
S R O M A N E S Q U E G V B P M A X H F
Q J D O L A A F F V J J Q N A X Z H B E
E K W N H C U G M D H N O L Y R C N T U
H D G A U T J T A G Z E O S U R O U C D
E L A S T K D G H W E E S H A O N G A A
R N V T C T Q P A C A D L W C R O X D L
A I Z E N N M E T R A X D U N G E O N S
L T T R D X X U T S D P G U K P W S G D
D I E Y S D C U U R V E C Q B J M H U K
E U Z S X S J R E L R I R G K D D V I C
S N G M E B C I X I H N Y O J O E R L O
W M W C J O R B U T G R L W B V X P D M
M P M G Y T B Q O Y L I B P D E T E J Q
F J N E S M S G C A Y Y V G J C J A M K
Z Y B E L Q E Y V Q K F W A X O T S N Y
J D D S E I A I A T H Z I R U T F A A X
M A N O R N H Q L P S C Q M P E L N Y C
Z K B U G C H F Z Z Y N E O G S M T N Z
Z J O U S T I N G D Y X L R L J Q S H G
F R M E K K F R B J K N I G H T N Y D G
```

ARMOR	BARON	CHIVALRY
CRUSADES	DESTRIER	DOVECOTE
DUNGEON	ESCUTCHEON	FEUDAL
GARDEROBE	GOTHIC	GUILD
HERALD	JOUSTING	KNIGHT
MANOR	MONASTERY	PEASANTS
ROMANESQUE	SQUIRE	

Answers on page 307

What was the population of the world at the start of the sixteenth century?

In 1500, the world population was an estimated 450 million people.

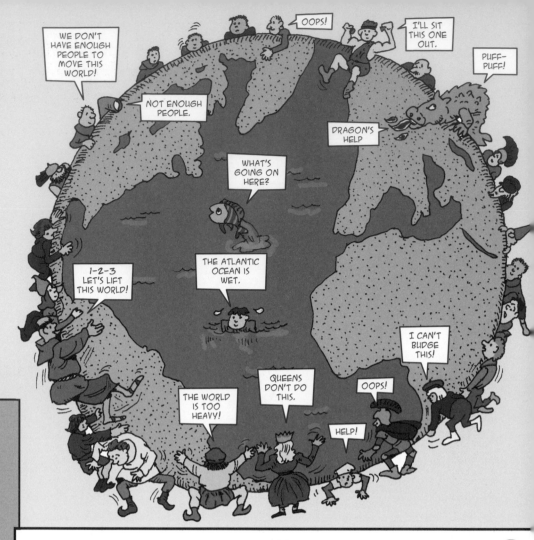

Who invented the first flushing toilet?

In the late sixteenth century, Sir John Harrington, a godson of England's Queen Elizabeth I, invented the first flushing toilet, which he named Ajax. One was even installed for his famous godmother's use!

What was the Renaissance?

In the late 1400s and early 1500s, European scholars and artists became more interested in the world around them. Their art and ideas began to reflect that, becoming more realistic and less religious. This time became known as the Renaissance. Historians consider the Renaissance the beginning of modern history. It began in northern Italy and then spread throughout Europe. In England there was an increase in literature and drama, and William Shakespeare wrote his plays during this time.

Botticelli paints the birth of Venus 1485

Who was Leonardo da Vinci?

Leonardo da Vinci was a leading artist and thinker during the Italian Renaissance. Born on April 15, 1452, in Italy, Leonardo was a painter, sculptor, and inventor. He was very interested in the laws of science and nature, which influenced his works of art and invention. He influenced many of the artists and intellectuals of his time.

What is the Mona Lisa?

The *Mona Lisa* is a famous portrait that was painted by Leonardo da Vinci sometime between 1503 and 1506. Art historians haven't always agreed on who is depicted in the portrait. The consensus is that the subject is Lisa del Giocondo, an Italian woman born in the Gherardini family who became the wife of a wealthy silk merchant from Florence. It's believed her husband commissioned the painting for the family's new home and to celebrate the birth of their son.

Who was Niccolò Machiavelli?

Niccolò Machiavelli was one of the most influential writers of the Renaissance. In 1513, he wrote *The Prince*, which served as a handbook for politicians. He advised rulers to be ruthless and self-serving, doing good only if it suited their needs.

Who was Michelangelo?

Michelangelo
David

Michelangelo, the most famous artist of the Italian Renaissance, is known for his artworks, including the *David* and *Pietà* statues and the ceiling frescoes he painted in the Sistine Chapel in Rome. As a young man he served as an apprentice to a painter before studying in the sculpture gardens of the Medici family. When he was still a teenager he went out on his own to start what would be an illustrious sculpting and painting career.

When was Saint Peter's Basilica built?

The building of the current Saint Peter's Basilica, in the Vatican in Rome, began in 1506. It was the idea of Pope Nicholas V during his reign in the late 1400s to replace the original fourth century church with a new one. Construction on the basilica stopped when Nicholas died, but a new phase began under Pope Julius II, and the building finally was consecrated (a kind of sacred dedication) in 1626.

WHAT WAS JACOPO PERI'S DAFNE?

In 1598 Jacopo Peri, an Italian music composer, wrote *Dafne*, which is considered the first opera. Peri set his music for *Dafne* to words written by the poet Ottavio Rinuccini.

Who was **Nicolaus Copernicus?**

Nicolaus Copernicus was a Polish astronomer. In Copernicus's time, most astronomers believed the theories of the solar system's movements that had been developed by the Greek mathematician Ptolemy more than 1,000 years earlier. Ptolemy stated that Earth was at the center of the universe and didn't move, and that all other heavenly bodies moved around Earth. But Copernicus thought Ptolemy was wrong. Between 1508 and 1514, Copernicus first suggested that Earth moved around the sun.

YOU GOT IT RIGHT!

WHO WAS GALILEO?

Galileo Galilei was a scientist and scholar whose studies have formed the basis for modern physics and astronomy. Born in Italy in 1564, Galileo became a mathematics professor. He constructed a series of telescopes and became convinced that the solar system revolved around the sun, as Copernicus had theorized. Because of his beliefs, the Church accused Galileo of heresy—having a belief that differs from the established beliefs—twice.

What did doctors think caused illness in the sixteenth century?

WHAT'S WRONG WITH ME, DOC?

DO YOU HAVE INSURANCE?

Doctors in the sixteenth century had little idea of how the human body worked. They could do little about disease—which infected and killed many people in the sixteenth century—because they didn't know what caused diseases. Doctors thought the body was made up of four "humors," or fluids. The four humors were: blood; phlegm; choler or yellow bile; and melancholy or black bile. If all four humors were balanced, you were healthy—but if you had too much of one humor, you fell ill.

LEONARDO DA VINCI

LEARN ABOUT LEONARDO DA VINCI AS YOU LOOK FOR THESE FUN ITEMS:

- ❏ Balloon
- ❏ Banana peel
- ❏ Birds (2)
- ❏ Bone
- ❏ Candles (13)
- ❏ Cane
- ❏ Chef
- ❏ Crown
- ❏ Doctor
- ❏ Duck
- ❏ Easel
- ❏ Feather
- ❏ Flowerpot
- ❏ Flying bat

- ❏ Ghost
- ❏ Graduate
- ❏ *La Gioconda*
- ❏ Ladder
- ❏ Lifesaver
- ❏ Lost shoe
- ❏ Mouse
- ❏ Paintbrush
- ❏ Paint bucket
- ❏ Painted egg
- ❏ Paper airplane
- ❏ Pencil
- ❏ Pizza
- ❏ Screwdriver

- ❏ Skull
- ❏ Snowman
- ❏ Stool
- ❏ Wizard

Answers on page 308

SKETCH FOR AN EQUESTRIAN STATUE

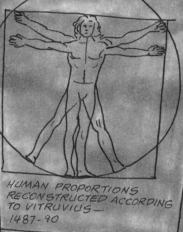

HUMAN PROPORTIONS RECONSTRUCTED ACCORDING TO VITRUVIUS— 1487-90

PLAN FOR A CHURCH— 1487-89

ANATOMY-MUSCLES OF UPPER LIMB

LEONARDO WAS ALSO AN ARCHITECT, MUSICIAN, MATHEMATICIAN, AND SCULPTOR.

HE'S GOING TO PAINT MY PORTRAIT.

"RENAISSANCE" MEANS "REBIRTH."

IN 1482, HE BECAME COURT ARTIST FOR THE DUKE OF MILAN.

AS A MILITARY ENGINEER FOR THE DUKE, HE DESIGNED A MOVABLE BRIDGE, DIFFERENT TYPES OF LADDERS FOR STORMING AND CLIMBING CASTLE WALLS, ARTILLERY, AND GUNS.

MACHINE FOR MAKING CONCAVE MIRRORS

WELL PUMP

ANATOMY IS THE STUDY OF THE STRUCTURE OF THE BODY.

HIS ARE THE FIRST ACCURATE DRAWINGS OF ANATOMY.

THE FIRST SUCCESSFUL HELICOPTER, DESIGNED IN THE 1930S, WAS BASED ON LEONARDO'S DRAWINGS.

HIS PAINTINGS ARE GRACEFUL, CALM, AND DELICATE.

HE EXPLORED HUMAN ANATOMY AND PERSPECTIVE.

I'M LOST!

HE MADE MAPS OF EUROPE

HE BASED HIS DRAWINGS ON THE ACTION OF A SCREW.

HE HAS GREAT POWERS OF OBSERVATION.

HE RECORDED HIS IDEAS OF ART, SCIENCE, AND ENGINEERING IN NOTEBOOKS.

HE WROTE HIS NOTES BACKWARD SO THEY CAN ONLY BE READ USING A MIRROR.

YOU ARE HERE X

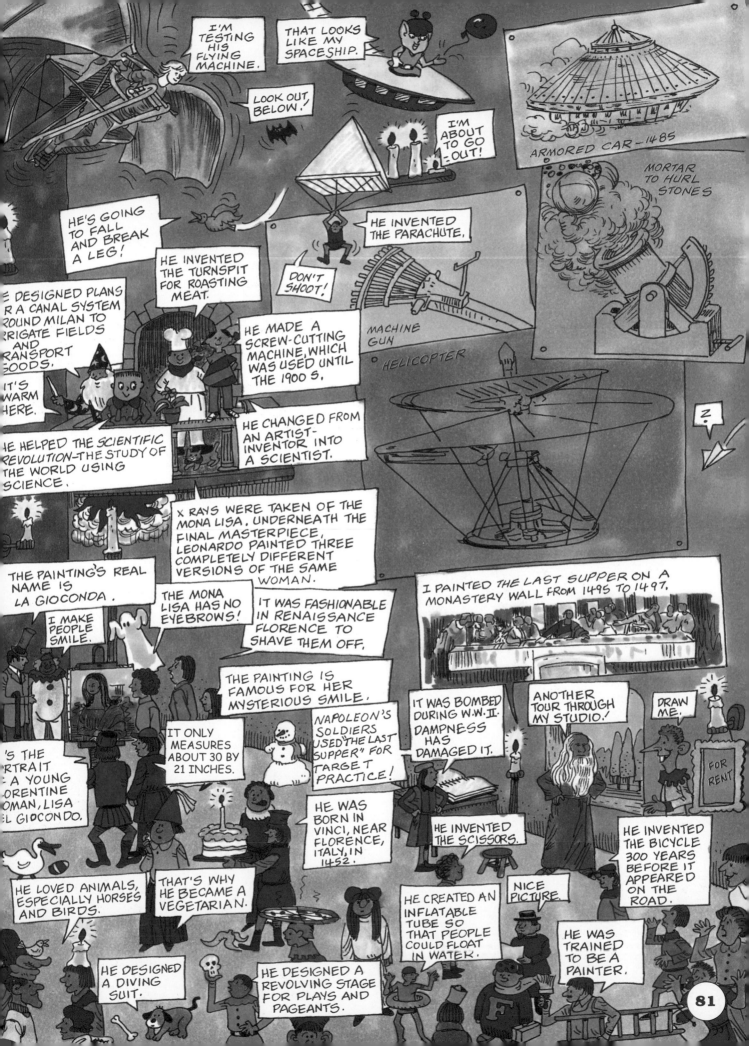

What book is said to have launched the modern study of anatomy?

The seven-volume *De Humani Corporis Fabrica* (On the Structure of the Human Body), which was written by 28-year-old Andreas Vesalius in the mid-sixteenth century. Anatomy is the study of the human body. An Italian doctor, Vesalius dissected human bodies and published his findings in this important set of books, 600 pages long and illustrated with engravings, in 1543.

HOW DID DOCTORS THINK THE PLAGUE WAS SPREAD?

Doctors thought the plague was caused by poisonous vapors, which they believed floated through the air and were absorbed into the skin.

What was a wise woman?

Seeing a doctor was expensive in the sixteenth century, so many people saw a local healer, called a wise woman, if they were sick. Wise women knew a lot about different herbs that were thought to cure many ailments, but oftentimes these cures didn't work.

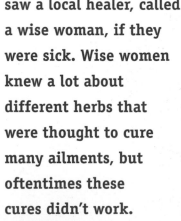

What was the average life span in the sixteenth century?

The average life span in the sixteenth century was short—certainly much shorter than today's. At birth, the average life expectancy was only 35. Of all the people born in the sixteenth century, between one-third and one-half died before the age of 16. But some people did live to be 50, 60, 70, and even 80.

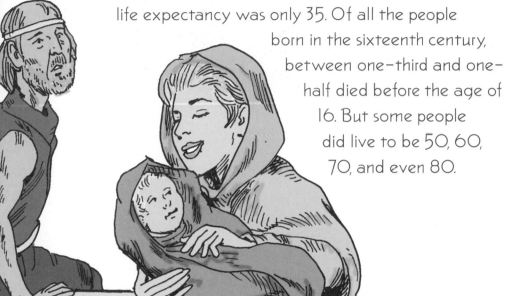

WHAT ARE TUDOR HOUSES?

Tudor houses were built while the Tudors (including King Henry VIII and Queen Elizabeth I) ruled in England. The houses were black and white—the timber frame would be painted black, and the spaces between were covered with lime to make them look white. The timber beams were uneven because they were cut by hand. Roofs were steeply pitched and covered with clay tiles or thatch.

Who was Nostradamus?

Nostradamus was born in France in 1503. His birth name was Michel de Nostredame, but he later began using a Latin version of his name–Nostradamus. He studied medicine and became a doctor, specializing in treating the plague. He made predictions about the future and wrote them down in a book called *The Prophecies*. Even today, some people believe his predictions have come true or will come true in the future.

When did people get married in the sixteenth century?

Among the upper classes, people married young—many girls married when they were only 15 or 16, while boys married at 18 to 21. Children from rich families had arranged marriages, which means their parents or their families decided who they would marry. Children from poor families had more choice over whom to marry and also tended to be older.

What were Bartholomew Babies?

Children of the 1600s played with wooden dolls that were called Bartholomew Babies because they were sold at the annual Bartholomew Fair in London. The dolls were carved of wood and typically had no arms, though some had leather arms. They were sold painted and dressed in the clothing of the time.

What was the Statute of Artificers?

An English law passed in 1563, the Statute of Artificers set regulations for prices, training, and hiring practices within craft guilds. A man or woman could not work in a guild-run trade unless they had apprenticed for seven years. For women, however, this rule often was not enforced. Very often the guilds let male members employ their wives and daughters, and often if a craftsman died his widow carried on his trade.

How did people in the sixteenth century keep track of the months of the year?

Calendars and prayer books from the sixteenth century show the way that people measured out the year, often according to the seasons and agricultural cycles. Calendars had pictures to show what time of year it was—for example, a farmer pruning new vines in spring, harvesting wheat in summer, and feeding pigs in fall that are later slaughtered in winter.

EAT UP!

I THINK FALL IS NEAR!

WHAT IS THE GREGORIAN CALENDAR?

The Gregorian calendar is sometimes known as the Western calendar because it is used throughout the Western world today. It was named after Pope Gregory XIII, who introduced it in 1582.

When was the Gregorian calendar adopted?

The Gregorian calendar was first adopted in some countries in Europe in 1582; England and America switched in 1752. It had a 365-day year divided into twelve months, and even accounted for leap years.

JANUARY						
				5	6	7
1	2	3	4	12	13	14
8	9	10	11	19	20	21
15	16	17	18	26	27	28
22	23	24	25			
29	30	31				

HAPPY New Year!

When did England hold its first national lottery?

It was held in 1567 by issue of Queen Elizabeth. The lottery was held to raise money to build ships and develop ports of sea, so that England could expand its export business. Tickets cost ten shillings each, which was more money than the average citizen could afford. The first prize was large and was paid in money, plate (silverware and other metal items), tapestries, and cloth. To encourage people to buy tickets, all ticket holders were told they would not be arrested for minor crimes.

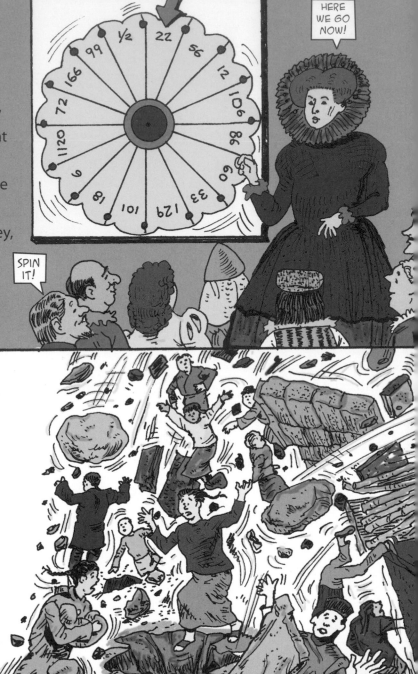

WHAT IS CONSIDERED THE DEADLIEST EARTHQUAKE IN HISTORY?

In January 1556, an earthquake in Shaanxi, China, killed an estimated 830,000 people. The earthquake started at night and continued into the morning, happening in an area where a large number of people lived in poorly constructed homes and buildings. Huge cracks opened in the earth, and in many areas there were landslides. Much of the destruction was hundreds of miles away from the epicenter of the earthquake.

Who invented the first violin?

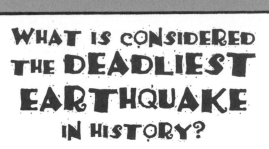

The kind of violin still in use today was invented in 1564 by Andrea Amati, an Italian instrument-maker.

WHAT WERE THE FIRST WATCHES LIKE?

The first watches were spherical metal objects made in the 1500s. They were about three inches across and hung on a ribbon, often around someone's neck. These first watches had a single hand that made its way around a dial marked with the division of 12 hours. Watches were worn more as a piece of jewelry than as a useful tool. Many of these first watches were decorated in colorful enamel.

What was petty school?

Only boys were educated in schools in the sixteenth century. They started at a preschool called petty school, and moved onto grammar school when they were about seven years old. They were taught respect for their elders, how to read and write English, table manners, and the catechism— a book detailing Christian faith.

What was a hornbook?

Children in the sixteenth century learned the basics for reading and writing with something called a hornbook, but it wasn't a book at all. A hornbook was a wooden board with a handle. A sheet of paper with the alphabet and a prayer written on it was tacked to the board. The paper usually was protected by a transparent slice of animal horn, which is how the hornbook got its name. A hole was made in the handle so a piece of leather could be tied to it, and the student could loop his hornbook through his belt or around his neck.

Who was Bernaby Fitzpatrick?

When schoolchildren of sixteenth-century England misbehaved, their teachers would beat them with a birch cane. The teachers of Henry VIII's son Edward, who would become King Edward VI when he was nine years old, were not permitted to beat the future king. Instead they punished another student, named Bernaby Fitzpatrick. He was called a whipping boy.

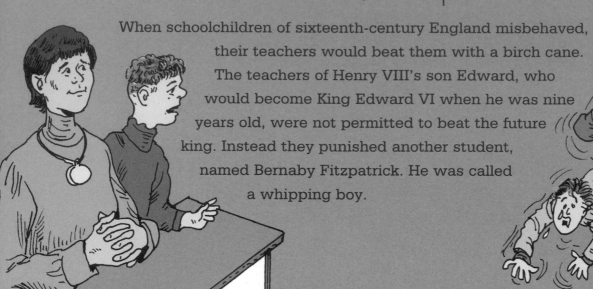

What was a dame school?

Dame schools were for young village children. The women who ran the schools taught the children the letters of the alphabet and sometimes how to read.

What were breeches, doublets, and jerkins?

Men in the sixteenth century wore short, trouser-like garments called breeches. They also wore a tight-fitting jacket called a doublet, over which they wore another jacket called a jerkin. Many men wore a gown, cape, or cloak over the jerkin. Instead of a doublet, working men wore a loose top because it was easier to move in. Some men wore a leather jerkin, called a buff jerkin.

WHAT WAS A
FARTHINGALE?

Many women wore a frame under their dresses called a farthingale. A farthingale would be made of whalebone or wood. In addition to a farthingale, some women would wear a padded roll around the waist, called a bum roll, to make their skirts flare out even more.

What did people use to dye their clothing?

People used mostly vegetable dyes to color their clothing. For example, they used walnuts to dye clothes brown. The most expensive dyes were bright red, purple, and deep blue. Poor people often wore clothing that was dyed brown, yellow, or light blue.

WHAT WAS A RUFF?

A ruff was a large, decorative frill, often made with lace, worn around the neck.

89

What were common fields?

Common fields were fields in sixteenth-century towns and villages where all the local people had the right to let their animals graze.

WHAT DID PEOPLE EAT IN THE SIXTEENTH CENTURY?

Rich people

What you ate in the sixteenth century depended on how wealthy you were. The poor ate mainly vegetables because they could farm them, and they weren't as expensive. Rich people ate more meat and fewer vegetables. Everyone ate bread, but the wealthy ate bread made from fine white flour, while the poor ate coarse bread made from barley or rye. On certain days, people ate fish instead of meat for religious reasons.

Poor people

How was food stored in the sixteenth century?

There were no refrigerators or freezers in the sixteenth century. Meat was preserved in barrels of salty water or hung in chimneys and smoked. Fruit and vegetables were stored in cold cellars and barns.

WHAT WERE TASTERS?

During the sixteenth century, some of the wealthiest and highest-ranking members of society had food tasters test their meals for them. Tasters would try the food first to see whether it had been poisoned.

WHAT WAS FRUMENTY?

Frumenty was a thick pudding made with cracked wheat grains and milk (sometimes almond milk), and with additions such as egg yolks and a spice, like saffron, for added color and taste.

WHAT WAS POTTAGE?

Pottage was a soup often eaten by the poor. It was made of vegetables and grains, but there were many variations. One recipe called for peas, milk, egg yolks, breadcrumbs, and parsley.

What were considered good table manners in the sixteenth century?

Often a number of people would eat from one dish, so having clean hands was important. People were told to wash their hands out in the open where everyone could see. They were also warned not to put their fingers in their ears or their hair, or to blow their noses with their hands while eating.

WHAT DID PEOPLE USE TO EAT?

Just as the food you ate was based on your class, what you used to eat was as well. The wealthy liked to show off their gold and silver plates, while the middle classes had dishes and bowls made of pewter. Nobody used forks in sixteenth-century England—instead, people ate with knives, spoons, or their fingers. Poorer people ate with wooden spoons.

WHAT WAS A TRENCHER?

Because plates and utensils for eating were costly, many people would use a trencher, which was a slice of thick unleavened bread that served as a plate. The trencher was eventually replaced by a square piece of wood that more closely resembled a modern-day plate.

AAHCHEW!

WE WON'T HAVE TO WASH DISHES!

WHAT WERE CONQUISTADORS?

Conquistadors were soldiers and explorers who served the Portuguese and Spanish empires in the fifteenth, sixteenth, and seventeenth centuries. They conquered territory beyond Europe and established colonies in many areas of the world.

WHO WAS BALBOA?

Vasco Núñez de Balboa was born in Spain in 1475. An explorer and conquistador, Balboa led the first European expedition in the New World to the coast of the Pacific Ocean in 1513.

Who was Ferdinand Magellan?

Ferdinand Magellan was the captain of the first expedition to sail completely around the world. Magellan took five ships with him when he left Spain in 1519. A little more than a year later he found the passageway, now known as the Strait of Magellan, from the Atlantic Ocean to the Pacific Ocean at the southern tip of South America. Magellan did not realize the Pacific Ocean would be so large—he expected Asia to be just a few hundred miles from South America. Instead, he traveled 12,600 miles before reaching land.

93

WHO WAS SIR FRANCIS DRAKE?

Francis Drake was an English admiral. In 1577 he circumnavigated (sailed around) the globe. When he returned to England, Queen Elizabeth I made him a knight, and he became Sir Francis Drake.

WHAT WAS THE GOLDEN HIND?

The Golden Hind was the ship Francis Drake took on his journey around the globe.

Who was Sir Walter Raleigh?

Sir Walter Raleigh was an English explorer, soldier, and writer. He was a close friend of Queen Elizabeth I and served in her army. He was made a knight in 1585.

Who was Sir John Hawkins?

Sir John Hawkins was a cousin of Sir Francis Drake. In 1562 he became the first Englishman to trade in slaves, capturing people in western Africa and selling them in the West Indies.

What was the first English colony in America?

The first English colony in America was near Roanoke Island in what is now North Carolina. Sir Walter Raleigh founded the colony and named it Virginia.

What is scurvy?

Scurvy is an illness caused by the lack of vitamin C. It was common among sailors in the sixteenth century, who sailed for long periods of time without fresh fruit or vegetables on board. Many sailors died of scurvy.

WHAT IS AN ASTROLABE?

An astrolabe is a tool used by sailors starting in the fifteenth century. One thing the astrolabe helped them measure was the sun's angle above the horizon. The sailors would then look up the angle on a table that would tell them how far north or south of the equator they were.

Who was responsible for creating one of the first atlases?

Christopher Saxton, a cartographer, or mapmaker. He created maps of 35 counties in England and Wales. He produced the colored maps and his work set a new standard of mapmaking in Britain.

WHO WAS MARTIN LUTHER?

Martin Luther was a German monk and scholar who, in 1517, wrote a document called "Ninety-five Theses" that attacked the Catholic Church and its corrupt practice of "selling indulgences to absolve sin." Luther further developed two central beliefs: that the Bible was the foremost religious authority and that faith was more important than actions. His theories sparked the division of the Catholic Church and the Protestant Reformation. Luther's writings changed the course of religious history in the West; from them Protestantism emerged.

WHO WERE THE JESUITS?

On August 15, 1534, in Paris, France, a former soldier named Ignatius Loyola and six of his fellow university students, including Francis Xavier, created the Society of Jesus. They made vows of chastity, obedience, and poverty, and pledged to make a pilgrimage to Jerusalem. The members of this all-male Roman Catholic religious order are known as the Jesuits.

IGNATIUS LOYOLA

FRANCIS XAVIER

Who was William Tyndale?

NEW TESTAMENT OF THE BIBLE

William Tyndale was an ordained priest in England in the early 1500s. He was a strong supporter of church reform, which was very controversial. In 1525 he translated the New Testament of the Bible into English, which was strictly forbidden. He worked on a translation of the Old Testament but was put to death for doing so before it was completed. Still, his work was the starting point for all English translations of the Bible, including the King James Version of 1611.

WHAT WAS HAMPTON COURT?

Hampton Court was the most significant palace of sixteenth-century England, home to Henry VIII and other Tudor monarchs. It is located thirteen miles southwest of London on the north bank of the River Thames. The Thames is the longest river in England.

WHO WAS HENRY VIII?

Henry was the second son of King Henry VII and Elizabeth of York. After the death of his older brother, Arthur, Henry became heir to the English throne. He was crowned king when he was 18 years old. He was known to love hunting and dancing.

Who was Catherine of Aragon?

Catherine of Aragon was the daughter of Ferdinand and Isabella of Spain. She was married to Henry's brother, Arthur, before he died in 1502. Soon after becoming king, Henry VIII asked the pope to grant him special permission to marry Catherine, his brother's widow.

Why was **Henry** called the **father** of the **Royal Navy?**

When Henry became king, there were only five royal warships. By the time he died, he had built up his naval fleet to around 50 ships. He refitted several boats with guns, built the first naval dock in Britain, and established the Navy Board, which set up the administrative machinery for the control of the fleet.

Who was Anne Boleyn?

Henry VIII and Catherine of Aragon had one daughter, Mary, and no male heirs to the throne. Having a male heir to the throne was very important to Henry. When Catherine was in her forties, Henry asked an English church official, Cardinal Wolsey, to appeal to the pope for an annulment, which would have declared his marriage to Catherine over. The pope refused to annul the marriage, so Henry broke away from the Catholic Church and married the now-pregnant Anne Boleyn in a secret ceremony.

What was the Great Bible?

Henry VIII made every church purchase a copy of an English-language Bible and place it somewhere in the church for all to see and read. To meet this demand, an edition called the Great Bible was published. The Great Bible got its name because of its size.

What was a lady-in-waiting?

A lady-in-waiting was an important member of the royal court, helping the queen (or queen consort) with everything from dressing to advice. Ladies-in-waiting were selected from high-ranking noble families.

Who was Mary I?

Mary Tudor was the only child of King Henry VIII and his first wife, Catherine of Aragon. She became Queen Mary I in 1553 when she was 37 years old. She was the first queen regnant of England and Ireland. Mary was a devout Catholic. When her half-brother, Edward, died and she assumed the throne, she inherited a Protestant kingdom. Mary got rid of many of the religious rules made by her father and half-brother—the two previous kings—and replaced them with Catholic laws. During her reign a number of Protestants were tortured or killed, which made her unpopular and earned her the nickname "Bloody Mary."

Why was Queen Mary I of England called "queen regnant"?

Queen regnant meant that she was a queen reigning in her own right rather than becoming queen consort by marrying a king.

Did Mary I have any children?

Mary married Philip II, king of Spain. However, they never had children. When Mary died in 1558, her half-sister, Elizabeth, became queen.

PHILIP, KING OF SPAIN

MARY I

Who were Edward and Elizabeth?

Two of Henry VIII's children. Elizabeth was the daughter of Henry and Anne Boleyn—she eventually became Queen Elizabeth I. After Anne Boleyn, Henry married Jane Seymour, and together they had Edward, who later became King Edward VI. Jane Seymour died shortly after Edward was born.

AFTER MARY, HOW LONG DID ELIZABETH I RULE ENGLAND?

Elizabeth I ruled for 44 years, until she died in 1603. Her death ended the rule of the House of Tudor, a royal family that had ruled England since the late 1400s.

Who ruled England after Elizabeth I?

James I, the son of Elizabeth's former rival, Mary Stuart, became king of England upon Elizabeth I's death.

What was the Elizabethan Age?

The Elizabethan Age was the period during the reign of Queen Elizabeth I. It was a very prosperous and important time for England. English poetry, music, literature, and theater grew in importance, and it was a period of exploration of other countries and lands.

What was Spirits of Saturn?

Spirits of Saturn was a paste used as makeup to turn Queen Elizabeth's skin pale white. However, Spirits of Saturn, made by mixing white lead—a poison—with vinegar probably made Elizabeth quite sick.

What was the Spanish Armada?

The Spanish Armada was a navy fleet sent by King Philip II of Spain to invade England during Elizabeth I's reign. It had 130 ships, 2,500 guns, and 30,000 soldiers and sailors.

Why did King Philip II of Spain attack England in 1588?

King Philip was angry with Queen Elizabeth because she hadn't punished Sir Francis Drake and other English sailors for attacking Spanish ships. Also, after Henry VIII split from the church of Rome, King Philip felt it was his duty to convert England back to Catholicism. As many as 15,000 Spaniards died during the famous battle and its aftermath. Only about 100 English soldiers lost their lives in battle.

WHAT WAS HENRY VIII'S FAVORITE WARSHIP?

The Mary Rose, which was built in 1509 and named for Henry's favorite sister, Mary, and the Tudor emblem of the rose.

Who was James Burbage?

James Burbage built the first permanent theater for live plays in 1576. Before Burbage opened The Theatre, actors performed mainly in market squares or inn courtyards. But as plays became more popular, there became a need for venues specifically for performances. Other playhouses followed Burbage's first theater.

WHAT WERE GROUNDLINGS?

In a sixteenth- and seventeenth-century theater, the best seats were in covered galleries. Those who could afford them were protected from the weather, but poor spectators stood on the ground in the open air. They were called ground- lings. The wealthiest theater patrons got to sit in rooms above the stage!

Who is known as England's national poet?

William Shakespeare. Known as England's national poet, he has had more theatrical works performed than any other playwright.

Who was William Shakespeare?

Shakespeare was an Elizabethan Age playwright who is still considered the greatest English-speaking writer in history. He was born in Stratford-upon-Avon, a busy town 100 miles from London, in 1564. By 1592, when he was 28 years old, he had written several plays and was living in London to pursue writing and acting. Even today, Shakespeare's true identity is something not everyone can agree on. Some historians think Shakespeare was actually several authors instead of just one.

How many plays are attributed to Shakespeare?

Shakespeare wrote at least 37 plays and a collection of sonnets (poems).

ROMEO AND JULIET

OTHELLO

HAMLET

THE TEMPEST

JULIUS CAESAR

A MIDSUMMER NIGHT'S DREAM

MUCH ADO ABOUT NOTHING

WHAT WAS THE GLOBE THEATRE?

The Globe Theatre was built in 1599, assembled from wood taken from The Theatre, the first theater in London. Shakespeare was one of the co-owners of the Globe, and beginning in late 1599, it became the primary home of the acting company that employed him as actor and writer.

WHO WAS HANS LIPPERSHEY?

Hans Lippershey lived in the Netherlands in the early seventeenth century. He made eyeglasses for a living, but is often credited with inventing the first telescope in 1608. He may not have been the first person to actually make a telescope, but he was the first to make the telescope a widely known invention.

What was the Dutch East India Company?

The Dutch East India Company was founded in 1602 by the Dutch to protect their trade in the Indian Ocean. Initially granted a 21-year monopoly to pursue trading in Asia, it helped the Dutch build a powerful trading empire in the East Indies and was in business until 1799.

WHEN DID QUEEN ELIZABETH I DIE?

Queen Elizabeth I died in 1603. Because Elizabeth did not have any children of her own, King James VI of Scotland— the only son of Elizabeth's cousin, Mary I, queen of Scots—became James I, king of England, Ireland, and Scotland.

WHAT WAS THE KING JAMES BIBLE?

In 1604 the new king—James I—agreed to honor the English people's request for an official translation of the Bible. This translation, known as the King James Bible, took the place of three other English versions: The Geneva Bible, the Great Bible, and the Bishops' Bible.

Who was Rembrandt?

Rembrandt van Rijn, born in 1606, was a seventeenth-century Dutch painter and artist. He is best known for his scenes from the Bible and for portraits, including self-portraits, as well as his unique use of shadow and light.

What was Jamestown?

Jamestown was the first permanent English colony to be settled in America. It was founded in Virginia in 1607, 13 years before the Pilgrims landed at Plymouth in Massachusetts.

What was the Virginia Company of London?

The Virginia Company of London was a group of investors who sponsored the expedition to Jamestown. It was formed in 1606 under the direction of King James I.

What were the names of the ships that first sailed to Jamestown?

The Susan Constant,
the Godspeed,
and the Discovery
left England for Jamestown
in December 1606.

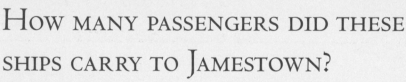

JAMESTOWN

THAT'S THE SUSAN CONSTANT.

THE GODSPEED AND DISCOVERY ARE FOLLOWING!

HOW MANY PASSENGERS DID THESE SHIPS CARRY TO JAMESTOWN?

One hundred and five passengers departed England on the Susan Constant, the Godspeed, and the Discovery, but one of them died during the voyage.

ALL ABOARD!

THEY ARE ALL OFF TO JAMESTOWN.

WHEN DID THE SHIPS ARRIVE IN JAMESTOWN?

The three ships left England in December 1606 and reached the Virginia coast in late April 1607.

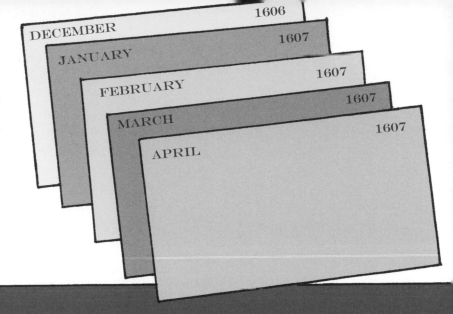

DECEMBER 1606

JANUARY 1607

FEBRUARY 1607

MARCH 1607

APRIL 1607

WHO WAS CAPTAIN CHRISTOPHER NEWPORT?

Captain Christopher Newport led the expedition to Jamestown.

When did the first women arrive in Jamestown?

Two Englishwomen arrived in Jamestown in 1608. While more followed in later years, men outnumbered women in Jamestown for most of the seventeenth century.

Who was Captain John Smith?

Captain John Smith became the leader of Jamestown in September 1608. He established a "no work, no food" policy to encourage the upper-class Englishmen who settled Jamestown to help with the labor and farming necessary to run the colony. He traded with the Powhatan for food. He was injured in the fall of 1609 and left Jamestown for England. He later returned to the New World, exploring the New England coast, but never returned to Virginia.

WHO WAS POWHATAN?

Powhatan was the leader of a group of Algonquian-speaking Native American tribes: his people were also called the Powhatan. Jamestown was established in Powhatan's territory. This caused a lot of tension between the English settlers and the native people. even though they did trade with each other.

What was the "starving time"?

The "starving time" was a period after John Smith left Jamestown to go back to England. The English colonists and the Powhatan fought a series of skirmishes, and the native people stopped bringing food supplies to the colony. Most of the settlers died of disease and starvation. The starving time ended when a group of new settlers arrived in Jamestown with supplies and set up a stronger government.

How did the colonists make money?

Having failed to find the gold that was supposed to make a profit for the Virginia Company, the settlers tried glassmaking, lumber production, and other industries. But it wasn't until the settlers began growing tobacco (first planted in 1612) that they found a profitable trade, and the colony developed quickly. Tobacco was considered a "cash crop"—it was easy to grow and ship back to England, and it made money for the settlement.

What was the House of Burgesses?

The House of Burgesses was the first legislature in the English colonies. It first met on July 30, 1619, at a church in Jamestown. The first item the House of Burgesses discussed was the minimum price of tobacco.

Who was John Rolfe?

John Rolfe was one of the English colonists who came to Jamestown in 1610, and was the first to grow tobacco there. In 1614 Rolfe married Powhatan's daughter, Matoaka—who was better known by her nickname, Pocahontas. Pocahontas had been kidnapped by the English settlers and had converted to Christianity before she married John Rolfe. They had one son before Pocahontas died on a trip to England.

HOW WAS THE HOUSE OF BURGESSES ORGANIZED?

The House of Burgesses was a representative government: Its 22 members were elected by voters; only men over the age of 17 who owned land in the colony could vote. There were also six councillors and a governor. The Virginia Company originally appointed the governor, but later England took more control in Virginia, restricting the powers of the House of Burgesses.

Who was Samuel de Champlain?

Samuel de Champlain was a French explorer. He began exploring North America in the early seventeenth century and established the city of Quebec in New France, which today is known as Canada.

Who was Henry Hudson?

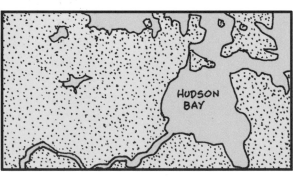

HUDSON BAY

Henry Hudson was an English explorer. He made two unsuccessful sailing voyages in search of an ice-free passage through the Arctic Ocean to Asia. On his third voyage, he made it to North America and sailed up the Hudson River, and on his fourth voyage, he found a large body of water in Canada, which later was named Hudson Bay.

WHAT HAPPENED IN LONDON IN 1666?

The Great Fire of London tore through the City district in early September 1666, destroying much of the municipal center and thousands of homes. It came less than a year after a plague had killed thousands of Londoners.

WHERE DID THE GREAT FIRE OF LONDON START?

The Great Fire of London started in a bakery on—strangely enough—Pudding Lane.

WHAT STARTED THE GREAT FIRE OF LONDON?

Thomas Farynor, the king's baker, insisted that he'd put out his ovens at the end of the working day, but somehow his house—which was made of wood, like most houses at that time—ignited during the night of September 2, 1666. Once the fire started, it spread quickly thanks to wind and a sustained drought.

What was King Charles II's response to the fire?

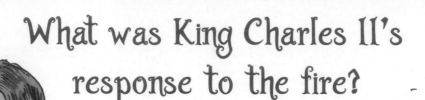

The king had been criticized for leaving London during the plague, but he stayed during the fire. He wanted to save the city, so he ordered firebreaks. To make these required knocking down good buildings in order to starve the fire of the wood it needed to keep burning. Charles also ordered stores of food that were being saved for the Royal Navy to be given to people who were fleeing the city to escape the fire.

How HOT was the heat from the fire?

It is said that the heat created by the fire was so great that it melted the lead roof of the old Saint Paul's Cathedral. People said they saw the lead flowing through the streets. As hot and as big as the fire was, only six people are recorded to have died in the inferno, though many historians doubt that number.

How was the fire eventually extinguished?

The wind that helped fan the Great Fire of London turned, sending the flames back toward areas already burned. When the fire had nothing left to burn, it eventually died out.

WHO WAS CHRISTOPHER WREN?

Christopher Wren was an architect who lived in London in the seventeenth century. When the Great Fire of London destroyed much of the city district, he drew up plans to rebuild the whole area. While those plans initially were rejected, Christopher Wren did oversee the design of 52 new churches in the city, as well as the famous replacement of Saint Paul's Cathedral. In 1669 he became the king's surveyor and had an overseeing role in London's rebuilding; he was made a knight in 1673.

Who was Mother Goose?

Nobody knows if Mother Goose really existed. In 1697, French author Charles Perrault published a collection of fairy stories—including *Little Red Riding Hood* and *Blue Beard*—that had the subtitle, *Tales of My Mother Goose*.

What famous nursery rhyme may be related to the Great Plague that hit London in 1664?

Some folklore scholars think the song "Ring around the Rosie," or "Ring-a-Ring of Roses," details the symptoms of the plague that swept through London from late 1664 to 1666. They say the first line (and title) of the poem refers to red, rash-type blotches that were seen on the skin of people with the plague. The second line ("a pocket full of posies") refers to the belief that scented flowers could overpower plague germs, which people thought were spread by a poisonous gas that floated through the air. These scholars say the last lines—"Ashes! Ashes! We all fall down!"—refer to the final stages of the plague: a sneezing fit that led to the person's death.

What were plague doctors?

Plague doctors—some of whom were not trained doctors at all—went from house to house to assess whether the people inside had the plague. Many traditional doctors had fled London for their own safety, so these plague doctors were in charge of deciding whether to chain a home shut to protect the city from the diseased people inside. A red cross would then be painted on the door, and the people inside wouldn't be allowed outside for 40 days.

How was English society organized in the seventeenth century?

At the top of English society were the nobility, and below them were the gentry, made up of gentlemen and their families. Below them were yeomen—farmers who owned their own land. Below the yeomen was the rest of the population, made up of tradespeople, craftsmen, tenant farmers (who did not own their own land), and laborers.

What was a hackney carriage?

People in the seventeenth century still used their feet as transportation most of the time and usually walked to places. But starting in the early 1600s, if they could afford it, they could hire a horse-drawn carriage called a hackney carriage to ferry them around.

What new types of furniture were introduced in the seventeenth century?

In the mid-seventeenth century, chests of drawers (what we sometimes call dressers) were introduced in London, and the grandfather clock (then called a longcase clock) was invented in 1670. Later in the century the kind of bookcase still used today was introduced. Chairs also became more comfortable—upholstered chairs and armchairs became popular.

STORE IT IN HERE!

HAVE A SEAT!

WHERE'S THE BABY?

TICK-TOCK-TICK-TOCK!

I'M THE FIRST MOUSE THAT RAN UP THE CLOCK!

What was *The Ladies Mercury?*

The Ladies Mercury is considered the first women's magazine, published in 1693. It was only a single sheet and lasted just four issues.

WHEN DID MAIL SERVICE START IN ENGLAND?

Established in 1516, the royal post was initially used only to carry mail for the monarchy. However, beginning in 1635, King Charles I allowed anyone to use his messengers to deliver mail, with the postage paid by the recipient. He did this to raise money, and it became the start of the Royal Mail's public letter service.

What were turnpike roads?

In 1663, turnpike roads opened in England. They were roads that people had to pay to use; the money was used to maintain the roads.

Who was William Harvey?

William Harvey was an English physician who was the first to correctly explain how blood circulates through the body and the role the heart has in that process.

Who was El Greco?

El Greco was a Greek-born artist who lived in Spain and whose painting helped define the Spanish Renaissance. Some of his works seem to foreshadow the much later art styles Expressionism and Cubism—both of which distort reality. El Greco influenced other artists for years after his death.

Who were the Pilgrims?

The Pilgrims were part of a group of people who left England on a sailing ship in the seventeenth century to escape religious persecution, or punishment for their spiritual beliefs.

Where did the Pilgrims sail?

After leaving Plymouth, England, on September 16, 1620, the Pilgrims' ship reached Plymouth Harbor, just west of what today is Cape Cod, Massachusetts, on December 21, 1620.

How long did it take to sail from England to Plymouth Harbor?

It took 66 days for the Pilgrims to sail across the Atlantic. They first stopped at what is now Provincetown, on the tip of Cape Cod. A little over a month later they arrived in Plymouth Harbor.

Why were the Pilgrims called "Separatists"?

The Pilgrims were Separatists from the Church of England, which means they had different beliefs from most of the English people. In 1606, some of the earliest known of these Separatists formed their own church in a small village in England named Scrooby.

What was the Church of England?

The Church of England became the national religion of England after Henry VIII broke off relations with the Roman Catholic Church. It was overseen by the government, so in the Pilgrims' time, King James I was the head of both the country and the church. That meant if a group of people, like the Separatists, didn't go to their local Church of England services they were disobeying the king, and this was considered treason.

WHO WAS JOHN ROBINSON?

John Robinson was the Pilgrims' pastor before part of the group sailed to Plymouth Harbor. A group of the Separatists, including John Robinson, had gone to Holland in 1608. But the Pilgrims were poor in Holland, making barely enough money to survive. So even though they had religious freedom, a group of them decided to leave Holland (and Robinson) behind 12 years later and sail to North America.

Why didn't the Pilgrims just sail to Jamestown and join the Jamestown colony?

The Pilgrims may have been afraid the English people who lived in Jamestown wouldn't accept them because of their religious beliefs. Instead, they were given a grant to settle an area on the Hudson River, near what is now New York City. In Holland they were able to raise enough money for a small ship, called the Speedwell, which they used to sail back to England to meet with other people also going to the new colony.

What was the Mayflower?

When the Pilgrims returned to England, they planned to sail to the colony in the Speedwell in the company of a bigger ship called the Mayflower. The Speedwell proved unseaworthy, and the Mayflower was the ship that eventually brought the Pilgrims and several dozen other people to America. It left England on September 16, 1620, with 102 passengers. In the 66 days it took to make the first leg of the voyage, two people died and one person was born. Even though these colonists had been given land in the northern part of the Virginia Colony (an area now in New York), rough seas changed their course, and the Mayflower made landfall in what is now Massachusetts.

What was the Mayflower Compact?

The Mayflower Compact was a document signed by forty-one male passengers of the Mayflower on November 21, 1620. This agreement framed a temporary government, and by signing it the 41 men agreed to be bound by its laws. The Mayflower Compact became the basis of government for the Plymouth Colony.

WHO WAS WILLIAM BRADFORD?

William Bradford was one of the original leaders of the Plymouth Colony. He was first elected governor of the colony in 1621 and was reelected 30 times. He may have been the first person to call the Separatists "Pilgrims." He wrote a book called *Of Plymouth Plantation* that is one of the most important histories of the settling of New England.

WHAT WAS THE FIRST WINTER LIKE IN THE PLYMOUTH COLONY?

The first winter in the Plymouth Colony was brutally hard, and more than 40 people died.

WHO LIVED IN PLYMOUTH BEFORE THE PILGRIMS?

The native inhabitants of the Plymouth Colony area were tribes of the native Wampanoag people, who had lived in the region for thousands of years before the Europeans arrived.

WHO WAS SAMOSET?

Samoset was a Native American who, when he first met the Plymouth colonists, said "Greetings, Englishmen." He had learned to speak English from English fishermen who had fished off the coast of his native land in Maine.

WHO WAS SQUANTO?

Like Samoset, Squanto was an English-speaking Native American who befriended the Plymouth colonists and eventually taught them how to grow food.

Who was Massasoit?

Massasoit was the chief of the Wampanoag tribe of Native Americans. Samoset introduced him to the Plymouth colonists. Massasoit and the colonists made a peace treaty that lasted for 50 years.

123

What did the **Native Americans** teach the **Plymouth colonists?**

The most important thing the Native Americans taught the settlers was how to grow squash, corn, and beans. They also showed the newcomers how to get sap from maple trees and where to fish and hunt beaver.

When was the first **Thanksgiving?**

In the autumn of 1621, after the Plymouth colonists' first successful corn harvest, a group of Native Americans joined them in a feast and celebration that lasted for three days. While nobody knows exactly what was served at this meal shared with the native people, historians think many of the dishes were prepared using traditional Wampanoag spices and cooking techniques.

Was there pumpkin pie at the first **Thanksgiving?**

Probably not. The settlers would not have had butter or wheat flour for a crust. And by the fall of 1621, the Mayflower's supply of sugar was running out, so the first Thanksgiving likely did not feature desserts, as today's meal does.

How many people participated in the first Thanksgiving feast?

Fifty-three colonists and ninety Wampanoag attended the first Thanksgiving feast.

WHAT DID THE PILGRIMS WEAR?

Pilgrims are depicted wearing buckles on their shoes and pointy hats, and white and black clothing. But buckles didn't come into fashion until later in the seventeenth century. Unless it was a special occasion, at which time black and white clothing would be acceptable, women typically wore red, dark green, brown, blue, violet, or gray, while men wore clothes that were white, beige, black, dark green, or brown.

What were the original 13 colonies?

The original 13 colonies, which eventually came together to form the United States, are:

New Hampshire
Massachusetts
Connecticut
Rhode Island
New York
New Jersey
Pennsylvania
Delaware
Maryland
Virginia
North Carolina
South Carolina
Georgia

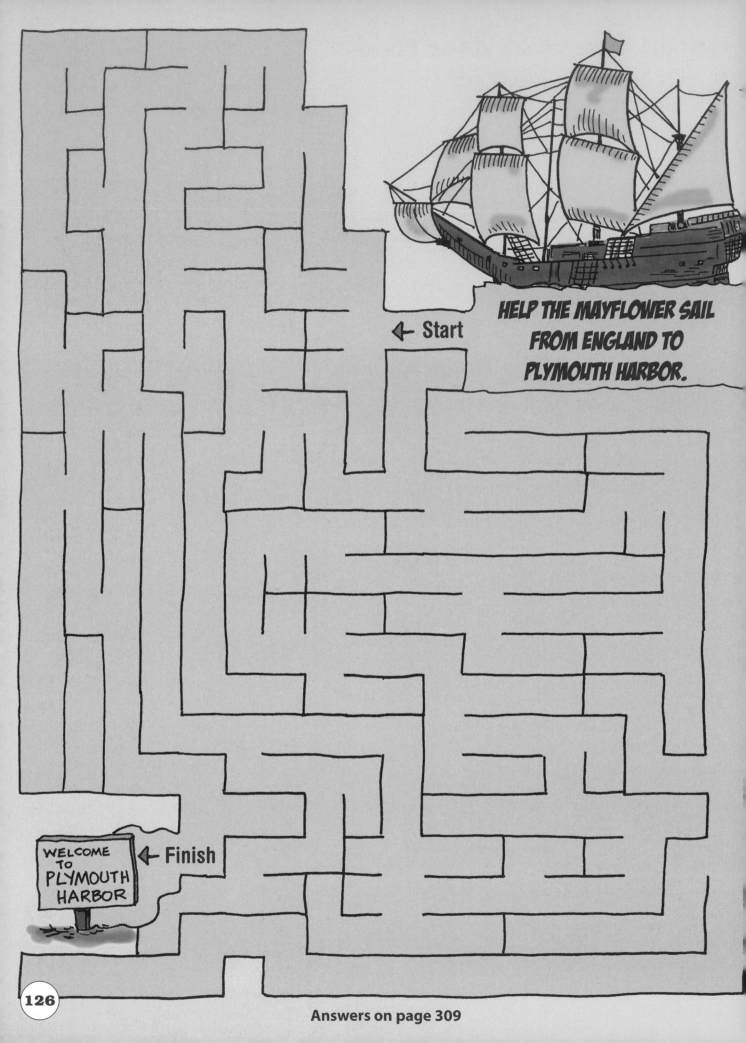

← Start

HELP THE MAYFLOWER SAIL FROM ENGLAND TO PLYMOUTH HARBOR.

WELCOME TO PLYMOUTH HARBOR

← Finish

Why did England decide to colonize North America, starting with the 13 colonies?

England sponsored voyages to colonize North America for financial reasons—the English hoped to find new sources of income in these new lands. They also hoped to counterbalance the expansion of other European nations abroad, and convert the native peoples to the Anglican religion (the Church of England).

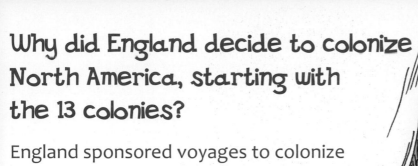

I MUST HAVE THOSE COLONIES!

HOW WERE THE COLONIES NAMED?

Many of the colonies were named for people. Maryland was named for Henrietta Maria, the wife of King Charles I. In 1664, England captured the territory between New England and Virginia from the Dutch (who called it New Netherland) and named it for King Charles II's brother, the duke of York. In 1680, the king granted land west of the Delaware River to William Penn, who named the colony "Penn's Woods," or Pennsylvania.

NEW YORK

PENNSYLVANIA

MARYLAND

Who was Miguel de Cervantes?

Miguel de Cervantes was one of Spain's most famous writers, and he created one of the world's greatest literary works—*Don Quixote*—in the early 1600s. *Don Quixote* tells the story of an elderly man who is so passionate about stories of brave knights that he sets out on his own adventures. Quixote gets so caught up in his fantasy that he convinces a poor peasant, Sancho Panza, to serve as his squire.

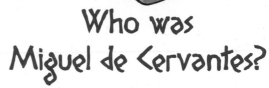

WHEN WAS THE THIRTY YEARS' WAR?

The Thirty Years' War took place from 1618 to 1648.

Why did the Thirty Years' War begin?

The Thirty Years' War began when Ferdinand II, who was the Holy Roman emperor as well as the king of Bohemia, tried to limit the religious activities of his Protestant subjects and force Catholicism on them, which caused them to rebel.

WHICH COUNTRIES WERE INVOLVED IN THE THIRTY YEARS' WAR?

The war involved the major powers of Europe at the time—including Sweden, France, Spain, and Austria. Most of the battles took place on what is now German soil.

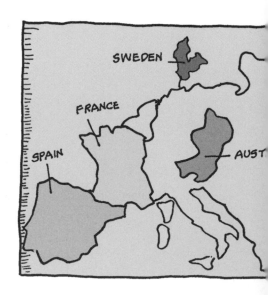

HOW DID THE THIRTY YEARS' WAR END?

The Thirty Years' War ended with a series of treaties called the Peace of Westphalia. Over its thirty years, the war reshaped the religion, politics, and power structure of Europe.

Peace of Westphalia

WHO WAS THE SUN KING?

France's Louis XIV was known as the Sun King. His reign lasted for 72 years, longer than the reign of any other king. In the time he ruled France, he presided over a golden age of art and literature, a large and glamorous court at the Palace of Versailles, and turned France into the dominant European power.

WHY WAS Louis XIV CALLED THE Sun King?

Louis XIV viewed himself as the direct representative of God, given a divine right to rule with absolute power—meaning he didn't want or need any help ruling the monarchy. He chose the sun as his symbol, implying that the entire realm orbited around him.

129

WHAT WAS VERSAILLES?

Versailles was Louis XIV's lavish palace, which is located about 14 miles southwest of Paris. It was known for its gardens, hall of mirrors, and stables that could house 2,000 horses!

Who was Robert LaSalle?

French explorer Robert LaSalle was born René-Robert Cavelier, Sieur de La Salle. He led an expedition down the Illinois and Mississippi Rivers, claiming the region for France. He named it Louisiana after King Louis XIV.

WHO WAS PETER THE GREAT?

Peter the Great was a Russian czar in the late seventeenth and early eighteenth centuries. He is known for his efforts to establish Russia as a great nation—he formed a strong navy, reorganized the army, reorganized schools, and exercised greater control over the Orthodox Church of Russia.

I'M GREAT... HOW ARE YOU?

When did the Salem witch trials begin?

The Salem witch trials began during the spring of 1692, after a group of young girls in Salem Village, Massachusetts, claimed to be possessed by the devil and accused several local women of witchcraft.

Who were Elizabeth (Betty) Parris and Abigail Williams?

In January 1692, nine-year-old Elizabeth (Betty) Parris and eleven-year-old Abigail Williams began experiencing violent fits that contorted their bodies and having uncontrollable outbursts of screaming. A local doctor diagnosed bewitchment.

WHO WAS BRIDGET BISHOP?

Bridget Bishop was the first person convicted by a special court that convened in Salem to hear the witch trials. She was hanged in June 1692.

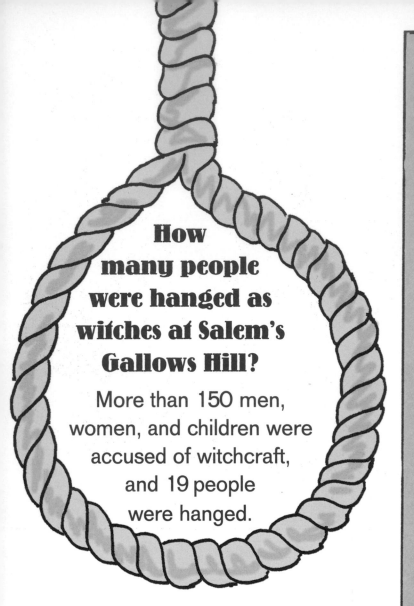

How many people were hanged as witches at Salem's Gallows Hill?

More than 150 men, women, and children were accused of witchcraft, and 19 people were hanged.

When was the first university in the United States founded?

Established in 1636 by vote of the Great and General Court of the Massachusetts Bay Colony, Harvard University is the oldest institution of higher learning in the United States.

WHO IS HARVARD UNIVERSITY NAMED FOR?

Harvard is named for John Harvard of Charlestown, the university's first benefactor, who left his library and half his estate to the institution when he died in 1638.

WHO WERE WILLIAM AND MARY?

King William III and Queen Mary II ruled England in the late seventeenth century. They signed a charter for a "perpetual College of Divinity, Philosophy, Languages and other good Arts and Sciences" to be founded in the Virginia Colony. The College of William and Mary was formed; it is the second-oldest college in America.

Who was Daniel Defoe?

Born in the seventeenth century, Daniel Defoe was an English novelist, pamphlet writer, and journalist best known for his novels, including *Robinson Crusoe*, which was based on several short essays he had written over the years.

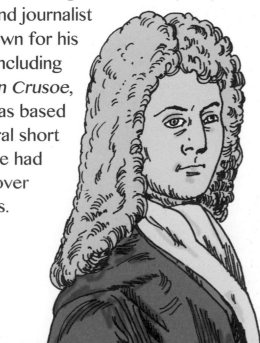

Who was Sir Isaac Newton?

Isaac Newton was an English physicist and mathematician. He was an important participant in the scientific revolution of the seventeenth century.

What did Sir Isaac Newton discover?

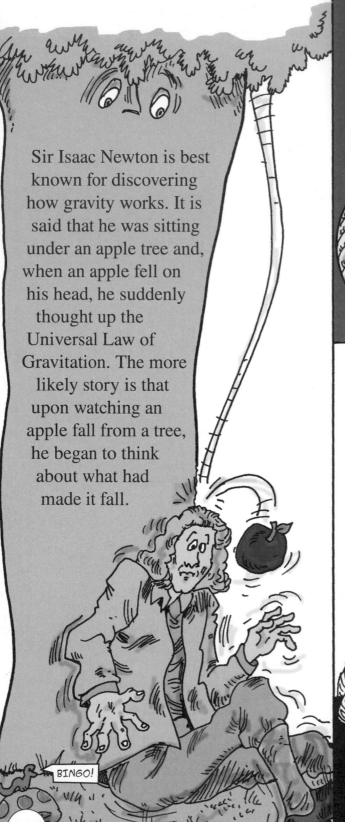

Sir Isaac Newton is best known for discovering how gravity works. It is said that he was sitting under an apple tree and, when an apple fell on his head, he suddenly thought up the Universal Law of Gravitation. The more likely story is that upon watching an apple fall from a tree, he began to think about what had made it fall.

BINGO!

Who was Johann Sebastian Bach?

Johann Sebastian Bach was a German musical composer. He composed classical music that is known for how complex and innovative it is.

Who was George Handel?

Like Bach, George Handel was a German musical composer born in the seventeenth century. He is best known for *Messiah*, which is an oratorio (a large concert piece with a sacred or religious theme). Handel composed both oratorios and music in another popular format, the opera.

SEVENTEENTH CENTURY
WORD SEARCH

Search for the seventeenth century words listed below.
Cirlcle horizontally, vertically, backwards, or diagonally
as you find each word.

```
P  M  J  C  H  R  S  A  T  N  O  H  A  C  O  P  E  E  U
V  E  R  S  A  I  L  L  E  S  U  M  A  R  Y  S  R  O  M
L  L  K  P  L  A  G  U  E  M  K  V  D  N  C  A  C  Y  A
F  A  O  U  L  Q  B  A  C  H  Z  E  X  Y  E  X  I  V  Y
X  S  S  Q  E  B  N  A  T  A  H  W  O  P  X  K  U  R  F
Y  Z  J  M  K  T  N  O  S  D  U  H  S  O  J  H  Q  U  L
M  R  L  Q  I  R  H  P  P  S  E  E  Q  O  C  T  H  C  O
X  B  E  Z  W  R  B  A  N  N  K  N  R  V  B  E  T  S  W
S  X  D  Q  K  T  G  W  N  A  O  L  R  Q  I  B  U  H  E
Q  C  N  O  K  E  O  L  H  K  O  T  C  O  V  A  O  Z  R
U  C  A  L  W  T  J  S  I  N  S  M  W  H  S  Z  M  P  H
A  J  H  P  D  A  T  U  D  P  N  G  B  E  Z  I  Y  K  K
N  D  I  E  M  N  V  O  N  J  S  U  I  L  N  L  L  W  N
T  Y  M  E  V  M  N  E  G  H  Z  A  P  V  X  E  P  Y  V
O  A  S  J  T  W  Y  N  O  L  O  C  Y  T  I  O  S  O  I
W  A  T  G  I  O  H  B  X  Y  V  D  W  W  T  N  I  Z  Y
V  L  X  O  G  C  H  Q  V  W  Z  I  J  Z  O  M  G  G  R
H  A  R  V  A  R  D  Q  O  V  Y  I  L  N  X  L  J  L  E
T  H  B  C  I  K  X  N  Q  J  A  M  E  S  T  O  W  N  N
```

BACH	HUDSON	NEWTON	SCURVY
COLONY	JAMES	PILGRIMS	SHAKESPEARE
ELIZABETH	JAMESTOWN	PLYMOUTH	SQUANTO
HANDEL	LONDON	POCAHONTAS	THANKSGIVING
HARVARD	MARY	POWHATAN	VERSAILLES
	MAYFLOWER	SALEM	

Answers on page 310

What was the population of Britain's American colonies in 1700?

The population of the British colonies in America in 1700 was probably between 250,000 and 275,000 people.

What was the **largest city** in the **American colonies** at the beginning of the **eighteenth century?**

Boston, with a total of about 7,000 inhabitants.

IT'S NOT OVER TILL IT'S OVER!

BOSTON WILL HAVE THREE PRO-TEAMS, SOON!

What were common jobs for people to have in the colonies?

Many people held jobs as blacksmiths, farmers, shoemakers, tailors, wheelwrights, cloth-makers, and printers. Everybody had to work in the colonies—it was considered a sin to be lazy.

HELP WANTED

A cooper performed a common job in the eighteenth century. Coopers made barrels for storing food, drink, and other items.

WHAT WAS A COOPER?

What was a schoolmaster?

In colonial days, a teacher was usually a man and was called a schoolmaster. Children attended Latin school and common school, where they learned to read and write.

What was a mobcap?

A mobcap was a pleated cloth bonnet with a ruffled brim that eighteenth-century women wore indoors. The mobcap protected their hair from dirt and dust, smoke from fireplaces, and grease from cooking. Women always wore hats while out in public.

137

Why did eighteenth-century men POWDER their WIGS?

Wealthy men in the eighteenth century wore wigs, most of which were made from goat or horse hair. They were never properly washed, so they often smelled bad and attracted lice. To get rid of the smell and bugs, men would use "powder" made of cornstarch and lavender in the wigs.

WHAT WERE WISKETS AND FROCK COATS?

A wisket was a waistcoat, which was a staple in the wardrobe of eighteenth-century men. The waistcoat was a sleeveless garment— like a vest—worn over a dress shirt. These were worn underneath a frock coat, which typically reached down to the knees.

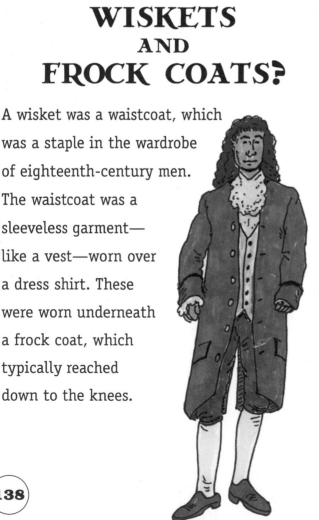

WHAT WAS A TRICORNE HAT?

A tricorne was a hat style worn by eighteenth-century men; it had turned up parts that shaded the wearer from the sun and also directed water away from the face when it rained. Tricornes were made from felt or beaver fur.

When did the AMERICAN COLONIES develop their own CURRENCY?

While still under British control, the colonists illegally opened a mint to make their own money. This first colonial mint was established in Boston, Massachusetts, in 1652.

What was Continental Currency?

Continental Currency was paper money issued in the colonies during the American Revolution, when the colonies fought to liberate themselves from British restrictions related to money.

When was the first bank chartered?

The First Bank of the United States was chartered in 1791 in Philadelphia. The bank, and the Coinage Act of 1792, established the start of the national American currency. Eventually it ended the practice of each state minting and using its own form of money.

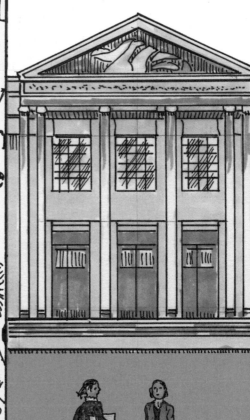

139

What was the New-England Primer?

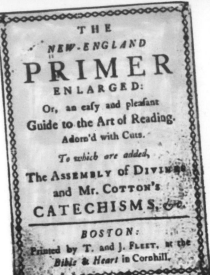

The New-England Primer was the book from which many eighteenth-century children in the colonies learned to read. It had a rhyme for each letter of the alphabet.

WHAT WAS QUEEN ANNE'S WAR?

Queen Anne's War started in 1702 and lasted for a decade; it was the second war in a series of wars fought between Great Britain and France in North America for control of the continent. After the British captured important French strongholds, Britain took control of Nova Scotia, Newfoundland, and the Hudson Bay (all in Canada) from France.

What was the Boston News-Letter?

The Boston News-Letter was the first successful newspaper in the colonies. It was first published on April 24, 1704.

Which state banned travel on Sunday?

Connecticut! In colonial Connecticut, travel on Sunday was prohibited unless you were traveling to attend church services.

WHAT WAS THE MOLASSES ACT?

The Molasses Act, a British law passed in 1733, forced the American colonists to pay heavy taxes on rum and molasses imported from the French and Spanish West Indies.

Who was John Peter Zenger?

John Peter Zenger was publisher of the *New York Weekly Journal*. In 1734, he was accused of libel, which means publishing statements about someone that are false and designed to hurt their reputation. He was acquitted (found not guilty), and his trial helped to establish the principle of freedom of the press in America.

Who was James Oglethorpe?

James Oglethorpe was a Londoner who served in the British Parliament before traveling to America and founding Savannah in 1733, the colony that later would become Georgia. In 1735, Georgia became the only one of the original 13 colonies to prohibit slavery.

WHEN DID THE U.S. SUPREME COURT FIRST CONVENE?

The first session of the U.S. Supreme Court convened in 1790.

What tradition ended when Justice William Cushing took the bench during the U.S. Supreme Court's first session?

HA-HA-HA-HA!

Wearing a wig! Just as England's judges had done, Justice Cushing took the bench during the first session of the U.S. Supreme Court wearing a fancy powdered wig. He was teased so much he stopped wearing his wig, ending that tradition.

I STILL LIKE MYSELF BETTER WITH A WIG!

How much was a U.S. Supreme Court justice paid?

In 1789, the chief justice's yearly salary was $4,000. Associate justices made $3,500. (In 2010, the chief justice earned $223,500 a year, while the associate justices got $213,900!)

WHO WAS BE JAMIN FRANKLI ?

Benjamin Franklin was an American Founding Father who was born in the early eighteenth century in Boston and was interested in electricity, mathematics, printing, and mapmaking. He organized America's first library for lending books to people, and one of the first volunteer fire departments. Additionally, he helped to draft the Declaration of Independence and the U.S. Constitution.

What did Benjamin Franklin show by using a kite?

In 1752, Benjamin Franklin flew a kite during a thunderstorm, demonstrating that lightning is a form of electricity.

What was the Treaty of Paris?

The Treaty of Paris, signed in 1763, ended the Seven Years' War, often called the French and Indian War in the United States. Under this treaty, France officially gave control of Canada to Britain.

WHAT WAS THE STAMP ACT OF 1765?

The Stamp Act was imposed on the colonies by British Parliament and placed a tax on newspapers, legal documents, playing cards, dice, almanacs, and pamphlets. This started the movement against "taxation without representation."

What did the colonists mean when they said "no taxation without representation"?

Many colonists believed that because they had no members in British Parliament, which governed from England while they were in North America, any laws Parliament passed taxing the colonists (like the Sugar Act and the Stamp Act) were illegal. Taxation without representation was one of the issues that started the American Revolution.

WHAT WAS THE QUARTERING ACT?

The Quartering Act required colonists to provide food and lodging to British troops stationed in the colonies.

Who was Patrick Henry?

Patrick Henry was an influential American speaker and leader who outwardly opposed the British government. He helped draft the U.S. Bill of Rights and is best known for his quote, "Give me liberty or give me death!"

What was the Stamp Act Congress?

The Sons of Liberty were colonists who opposed the Stamp Act and other British laws. A few of them were part of the Stamp Act Congress, which was made up of delegates from nine of the colonies. They met in New York to organize a united response to the Stamp Act. The Stamp Act Congress sent a Declaration of Rights and Grievances to the British governing powers. Eventually the British government repealed the Stamp Act.

Who was Daniel Boone?

Daniel Boone led an expedition to forge a trail to the west through the Cumberland Gap, which is a pass through the Cumberland Plateau in the Appalachian Mountains, near the area where Tennessee, Kentucky, and Virginia meet. He settled an area he called Boonesborough in Kentucky.

Who was the first Postmaster General of the United States?

Benjamin Franklin.

What was the Declaratory Act?

The same day the British government called off the Stamp Act it passed the Declaratory Act, which stated that British Parliament had the right to make laws and tax the colonies. When the colonists protested the Stamp Act, they boycotted many British imports, which hurt British merchants and businesses. Parliament repealed the Stamp Act but wanted to send a message to the colonies with the Declaratory Act that the British government still had the right to tax them.

What was the
Tea Act?

The Tea Act said the colonies could buy tea from only one company, the East India Trading Company, and they had to pay high taxes on this tea. In the eighteenth century people drank a lot of tea. It was, therefore, a major source of income for the East India Trading Company, which was a British company. The Tea Act was one of the reasons the Boston Tea Party happened.

When was the
Boston Tea Party?

The Boston Tea Party took place on December 16, 1773, and it was one of the key events that led to the American Revolution.

What was the
Boston Tea Party?

The Boston Tea Party was a protest by American colonists against taxes imposed by the British government—it wasn't really a party at all. Colonists boarded three trade ships in Boston Harbor and threw the ships' cargo of tea overboard into the water. Some of the colonists dressed as Mohawk Indians to disguise themselves.

How much tea was *thrown* overboard?

Three hundred and forty-two chests of tea carried by the ships named the Dartmouth, the Eleanor, and the Beaver, were thrown overboard. It was about 90,000 pounds of tea and in today's money would be worth about $1.7 million!

THE BEAVER IS COMING!

THIS IS THE DARTMOUTH!

THIS IS THE ELEANOR!

WHO WAS SAMUEL ADAMS?

Samuel Adams was a member of the Massachusetts colonial government who helped organize opposition to the Stamp Act and the Tea Act, and influenced the Boston Tea Party. He also was selected to represent Massachusetts at the First Continental Congress.

What was the First Continental Congress?

The First Continental Congress was a meeting in 1774 of delegates from 12 of the 13 colonies (all except Georgia). They discussed their relationship with Britain and the Intolerable Acts, which the British Parliament had imposed on Boston as punishment for the Boston Tea Party.

Who was the First Commanding General of the Continental Army?

The Second Continental Congress, which met in 1775, established the Continental Army and named George Washington as the first commanding general.

What bird is the symbol of the United States?

The American bald eagle is the national bird and appears on the U.S. seal, designed in 1782. Ben Franklin later said that the turkey would have been a better choice.

I WOULD MAKE A SILLY SYMBOL!

Who was John Adams?

John Adams was one of the Founding Fathers of the United States and was the second U.S. president. He was a Massachusetts delegate to the Continental Congress, he fought for American independence, and he was a member of the group who worked on the Declaration of Independence. He and Thomas Jefferson were the only two signers of the declaration to become president.

Who was Thomas Jefferson?

Thomas Jefferson was the third president of the United States. He is known as a Founding Father of the United States, and was the main author of the Declaration of Independence.

What is Monticello?

Monticello was Thomas Jefferson's home, which he built and rebuilt over the course of four decades. Monticello is located in Albemarle County, Virginia, near where he was born. When he was 21, Jefferson inherited several thousand acres of land on his family's estate. This included a small hilltop he called Monticello (Italian for "little mountain"), and several years later he decided to build his home there.

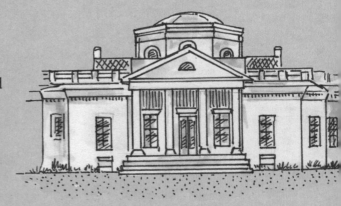

What is **important about Thomas Jefferson's book collection?**

Thomas Jefferson's books started a new collection at the Library of Congress after its original collection of books was destroyed in the War of 1812. Jefferson was in debt, so the U.S. Congress bought his collection, which totaled about 6,500 books.

What was the Committee of Five?

The Committee of Five was tasked in 1776 with writing a document explaining why the American colonies were declaring independence from Britain. This document was later called the Declaration of Independence. The five members were Benjamin Franklin, John Adams, Robert Livingston, Roger Sherman, and Thomas Jefferson, who was selected to write the first draft.

When was the Declaration of Independence presented?

The Committee of Five presented the original declaration to the Continental Congress on June 28, 1776. After a year of fighting between the 13 colonies and the British, the Second Continental Congress decided it was time for the colonies to officially declare their independence and break away from British rule. The Declaration of Independence was officially accepted a few days later.

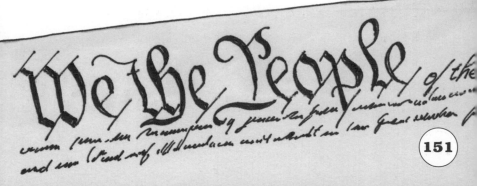

What did the *Declaration of Independence* say?

The Declaration of Independence explained why the colonies wanted freedom and listed the unjust things the British king had done to the colonies. One of the most notable statements in history can be found in the Declaration of Independence:

We hold these truths to be self-evident, that all men are created equal, that they are endowed by their Creator with certain unalienable Rights, that among these are Life, Liberty and the pursuit of Happiness.

On what day did Congress adopt the Declaration of Independence?

July 4, 1776— a day the United States still celebrates as Independence Day.

WHAT WAS THE BOSTON MASSACRE?

In March 1770, British troops fired their weapons at a group of men and boys throwing snowballs at them. Three people in the crowd—Crispus Attucks, James Caldwell, and Samuel Gray—were killed, and two other men who were injured later died. John Adams, who was a lawyer, defended the soldiers when they went to court, saying that the crowd had started the fight with the soldiers and the soldiers had a right to defend themselves.

WHAT WAS THE FLAG RESOLUTION?

In 1777, the Second Continental Congress passed the Flag Resolution, describing the flag that would represent the 13 newly united states. The Flag Resolution was passed on June 14, which is celebrated today as Flag Day, and said the U.S. flag would have 13 red and white alternating stripes and that there would be a blue area with 13 white stars.

Who was Betsy Ross?

Betsy Ross was a scamstress. Legend has it that she made the first American flag based on a sketch drawn by George Washington. No one knows for sure whether that story is true.

Who was John Paul Jones?

He was the first naval hero in U.S. history, and he is considered the father of the U.S. Navy. His reputation was made in a sea battle he fought against the British on September 23, 1779, during the American Revolution.

Jones's ship attacked a much larger British ship. The two ships dueled for hours and Jones's ship was badly damaged. Yet, when the British captain called for him to surrender, he replied, "I have not yet begun to fight!" and he finally won the battle.

153

WHEN DID THE AMERICAN REVOLUTIONARY WAR START?

The first shot of the American Revolutionary War, which was fought to free the colonies from British rule, was fired on April 19, 1775. It happened at what is now known as the Battle of Lexington, in Massachusetts. Nobody knows whether an American or a British soldier fired the first shot. The phrase "the shot heard round the world" is from a poem by Ralph Waldo Emerson about the battle in nearby Concord later that same day.

Who spoke the words, "The British are coming"?

Paul Revere. Before the American Revolutionary War began, the British Army was stationed in Boston and planning to attack the colonists. Paul Revere, a silversmith, and another rider named William Dawes were sent on horseback to warn Samuel Adams and John Hancock about the attack. The two riders went different ways so one or the other would make it to Lexington, where Adams and Hancock were stationed. Stories say that Revere yelled "The British are coming!"—but it's more likely he whispered it, as he didn't want to get caught.

THE BRITISH ARE COMING!

Who was John Hancock?

John Hancock was the first person to sign the Declaration of Independence—his signature is an impressive five inches long! He started out as a businessman but got involved in the American Revolutionary War and became president of the Continental Congress.

WHAT WERE LOYALISTS?

Loyalists were those people in the American colonies who didn't want to break away from the British but wanted to remain British citizens. During the American Revolutionary War, colonists were divided into two groups—patriots and loyalists.

WHAT WERE PATRIOTS?

Patriots wanted the American colonies to be independent from Britain—they wanted their own country called the United States.

WHAT WAS A MILITIA?

A militia was a group of local men who were ready to defend their homeland if needed but weren't regularly soldiers. Militias trained only a few times a year. Most men between the ages of 16 and 65 were in their local militia. Some militiamen were patriots and fought for American independence.

What was the Continental Army?

The Continental Army was the first real army of the United States. The army was made up of paid volunteers who, like today's soldiers, enlisted for a period of time. They had to commit to at least one year.

What was George Washington, commander of the Continental Army, known for being good at?

He was considered one of the best horsemen of his time.

HOW MUCH WERE SOLDIERS PAID IN THE CONTINENTAL ARMY?

Soldiers who enlisted in the Continental Army were promised a sum of money or a plot of land at the end of their service. They also were paid a monthly salary: privates earned about $6 a month, sergeants $8, and captains $20. Soldiers had to use their own money to buy their uniforms and weapons.

How many soldiers fought in the American Revolutionary War?

As many as 150,000 men fought for the American side in the war, many of them in local militias. The largest number of soldiers serving in the Continental Army at any one time was about 17,000.

What was a musket?

A musket was the main weapon used by a soldier in the American Revolutionary War. Muskets fired lead balls and, because they were not very accurate, many soldiers would fire their muskets at the same time in an effort to cover a wide area. When enemy soldiers were within close range, a solder would attach a sharp blade to the end of his musket (called a bayonet) and use that to fight.

What did American soldiers wear?

Most soldiers didn't have uniforms—they wore whatever clothes they had. In 1775, Congress adopted brown as the official color of the uniforms. But brown material was hard to find, so often the soldiers within the same regiment tried to wear the same color, like blue or gray, so their fellow soldiers could tell them apart from the enemy.

Colonial America

- Antenna
- Baseball
- Basket
- Bell
- Ben Franklin
- Betsy Ross
- Bone
- Broom
- Bucket
- Candles (2)
- Cannonballs (4)
- Cats (2)
- Chicken
- Clock
- Dogs (2)
- Drums (3)
- Duck
- Ear of corn
- Flower vase
- Horses (4)
- Kites (2)
- Lamppost
- Mouse
- One dollar bill
- Saw
- Spinning wheel

Answers on page 311

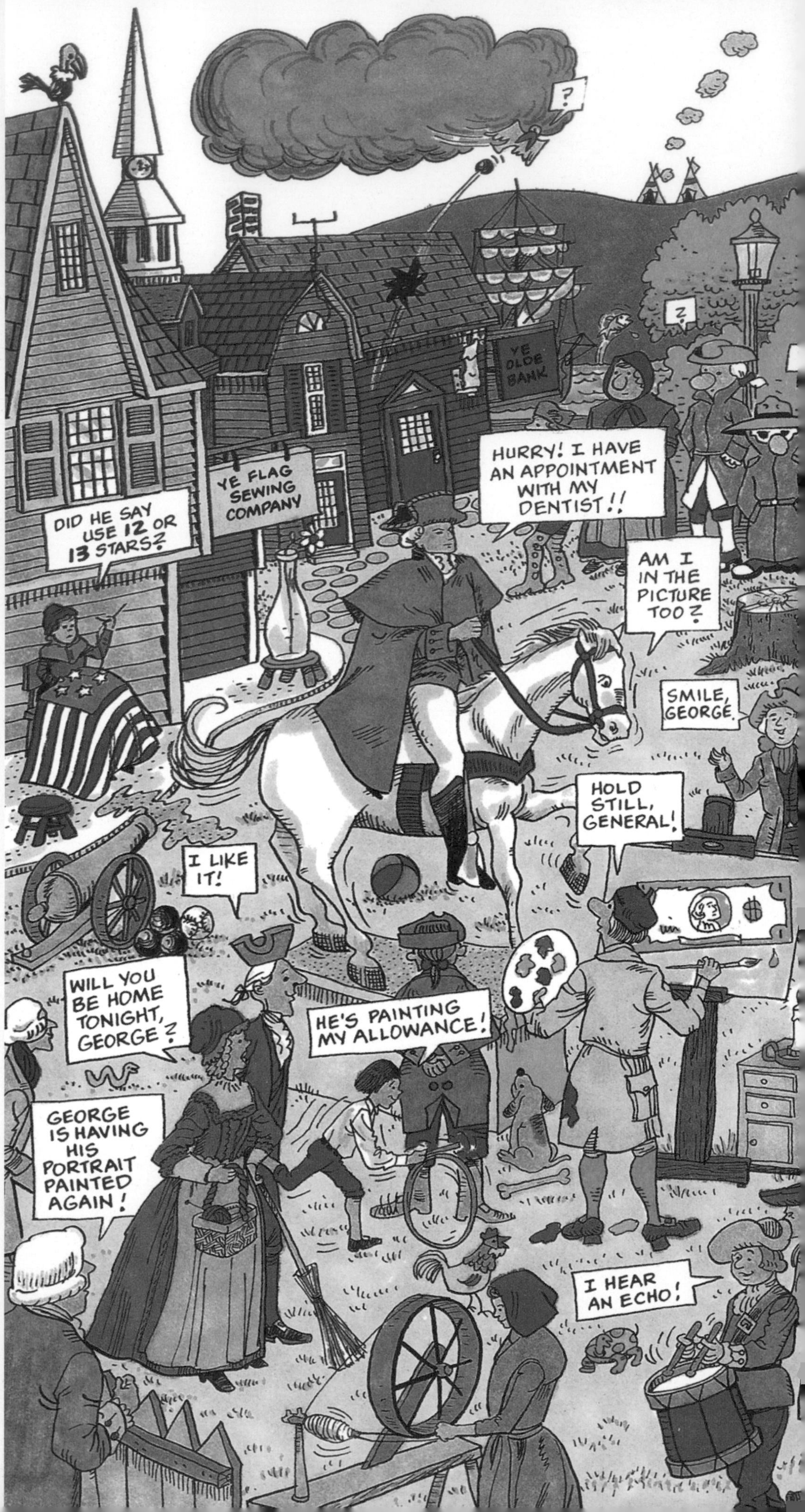

WHAT WERE "LOBSTER BACKS"?

Soldiers in the British army were called "lobster backs" or "red coats" because of their bright red coats, even though some troops wore blue uniforms during the American Revolutionary War.

WHO WERE THE MINUTEMEN?

Minutemen were members of the Massachusetts militia who were prepared to fight at a moment's notice.

What is the Bill of Rights?

The Bill of Rights contains the first 10 amendments (changes or additions) to the U.S. Constitution. In 1791, the Bill of Rights was ratified—or approved— and it outlines the basic rights and freedoms of Americans. Today the U.S. Constitution has 27 amendments.

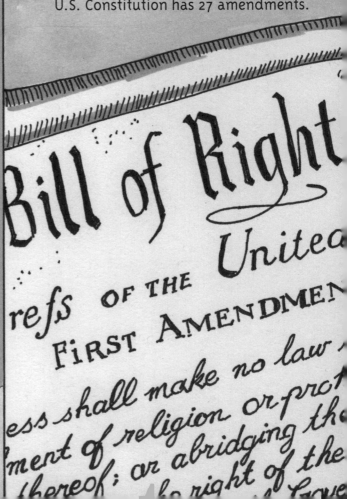

What is the U.S. Constitution?

The first constitution drafted by the new American states was called the Articles of Confederation. Six years after the Articles of Confederation was written, the Constitutional Convention, a gathering of representatives from most of the states, met to discuss changes to them. They decided instead to draft an entirely new constitution, which would define the U.S. government; it was agreed that this federal government would run the country but would not infringe on a person's or a state's rights. In order to keep a balance of power in the government, the writers of the constitution created three branches of government—executive, legislative, and judicial.

What was the Virginia Plan?

The Virginia Plan was one of two competing plans for the Constitution. It was written by James Madison, who often is called the Father of the Constitution because so many of his ideas went into the writing of the document. The Virginia Plan represented the wishes of the larger states, and said that a state's population or wealth should determine the number of representatives the state had in Congress.

What was the New Jersey Plan?

THE STATE OF NEW JERSEY

The New Jersey Plan was the second competing plan for the Constitution. It was written by William Paterson, who was from New Jersey. It represented smaller states and said each state should have the same number of representatives.

What was the Great Compromise?

The Great Compromise said that the U.S. Congress would have two parts, which we usually call the House and the Senate. The number of representatives each state had in the House would be based on the state's population, but each state would have the same number of representatives—two—in the Senate.

How many states needed to accept the U.S. Constitution before it could go into affect?

In order for the Constitution to be ratified, or accepted and put into place, nine of the thirteen states needed to ratify it. The first state to ratify it was Delaware, and the last was Rhode Island.

WHO WAS THE FIRST PRESIDENT OF THE UNITED STATES?

In addition to being leader of the Continental Army, George Washington was the first president of the United States. He helped create the role of president and established traditions of the presidency that continue to be followed today.

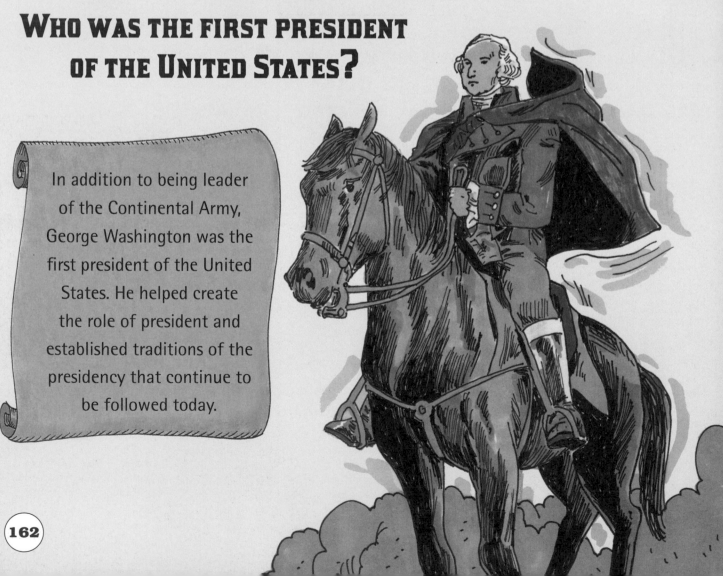

Did George Washington live in Washington?

No. Even though the capital of the United States is named for him, in Washington's first year as president the capital was New York City, and then it moved to Philadelphia, Pennsylvania.

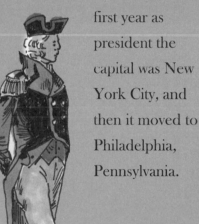

What was *Common Sense*, and who wrote it?

Thomas Paine was a writer and during the American Revolution he wrote a pamphlet called *Common Sense*, which argued that the colonies should break away from the British. Thomas wrote in a way that most people could understand, and his pamphlet influenced many people to decide that being an independent nation was best for the colonies.

WHAT WAS VALLEY FORGE?

The American Continental Army camped at Valley Forge during the winter of 1777 and 1778. Valley Forge is located in the southeastern corner of Pennsylvania, about 25 miles northwest of Philadelphia. While spending the winter at Valley Forge, the American forces banded together to become a true fighting unit, so Valley Forge is sometimes called the birthplace of the American army.

Who were the Green Mountain Boys?

The Green Mountain Boys was a group of militiamen from Vermont led by Ethan Allen. They planned to take over Fort Ticonderoga, a fort in upstate New York, from the British. Colonel Benedict Arnold from Connecticut joined the group, and he and Ethan Allen established a joint command.

Who was Benedict Arnold?

Benedict Arnold was a member of the Sons of Liberty in Connecticut. He became a general in the Continental Army during the American Revolutionary War. Ultimately, he began to reveal American strategy to the British, and plotted to help them take over West Point. Eventually Arnold managed to betray both the Americans and the British. Even today, the name "Benedict Arnold" often means "traitor."

Where did the Battle of Bunker Hill happen?

Not on Bunker Hill! There were two hills in Boston that the British wanted to take over—one was Breeds Hill and one was Bunker Hill. If the British captured these hills, they could bombard the Americans from their heights. Even though it's called the Battle of Bunker Hill, it actually took place mostly on Breeds Hill.

DON'T SHOOT 'TILL YOU SEE THE WHITES OF THEIR EYES!

WHO WERE THE HESSIAN SOLDIERS?

The Hessian soldiers were German soldiers that the British hired to fight for them in the American Revolution. There were about 30,000 of these soldiers, who got their name from the area of Hesse-Kassel, where many of them were from.

What were Durham boats?

Durham boats were designed to carry heavy loads and were named for a Pennsylvania ironworks company that used them. One of the most important victories for the Continental Army took place when George Washington and his men crossed the Delaware River to attack Hessian troops in Trenton, New Jersey, on Christmas Day in 1776. This victory helped turn the war in the American's favor. Boats from all over the area were used to take the army across the river, and many of these were Durham boats.

What was the Peace of Paris?

The Peace of Paris officially ended the American Revolutionary War, and included the official peace treaty between the United States and Britain. It was signed on September 3, 1783.

How was Thomas Jefferson elected president in 1801?

Jefferson and his running mate, Aaron Burr, received the same number of electoral votes. The outcome of the election was taken to the House of Representatives, and Jefferson was elected after six days of voting and thirty-six ballots, becoming the third president of the United States.

Who was Napoleon Bonaparte?

Napoleon Bonaparte was a military general and the first emperor of France. He is one of the most recognized and infamous leaders in history, known for revolutionizing military organization and training, and for conquering much of Europe in the early nineteenth century.

When was the United Kingdom formed?

On January 1, 1801, the Kingdom of Great Britain and the Kingdom of Ireland combined to form the United Kingdom of Great Britain and Ireland.

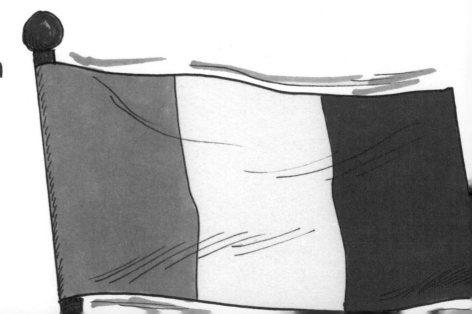

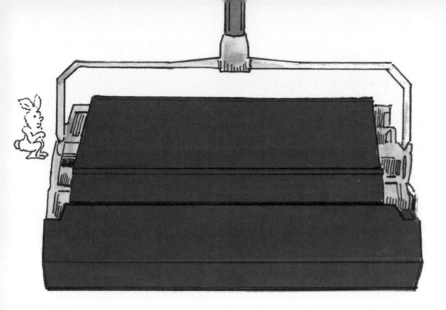

What seventeeth-century invention started a revolution in housecleaning?

The carpet sweeper!
Its creation introduced in 1870 a multitude of new labor-saving appliances. Prior to the invention of the carpet sweeper, most women used a broom and a carpet beater to clean the floors and carpets of their homes.

Who was *Mark Twain?*

Mark Twain's real name was Samuel L. Clemens; Mark Twain was his pen name. He wrote several famous novels in the nineteenth century, including *The Adventures of Tom Sawyer* and *The Adventures of Huckleberry Finn*.

What became the largest city in the world in the nineteenth century?

By the end of the nineteenth century, London had become the largest city in the world. At the beginning of the century, in 1801, the British flag—also known as the Union Jack—was amended and officially adopted as the flag of the United Kingdom of Great Britain and Ireland.

What was the Louisiana Purchase?

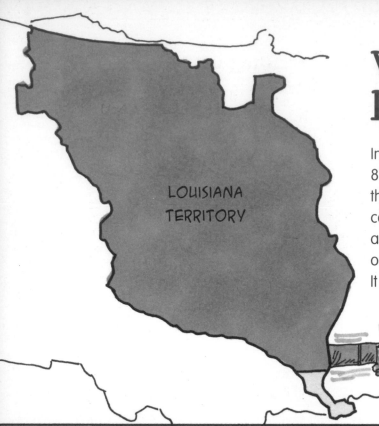

LOUISIANA TERRITORY

In 1803, Thomas Jefferson purchased approximately 828,000 square miles of land from France, doubling the size of the United States at that time. This land was called the Louisiana Territory. This was a very important achievement for Thomas Jefferson; 15 more states, all or in part, were eventually created from this land. It cost the United States $15 million.

Who were **Lewis and Clark?**

Captain Meriwether Lewis was Thomas Jefferson's private secretary. Jefferson put him in charge of the expedition to explore the Louisiana Territory. Lewis asked his friend, Lieutenant William Clark, to help. Lewis, Clark, and their band of about 30 explorers left Saint Louis, Missouri, on May 14, 1804. They started out traveling up the Missouri River into what is today the state of Montana, where they encountered the Great Falls, crossed the Rocky Mountains, and finally reached the Pacific Ocean. Their westward expedition took more than a year, and it took them six months to return home.

WHO WAS SACAGAWEA?

Lewis and Clark met Native Americans from a number tribes along the way, many of whom they made friends with, including Sacagawea, a Shoshone who was the wife of a French Canadian fur trapper. Sacagawea joined the expedition as an interpreter and guide, and was the only woman on Lewis and Clark's expedition.

Who was Beethoven?

Ludwig van Beethoven was a German composer who lived in the late eighteenth and early nineteenth century. While famous for his musical compositions, Beethoven is also known for becoming deaf later in his life.

When and where did the world's first municipal park open?

The first public man-made park, complete with lakes and fields, opened in England in 1847. This park started a trend in Victorian England, as people enjoyed having open spaces near urban centers.

What was the Victorian Age?

The Victorian Age was a period of time in British history when Victoria was queen. This period lasted from 1837 until Queen Victoria's death in 1901. It was a time of peace and stability for England.

What did a Philadelphia shoemaker design in 1822 that changed how people wore shoes?

In much of the world in the nineteenth century, the two shoes of a pair were identical and could go on either foot.

In 1822, a shoemaker in Philadelphia became the first cobbler of the time to make left- and right-footed shoes.

WHAT NATIONAL LANDMARK WAS UNVEILED IN 1886?

The Statue of Liberty, which was a gift to the United States from France, was unveiled in New York Harbor in 1886.

What was the National Road?

The National Road, also called the Cumberland Road, was the main route for settlers moving westward and for farmers from the West to ship crops to cities in the East. Construction on the National Road began in 1811. By the time it was completed, in 1837, the National Road ran from Cumberland, Maryland to Vandalia, Illinois.

WHAT WAS THE CLERMONT?

The Clermont was a steamboat built by Robert Fulton. On August 17, 1807, it made its first trip from New York City to Albany, New York. It traveled at a speed of only five miles an hour, and the travel took 32 hours, but the journey began a new era of steam-powered transportation.

When did Florida become a part of the United States?

What is now the state of Florida was claimed by Britain in 1763, but was ceded to Spain 20 years later.

In 1819, the United States annexed Florida, and it became a state in 1845.

What was the War of 1812?

The United States declared war on Great Britain on June 18, 1812, after the British had been interfering with American trade and forcing American sailors to serve in the British navy. This started the War of 1812. On December 24, 1814, a peace treaty ending the War of 1812 was signed in Ghent, Belgium, which gave it its name, the Treaty of Ghent.

What was William Henry Harrison known for?

William Henry Harrison became famous for his victory over Native Americans at the Battle of Tippecanoe and his time as a general in the army during the War of 1812. But he may be most famous for the length of time he served as president of the United States: he served the shortest term of any U.S. president because he died of pneumonia one month after taking office.

What were the Napoleonic Wars?

The Napoleonic Wars were a series of wars fought between Napoleon and his French empire and a group of opposing European forces led by Great Britain.

Why did the British set fire to the White House and the Capitol?

On August 24, 1814, the British set fire to the White House and the U.S. Capitol in retaliation for an earlier American raid on York, Ontario (now Toronto). After the British burned the president's house in 1814, it was finally repaired in 1817 and given a new coat of white paint—and thus came to be known as the White House!

What was the Battle of Waterloo?

The Battle of Waterloo happened on June 18, 1815, and was Napoleon's last battle. It was fought near Waterloo, which today is in Belgium. Napoleon was defeated by a combination of British and Prussian forces. After his defeat, he gave up his power and later died in exile.

Who was Francis Scott Key?

Francis Scott Key was a lawyer who, while aboard a British warship, saw the British attack on Fort McHenry, Maryland, during the War of 1812. The British lost the battle, and the sight inspired Key to write a poem called "The Star-Spangled Banner," which became the U.S. national anthem.

Who was Charles Dickens?

Charles Dickens, born in England in 1812, was a British author who wrote numerous stories, many of which are now considered classics, including *Oliver Twist, A Christmas Carol, A Tale of Two Cities,* and *Great Expectations.* He died in 1870, leaving his final novel unfinished.

WHO WAS LOUIS PASTEUR?

Louis Pasteur was a French chemist who, in the mid-nineteenth century, discovered that microbes (tiny organisms) would cause certain beverages such as wine and milk to sour, and developed the process of pasteurization to prevent it. The process of pasteurization involves heating beverages in order to kill the microorganisms. He devoted much of his career to studying germs and developing vaccines, including the vaccine for rabies.

WHAT WAS THE INDUSTRIAL REVOLUTION?

The Industrial Revolution took place during the eighteenth and nineteenth centuries. During the Industrial Revolution, rural farming societies became more industrialized and urban. Prior to the Industrial Revolution, people used hand tools and basic machines. With industrialization came a shift to powered machines that did specific jobs, as well as factories and mass production. Francis Cabot Lowell opened the first factory in the United States able to turn raw cotton into cloth using power machinery.

Who was General Andrew Jackson?

Andrew Jackson was the seventh president of the United States. Prior to that, however, he fought in the War of 1812. He stopped a British attack at the Battle of New Orleans, which occurred after the war was over—but the news that a peace treaty had been signed (it took place in Belgium) hadn't reached the United States yet. During this final battle, the British had more than 2,000 casualties (dead and wounded), while the U.S. forces had just 71.

WHAT IS THE ERIE CANAL?

On July 4, 1817, construction began on the Erie Canal, which was designed to connect the Great Lakes to the Hudson River in New York. It officially opened in 1825. The canal was four feet deep and forty feet wide. It was enlarged between 1835 and 1862 to seventy feet wide and seven feet deep.

What happened in 1819 that affected the practice of putting people in prison if they had financial debt?

In 1819 there was a financial panic throughout the United States, which caused the country's first major economic depression. This led the government to establish relief measures for people in debt, and about 15 years later, the United States ended the practice of imprisoning people for not being able to pay their debts.

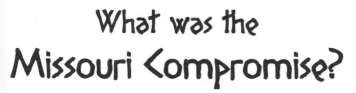

What was the Missouri Compromise?

At the time of the Missouri Compromise of 1820, the United States included both free states, which were antislavery, and slave states, which were pro-slavery. In 1817, Missouri asked to be admitted to the union, and the House of Representatives agreed, provided it be a free state. The Senate refused to agree to those terms. Congress settled the dispute with a compromise that allowed Missouri to be a slave state, admitted Maine as a free state, and drew an imaginary line across the former Louisiana Territory making regions north of the line free.

WHAT WAS THE MONROE DOCTRINE?

The Monroe Doctrine was the beginning of U.S. foreign policy. In December 1823, President James Monroe stated that the "American continents" could no longer be colonized by Europe. President Monroe even threatened force if Europe continued to try to colonize the Americas.

WHAT WERE THE OPIUM WARS?

The Opium Wars were a series of wars fought in the mid-nineteenth century between Great Britain (and later France) and China over differences in opinion over diplomatic relations and trade relations, specifically the trading of opium, which China wanted to end.

WHAT WAS THE CRIMEAN WAR?

The Crimean War was a war fought between Russia and an alliance of France, Britain, the Ottoman Empire, and Sardinia. The conflict primarily was fought over issues of religion, and Russia eventually ended up losing in 1856. However, it was one of the first "modern" wars, as railways, telegraphs, and other technology were used throughout the war. It is also famous for the use of modern medical practices to treat the wounded, and it was one of the first wars to be documented in writing and with photographs.

Who was Florence Nightingale?

Florence Nightingale, a British woman born in Italy in 1820, pioneered modern medical care during the Crimean War to improve the conditions at British war hospitals. She also founded London's Saint Thomas' Hospital and the Nightingale Training School for nurses, which helped to establish nursing as a profession.

What was the Kansas-Nebraska Act?

The Kansas-Nebraska Act was passed in 1854. It allowed for "popular sovereignty," which meant that settlers of a territory could decide whether or not to allow slavery within the new region's borders. The Kansas-Nebraska Act helped contribute to the beginning of the Civil War because it caused tensions between antislavery and pro-slavery forces, some of which turned violent.

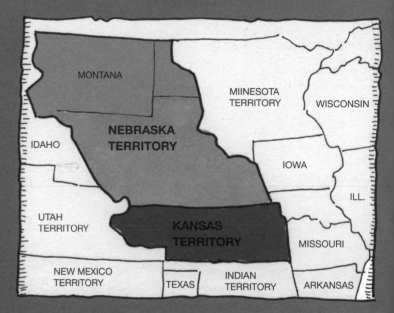

What is Manifest Destiny?

In the nineteenth century, the United States began to expand westward, past the original 13 colonies toward the Pacific Ocean. Many people living in the United States at the time believed it was the country's "destiny" to stretch to the Pacific, and this belief became known as Manifest Destiny.

When was the first North American transcontinental railroad built?

The first transcontinental railroad, stretching from the East Coast to the West Coast, was completed when the 1,800-mile link from California to Omaha, Nebraska was built between 1863 and 1869. Railroads moved people in a way that was safer, faster, and cheaper than wagon travel, and they also moved mail and supplies.

What were the two new main railway lines called?

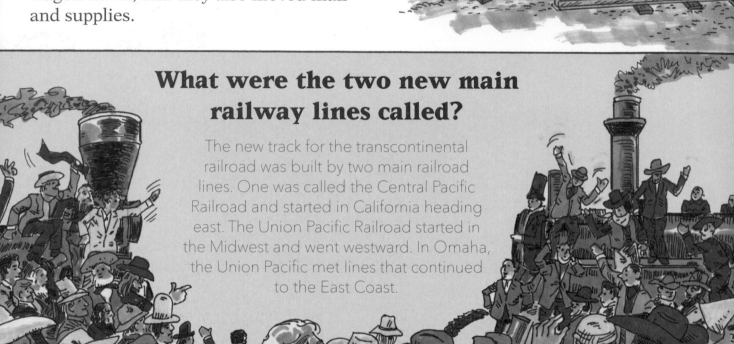

The new track for the transcontinental railroad was built by two main railroad lines. One was called the Central Pacific Railroad and started in California heading east. The Union Pacific Railroad started in the Midwest and went westward. In Omaha, the Union Pacific met lines that continued to the East Coast.

WHERE DID THE TWO RAILWAYS FINALLY MEET?

The Central and Union Pacific railroads finally met at Promontory Summit, Utah, on May 10, 1869. The final spike, driven into the ground by the head of Union Pacific (a former governor of California), was called the "Golden Spike."

WHAT WAS THE PONY EXPRESS?

The Pony Express was a mail delivery service. Sent by the Pony Express, mail could travel between Missouri and California in about 10 days, rather than the weeks it took when mail traveled by horse and carriage. The Pony Express had a planned route with a number of stops along the way where the riders changed horses. Every 100 miles or so the rider himself would be replaced, which kept the mail moving at a good speed.

WHAT WAS THE OREGON TRAIL?

The Oregon Trail was a major route that more than 300,000 people took when migrating west between about 1840 and 1869. Many of the travelers went in covered wagons and traveled in long wagon trains (one wagon following another). The Oregon Trail began in Independence, Missouri, and ended in Oregon City, Oregon. It was about 2,000 miles long.

OREGON

→ OREGON TRAIL

MEXICO   TEXAS

What was a prairie schooner?

A "prairie schooner" was another name for a covered wagon. From afar their cotton or linen canvas tops looked like sails, making them look like big sailboats called schooners skimming over the prairies of the West. The wagons were usually about ten feet long and four feet wide and were made of wood, with iron wrapped around the wooden wheels. Oxen, or sometimes mules or horses, pulled the wagons, which could weigh as much as 2,500 pounds.

What was the California Gold Rush?

Between 1848 and 1855, more than 300,000 people rushed to California to look for gold—this was the California Gold Rush. James Marshall first discovered gold at Sutter's Mill, near the city of Coloma, California.

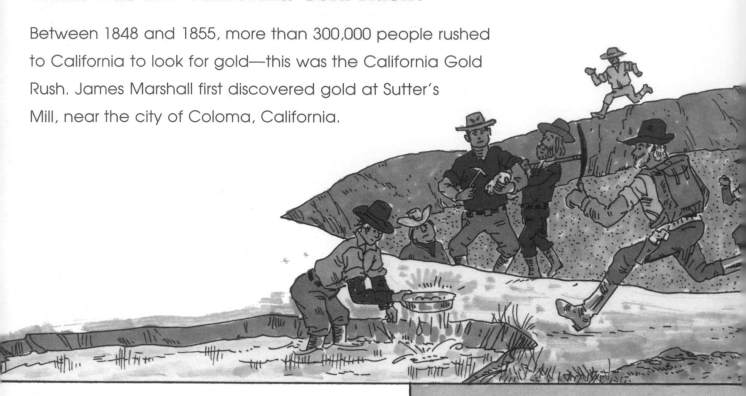

Who were the Forty-niners?

People who rushed to California in 1849 to find gold were called Forty-niners. Around 6,000 people came to the California gold fields in 1848, but about 80,000 arrived in 1849. These people, hoping to find gold and get rich, didn't come just from America; they came from all over the world, including places like China, Mexico, Europe, and Australia.

HOW DID MINERS LOOK FOR GOLD?

MANY OF THE MINERS USED A METHOD CALLED PANNING TO SEPARATE GOLD FROM DIRT AND GRAVEL. WHEN PANNING FOR GOLD, MINERS WOULD PUT GRAVEL AND WATER INTO A PAN AND THEN SHAKE IT BACK AND FORTH. GOLD IS HEAVY, SO IT WOULD FALL TO THE BOTTOM OF THE PAN. THE MINER WOULD BE ABLE TO SEPARATE OUT THE GOLD AND THROW OUT THE DIRT AND GRAVEL.

What were boomtowns and ghost towns?

I DON'T WANT TO LIVE HERE!

Whenever gold was discovered in a new place, miners would quickly move in and set up camp. Sometimes these camps would quickly grow into towns; these were called boomtowns. San Francisco, which began as a village of 50 people, is an example of a boomtown, growing to 30,000 residents in just a few years. However, many boomtowns were abandoned and eventually turned into ghost towns: when the gold ran out, the miners and the businesses that served them would pick up and leave to find the next gold strike.

What was the Battle of the Alamo?

The Battle of the Alamo was one of the most famous battles fought in the Texas war of independence from Mexico. The Mexican-American War, fought between the United States and Mexico, began 10 years later in 1846, lasting until 1848. While Mexico eventually lost the war and agreed to give the United States a large chunk of land that became all or part of eight states, the war was predominately fought over the territory of Texas.

What was the Homestead Act of 1862?

The Homestead Act was passed in 1862 to encourage independent farmers to move out West. Under the new law, an individual could get 160 acres of unoccupied land in the public domain. They could keep the land if they lived on it for five years and made improvements to it.

Search & Find®
for these fun
items in the

American Gold Rush

- Arrow
- Bear
- Broom
- Butterfly
- Cactus
- Comb
- Empty can
- Feather
- Fish bone
- Football
- Frying pan
- Giant
- Golf club
- Guitar
- Hair bow
- Heart
- Horse
- Periscope
- Pumpkin
- Snail
- Snake
- Tombstone
- Top hat
- Wagon wheel
- Wealthy duck

Answers on page 312

182

183

What were Sooners?

One of the biggest rushes for unclaimed land occurred in Oklahoma on April 22, 1889. It is estimated that 50,000 people lined up to claim almost 2 million acres. They were allowed to enter the area to claim land at noon, but some people snuck onto the land early and hid in order to claim the best areas first. They were nicknamed "Sooners."

CAN YOU FIND 10 SOONERS THAT ARE HIDING HERE?

I'M NOT A SOONER!

What was the Trail of Tears?

In the 1830s, various tribes of Eastern Woodlands Indians signed agreements giving the United States control of their lands. A small group of Cherokees signed over all of the Cherokee land in return for land in Oklahoma plus $5 million. In 1838, the U.S. Army forced the people of the Cherokee nation to move from their homes in the Southeast to Oklahoma. This migration is called the Trail of Tears, and more than 4,000 Cherokee people died on the journey to Oklahoma.

Who were gunslingers?

The western United States in the nineteenth century is legendary for being lawless. Men carried guns to protect themselves. Gunslingers, gunmen, or gunfighters were names for both the outlaws who stole from people and the lawmen who tried to stop them—it truly was the Wild West! Some famous gunfighters were Wild Bill Hickock, Jesse James, Billy the Kid, and Wyatt Earp.

What was Butch Cassidy's Wild Bunch?

Butch Cassidy's Wild Bunch was a gang of famous gunfighters, horse thieves, and bank robbers. They included Butch Cassidy, Harry "Sundance Kid" Longabaugh, and Kid Curry. They were known for their exploits, including stealing $60,000.

Who was Louis Daguerre?

Louis Daguerre was a Frenchman who, in 1839, invented a process that captured photographic images, starting the era of photography. Daguerreotypes, as the photographs were called, were first made in the United States in September 1839.

SAY CHEESE!

Who was Gregor Mendel?

Gregor Mendel was a monk from Austria who, while experimenting in his garden, discovered the basic principles of heredity. His experiments became the basis for the modern studies of genetics and heredity.

WHAT WAS THE UNDERGROUND RAILROAD?

The Underground Railroad wasn't a railroad at all—it was a term used to describe the linked trail of people, homes, and hideouts that helped slaves from the southern United States escape to the free northern United States and Canada.

Who was Harriet Tubman?

Harriet Tubman was born a slave on a plantation in Maryland in the early 1820s. After she escaped from slavery in 1849, she became famous for working on the Underground Railroad. She may have helped as many as 300 slaves escape.

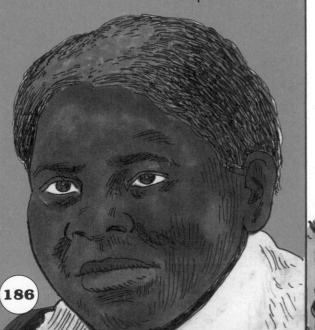

What was the Fugitive Slave Act of 1850?

The Fugitive Slave Act of 1850 stated that runaway slaves found in free states had to be returned to their owners in the South.

Who were abolitionists?

Abolitionists were people who wanted slavery made illegal and all slaves set free.

Who was Sojourner Truth?

Sojourner Truth was born Isabella Baumfree. She was a slave who later became an abolitionist and a women's rights activist.

Where was the first telegraph message sent?

Samuel F. B. Morse sent the first telegraph message from Washington, D.C., to Baltimore, Maryland, in 1844.

What was the Oregon Treaty?

The Oregon Treaty was signed in 1846 was between the United States and Great Britain. It set the western boundary between the United States and Canada at the 49th parallel (a line of latitude), giving the United States land that later would become parts of Oregon, Washington, Idaho, Montana, and Wyoming.

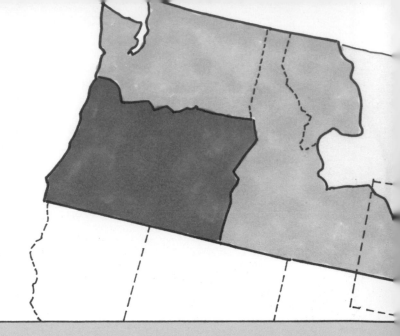

When did the **first public zoo** open in the **United States?**

The first public zoo— the Philadelphia Zoological Gardens— opened in 1874.

What was the **Irish Potato Famine?**

Between 1845 and 1849 much of the potato crop in Ireland was ruined, causing a period of starvation called the Irish Potato Famine. The lack of food led many Irish people to immigrate to other countries, including the United States.

Who was Marie Curie?

Marie Curie was born in Poland in 1867. She became the first woman to win a Nobel Prize, which she won in two different fields: physics and chemistry. The experiments she did with her husband, Pierre Curie, led to the discovery of polonium and radium and, eventually, the X-ray.

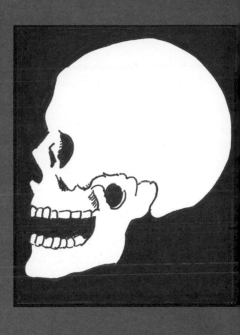

What happened in 1859 to change the way many Americans lived?

An oil well was drilled in Titusville, Pennsylvania, and this event changed the way many Americans lit their homes. Before oil from the ground, people mainly used whale oil (which comes from whale fat, or blubber) and candles to light their homes. Kerosene made from the new oil was used in lamps that replaced these older lighting methods in many American homes.

OIL WELL

Who was Henry David Thoreau?

Henry David Thoreau was a nineteenth-century essay writer and poet. He began writing nature poetry in the 1840s. From 1845 to 1847 he stayed in a wilderness cabin on Walden Pond in Concord, Massachusetts. His writing about his time there became his masterwork, *Walden*. He also was a dedicated abolitionist.

WHO WAS JOHN BROWN?

John Brown, an abolitionist, wanted to end slavery and help escaped slaves but was frustrated by the peaceful nature of the abolitionist movement. He thought that any method necessary—including violence—should be used to end slavery.

WHAT HAPPENED AT THE RAID ON HARPERS FERRY IN 1859?

John Brown believed that if he could organize the four million slaves living in the South and arm them with weapons, they would revolt and gain their freedom. His plan was to first take over the federal weapons arsenal in Harpers Ferry, which was then in the state of Virginia. The initial part of the raid was successful, however the local slaves Brown thought would help him and his 20 men fight the local townspeople never came to his aid. Brown was captured two days after the raid and was later hanged.

Who was Dred Scott?

Dred Scott was a slave who made history by waging a legal battle to gain his freedom. He had worked in two free states, so when he tried to buy his freedom and was denied, he took his case to the Missouri courts, in the state where he had been enslaved. He won in a lower state court, but the Missouri Supreme Court overturned the decision. The subsequent U.S. Supreme Court decision denying Scott's freedom was one of the acts that led to the start of the Civil War.

Who was Frederick Douglass?

Frederick Douglass was an abolitionist leader who was born into slavery. While enslaved he learned to read. At age 20, he escaped to the North, where he became a preacher and honed his public speaking skills. He used his talents to speak against slavery and for women's rights, as he believed in equal rights for all people. He wrote several autobiographies describing his life as a slave and afterwards.

Who was Elizabeth Cady Stanton?

SUSAN B. ANTHONY

Elizabeth Cady Stanton was one of the leaders of the women's suffrage (voting rights) movement. She believed women and men were created equal and should be treated the same under the law. Together, she and Susan B. Anthony, another civil rights leader, formed the National Woman Suffrage Association in 1869. They believed women should be given the right to vote.

Where did the Great Chicago Fire of 1871 start?

The Great Chicago Fire was one of the worst fire disasters in the history of the United States, and it all started in a small barn on Chicago's West Side. Legend has it that a cow kicked over a lantern in the barn and started the fire, but nobody knows for sure—it could have been a human or even a meteorite that caused the event. Most of the buildings in the area at that time were made of wood and more than 17,000 buildings over a stretch of land that covered less than four square miles were completely destroyed. An estimated 300 people died.

What did Alexander Graham Bell invent?

Alexander Graham Bell invented the telephone in 1876. He was interested in the science of sound because both his mother and wife were deaf. He had an assistant, Thomas Watson, who helped him develop the first telephone. The first words spoken over the telephone were by Alexander Graham Bell on March 10, 1876. They were, "Mr. Watson, come here, I want to see you."

What did Thomas Edison invent?

Thomas Edison invented hundreds of things and secured patents for more than a thousand inventions, but his most famous is the light bulb. He also started an electric company, which later merged with several other companies to become General Electric, one of the biggest corporations in the world today.

What was the Battle of the Little Bighorn in 1876?

Lieutenant Colonel George Custer of the U.S. cavalry attacked a gathering of Sioux tribes in a dispute over an area in the Black Hills of South Dakota. The Native Americans considered the area sacred ground, but the United States wanted to explore it for gold. Led by Sitting Bull, chief of one of the tribes, the Sioux refused to leave. Custer attacked, but he didn't realize how big Sitting Bull's army was, and the Sioux easily defeated Custer, who was killed along with his men.

Who was Booker T. Washington?

Booker T. Washington was born a slave and grew up during the Civil War. Once free, he put himself through school, became a teacher, and founded the Tuskegee Normal and Industrial Institute in Alabama (now known as Tuskegee University). The school focused on training African Americans in manual trades and agriculture.

What started the Civil War?

In early 1861, many of the states in the southern part of the United States decided they wanted to form their own country with a slavery-based economy. They called it the Confederate States of America. The states in the North didn't think the southern states had the right to leave the Union, and this started the Civil War. The Civil War and the major events leading up to the war lasted from 1860 to 1865. It was the deadliest war in American history, with around 210,000 soldiers killed in action and at least 625,000 total deaths, many from disease.

YANKEE

REBEL

Who was Harriet Beecher Stowe?

Harriet Beecher Stowe wrote a book called *Uncle Tom's Cabin*, which was published in 1852. It was a story about a slave named Tom. Though not a slave herself, Harriet Beecher Stowe was horrified by slavery and hoped her book would help others see why slavery needed to be abolished. It too was a catalyst for the Civil War, as it caused many people to join the abolitionist movement.

WHO WAS ABRAHAM LINCOLN?

Abraham Lincoln was the 16th and the tallest president of the United States (he was six feet four inches tall!). He is most famous for leading the country during the Civil War, and for helping the North defeat the South and keeping the country united. He pushed for freedom for all slaves and gave a very famous speech called the Gettysburg Address. Lincoln was assassinated by John Wilkes Booth while attending a play.

What did women do during the Civil War?

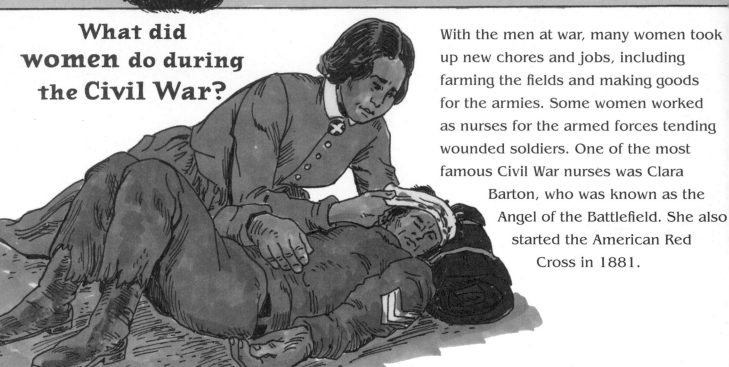

With the men at war, many women took up new chores and jobs, including farming the fields and making goods for the armies. Some women worked as nurses for the armed forces tending wounded soldiers. One of the most famous Civil War nurses was Clara Barton, who was known as the Angel of the Battlefield. She also started the American Red Cross in 1881.

WHAT WERE "THE BLUE" AND "THE GRAY"?

Not having consistent uniforms led to confusion on the battlefield, so the Union army wore blue uniforms and the Confederates wore gray, and they came to be known by their colors. The Union uniform consisted of a dark blue wool coat with light or dark blue trousers and a dark cap called a forage cap. Their shoes were ankle boots called brogans. Confederate uniforms consisted of a gray coat and trousers, though some ranks wore light blue trousers.

WHAT WAS THE EMANCIPATION PROCLAMATION?

The Emancipation Proclamation was an order given on January 1, 1863, by Abraham Lincoln to free the slaves. Slaves weren't immediately set free because the Emancipation Proclamation had limitations, but it did eventually set millions of slaves free.

WHAT BATTLE STARTED THE CIVIL WAR?

The Battle of Fort Sumter (April 12-14, 1861), which was on an island in South Carolina, started the Civil War. Many battles followed, including those at Shiloh, Antietam, Fredericksburg, and Gettysburg, led by famous generals, including Generals Ulysses S. Grant and Robert E. Lee.

Which battle ended the Civil War?

The Battle of Appomattox Court House in Virginia. In 1865, the Union Army began marching through Virginia and pushing back the remaining Confederate forces. General Robert E. Lee, leader of the Confederate Army of Northern Virginia, abandoned the capital of Richmond in the hopes of meeting up with more Confederate troops in North Carolina. But the Union Army soon cut off the Confederate retreat, and General Ulysses S. Grant, who led the Union forces, had the Confederate forces surrounded. The Confederates were outnumbered, so General Lee surrendered at Appomattox on April 9.

195

Nineteenth Century Word Search

Look for the nineteenth century words listed below. Circle horizontally, vertically, backwards, or diagonally as you find each word.

```
M N T W I O F Z D J A C K S O N V B Y
S P T D M S R E G N I L S N U G S R A
Z Y O X E N N N D W F Z N S F H O V Z
V I C X N O M I O M C M O E E S O L K
J N S Z D T C G U B B W S S X A N E J
S L M I E N L H G R O J I F E L E W C
K N U J L A N T L O N N R B Q H R I S
N E E R P T L I A W A L R S U A S S L
Q A G K X S U N S N P I A J N G C F N
I S P R C E E G S W A M H E D L S I H
E J P O U I E A R Y R U P C A A A H U
E E P N L D D L N C T K U R C W R R T
P F A V B E K E Y D E R K A T B M U P
B F S T M H A E Q D I A G X F F S M P
A E T U U Q I N Y E U A E R O H T W N
K R E B P A B J D R W Z Y A X A U R D
M S U M B P M A E E F C U Y S I L G K
N O R A T H Z L A S S E R R E U G A D
A N D N Z V I C T O R I A F B G X Z J
```

Bonaparte	Douglass	Mendel	Stanton
Brown	Gunslingers	Napolean	Thoreau
Clark	Harrison	Nightingale	Tubman
Curie	Jackson	Pasteur	Twain
Daguerre	Jefferson	Sacagawea	Victoria
Dickens	Key	Scott	
	Lewis	Sooners	

Answers on page 313

Name Matching

Match the nineteenth-century person with his or her description:

☐ Ulysses S. Grant

☐ Robert E. Lee

☐ Thomas Jefferson

☐ Samuel L. Clemens

☐ Napoleon

☐ Andrew Jackson

☐ Marie Curie

☐ Jesse James

☐ Harriet Tubman

☐ Dred Scott

☐ Susan B. Anthony

☐ Florence Nightingale

A. One of the famous gunslingers of the Wild West.

B. Pioneered modern medical practices during the Crimean War and helped establish nursing as a profession.

C. Went by the pen name Mark Twain; authored several famous novels including The Adventures of Tom Sawyer and Adventures of Huckleberry Finn.

D. Leader of Confederate forces during the Civil War.

E. Military general and the first emperor of France.

F. Leader of the Union forces during the Civil War.

G. Nobel prize winner in physics and chemistry.

H. Seventh president of the United States; general during the War of 1812.

I. Third president of the United States; had his presidency decided by the House of Representatives because of a tie.

J. A former slave who helped other slaves escape using the Underground Railroad.

K. A slave who made history by waging a legal battle to gain his freedom; his case went all the way to the U.S. Supreme Court.

L. One of the leaders of the women's voting-rights movement, along with Elizabeth Cady Stanton.

197

Answers on page 314

What early-American inventions rapidly changed everyday life in the twentieth century?

The telephone, the automobile, and the electric light. Even though they were all invented prior to the twentieth century, an industrial boom created plenty of jobs and, in general, Americans believed that the years ahead would be filled with peace and prosperity, and become progressively better.

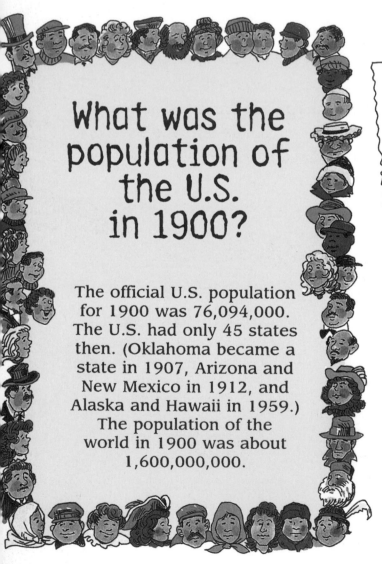

What was the population of the U.S. in 1900?

The official U.S. population for 1900 was 76,094,000. The U.S. had only 45 states then. (Oklahoma became a state in 1907, Arizona and New Mexico in 1912, and Alaska and Hawaii in 1959.) The population of the world in 1900 was about 1,600,000,000.

EVERYBODY SAY "CHEESE"!

WHAT WAS THE "BROWNIE" CAMERA?

The lightweight, box-shaped camera that made photography available to amateurs. In 1900, George Eastman's company, Eastman Kodak, released the easy-to-operate camera. The Brownie, which cost only $1, was a success for many years.

How did the hamburger and hot dog come to be?

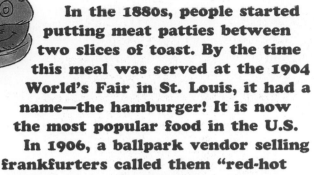

In the 1880s, people started putting meat patties between two slices of toast. By the time this meal was served at the 1904 World's Fair in St. Louis, it had a name—the hamburger! It is now the most popular food in the U.S.

In 1906, a ballpark vendor selling frankfurters called them "red-hot dachshund sausages," because they looked like the long-bodied dog. The name "hot dog" was born when a cartoonist drew a dachshund inside a long bun—but called it a hot dog because he didn't know how to spell dachshund!

WHO SENT THE FIRST TRANSATLANTIC WIRELESS RADIO MESSAGE?

Guglielmo Marconi, an Italian scientist and inventor. On December 12, 1901, he sent the first wireless transatlantic communication: He transmitted the Morse code letter *S* from England to Canada. Marconi's work, together with new understanding about radio waves, led to the development of modern radio.

WHAT AMAZING STUNT DID ANNA EDSON TAYLOR PERFORM?

In 1901, she rode safely over Niagara Falls in a wooden barrel! The Michigan schoolteacher was the first person to survive the 158-foot fall. (She suffered only a few bumps and bruises.) Taylor hoped that the stunt would win her money as well as fame, but a vaudeville tour that featured her and her 4½-foot-long barrel earned her very little. Taylor's advice on the daredevil stunt? "Don't try it!"

HOW DID THEODORE ROOSEVELT BECOME THE 26th U.S. PRESIDENT?

Roosevelt had been vice president for only six months when President William McKinley was shot and killed. Roosevelt took the oath of office and became president on September 14, 1901—six weeks before his 43rd birthday. He was the youngest person ever sworn in as U.S. president.

WAS THERE A **PING-PONG** CRAZE IN THE U.S.?

The game known as gossima failed to catch on—until its name was changed to Ping-Pong! Then families in the U.S. and Europe converted their tables into indoor tennis courts and catapulted this simple game into a popular pastime. The game (also known as table tennis) began in Britain but found a place in homes worldwide.

WHAT KIND OF MUSIC DID SCOTT JOPLIN WRITE?

Joplin wrote ragtime, a lively kind of music composed mainly for piano or small bands. Ragtime was very popular in the U.S. at the turn of the century. Joplin wrote or collaborated on more than 60 pieces of music, including two operas. One of his most famous compositions was called "The Entertainer." Joplin became known as the "King of Ragtime" and was an early influence on jazz music.

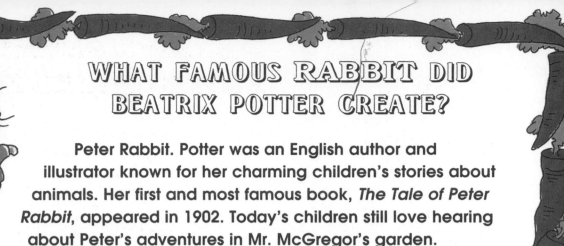

WHAT FAMOUS RABBIT DID BEATRIX POTTER CREATE?

Peter Rabbit. Potter was an English author and illustrator known for her charming children's stories about animals. Her first and most famous book, *The Tale of Peter Rabbit*, appeared in 1902. Today's children still love hearing about Peter's adventures in Mr. McGregor's garden.

HOW DID THE BARNUM AND BAILEY CIRCUS TRAVEL BETWEEN CONTINENTS?

In a ship resembling Noah's Ark. In 1902, lions, tigers, and elephants made the long sea journey from the U.S. to Europe, along with the famous Siamese twins, Eng and Chang. The Ringling brothers bought the circus in 1907, and turned it into "The Greatest Show on Earth."

What Was The Great Train Robbery?

An action-packed, 1903 western that was the first movie to tell an original story. The 10-minute film used stunt riders on horseback, chase scenes, and gunfights, none of which had ever been seen by film audiences. The clever editing gave the film a realistic look—another first in moviemaking. In one scene, an outlaw fired his pistol toward the camera, and the screen turned red! Audiences went wild.

WHERE WAS THE FIRST WORLD SERIES PLAYED?

Fans mobbed the Huntington Avenue ballpark in Boston, Massachusetts, in October 1903 to see the American League's Boston Pilgrims take on the National League's Pittsburgh Pirates. Boston won five games in the best-of-eight series. The winning players earned $1,182 each. (Today, some players earn more than that in a single inning!)

Who was the first woman to win a Nobel Prize?

Marie Curie. The Polish-born scientist shared the award for physics with her husband, Pierre Curie, and colleague, Antoine Becquerel, on December 10, 1903. The trio was recognized for its work studying radioactivity. Marie Curie won a second Nobel Prize in 1911, that time in chemistry. She is the only person to have won two Nobel Prizes!

WHICH WRIGHT BROTHER PILOTED THE FIRST AIRPLANE FLIGHT?

Orville Wright was at the controls during the first flight on December 17, 1903. The flight took place on a beach near Kitty Hawk, North Carolina. The Wright brothers' biplane flew 120 feet and was in the air for 12 seconds. They made three more flights that day. The longest (with Wilbur at the controls) traveled 852 feet in 59 seconds.

WHY DID SO MANY IMMIGRANTS COME TO THE UNITED STATES IN THE EARLY 1900s?

Most were poor and hoped that the U.S. would offer them a more prosperous way of life. Some left their homelands to escape from religious persecution. During the late 19th and early 20th centuries, millions of people, mainly from southern and eastern Europe, made the long voyage to the U.S. In 1904 alone, the U.S. admitted one million immigrants! The country continued to grow as a nation of many different cultures, traditions, and religions.

WHAT NEW DESSERT TREAT WAS SERVED AT THE ST. LOUIS WORLD'S FAIR?

The ice-cream cone. For the first time, vendors sold ice cream rolled in a waffle. The large crowds in the St. Louis heat ate them up! Fair visitors also enjoyed a new drink: iced tea. The 1904 fair, known as the Louisiana Purchase Exposition, celebrated the area's 100th anniversary as part of the United States.

HOLD THAT DOOR!

WHEN DID NEW YORK CITY'S UNDERGROUND RAILWAY OPEN?

Fifteen thousand people rode the rails on the new subway system's opening day, October 27, 1904. The first train took its passengers on a 9.1-mile trip (from City Hall in lower Manhattan to 145th Street) in 26 minutes—precisely on time. Riders admired the clean stations and the almost-silent ride provided by the olive-green cars.

WHERE DID THE FIRST NICKELODEON OPEN?

In Pittsburgh, Pennsylvania, in 1905. Usually, nickelodeons were stores that owners converted into movie theaters by installing chairs. A pianist played music that fit the action on the silent screen. These theaters were called nickelodeons because the admission fee was five cents.

WHAT WAS THE FIRST COUNTRY TO ALLOW FEMALE CITIZENS TO VOTE?

Finland granted women the vote in 1906, while it was still under Russian rule. The first fully independent country to grant equal voting rights was Norway, in 1913. The struggle for suffrage (voting rights for women) had begun at the first Women's Rights Convention in Seneca Falls, New York, in 1848. By 1900, that right had been won in several U.S. states and in New Zealand (then part of the British Empire). Not until 1920, when the 19th Amendment to the Constitution was passed, could U.S. women vote nationwide.

WHAT STARTED A THREE-DAY FIRE THAT DEVASTATED SAN FRANCISCO?

A severe earthquake. A few terrifying days in April 1906 were all it took to turn much of that thriving city into rubble. Thousands of panicked citizens fled. Others gathered in public squares and parks for safety. Damage estimates ran as high as $250 million. It was the worst disaster California had ever experienced.

WHO BECAME THE FIRST AFRICAN-AMERICAN HEAVYWEIGHT BOXING CHAMPION?

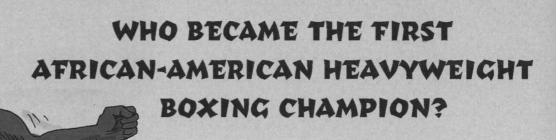

Jack Johnson of Galveston, Texas. He won by a TKO (technical knockout) on December 26, 1908, in Sydney, Australia. Although many white people were unhappy about a black man being boxing's champion, Johnson retained his title until 1915. He retired from the ring in 1928, after 112 professional bouts. He later appeared in vaudeville and carnival acts, and wrote two books about his life.

HOW WAS CELLOPHANE DISCOVERED?

By accident! A Swiss chemist named Jacques E. Brandenberger did it in 1908. Hoping to invent a stain-resistant tablecloth, he sprayed viscose on cloth. (Viscose is a thick, golden-brown solution taken from a plant fiber called cellulose.) Brandenberger found that he could peel the coating from the tablecloth in a thin, see-through sheet. Instead of inventing one useful household item, he had discovered another!

WHEN WAS THE FIRST MODEL T FORD BUILT?

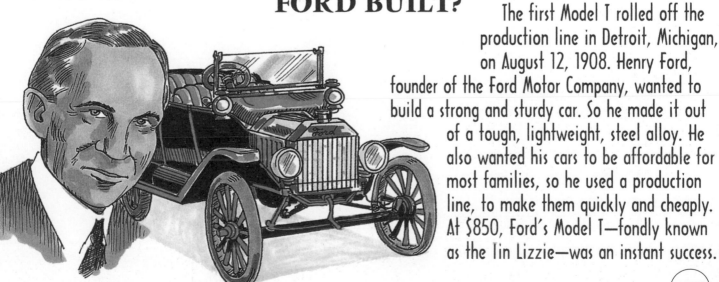

The first Model T rolled off the production line in Detroit, Michigan, on August 12, 1908. Henry Ford, founder of the Ford Motor Company, wanted to build a strong and sturdy car. So he made it out of a tough, lightweight, steel alloy. He also wanted his cars to be affordable for most families, so he used a production line, to make them quickly and cheaply. At $850, Ford's Model T—fondly known as the Tin Lizzie—was an instant success.

What were the years 1910 to 1919 most remembered for?

This decade was most remembered for the devastation of World War I, in which modern warfare was introduced.

WHY WERE PEOPLE AFRAID OF HALLEY'S COMET?

THE SKY IS FALLING!

The arrival of Halley's Comet in 1910 terrified many people. Some were convinced that the comet would release poisonous gases into the atmosphere. Others believed that it would cause a great earthquake. They were all wrong. The comet, named for astronomer Edmond Halley, reappears about every 76 years. Though a dramatic sight, it's too far away to damage our planet.

WHAT DOES NAACP STAND FOR?

National Association for the Advancement of Colored People. The NAACP is a civil-rights group dedicated to ending racial discrimination. Writer W. E. B. Du Bois (pictured) helped start the group in 1909, along with other Americans, both black and white. Today, it has hundreds of thousands of members.

HOW MANY PEOPLE WERE RESCUED FROM THE SINKING TITANIC?

Out of 2,340 passengers and crew members on board the *Titanic*, only 745 people were saved. The brand-new luxury liner hit an iceberg on April 15, 1912. There were not enough lifeboats to accommodate all the people aboard, many of whom were women and children. The ship and most of its passengers and crew did not survive the icy waters of the North Atlantic.

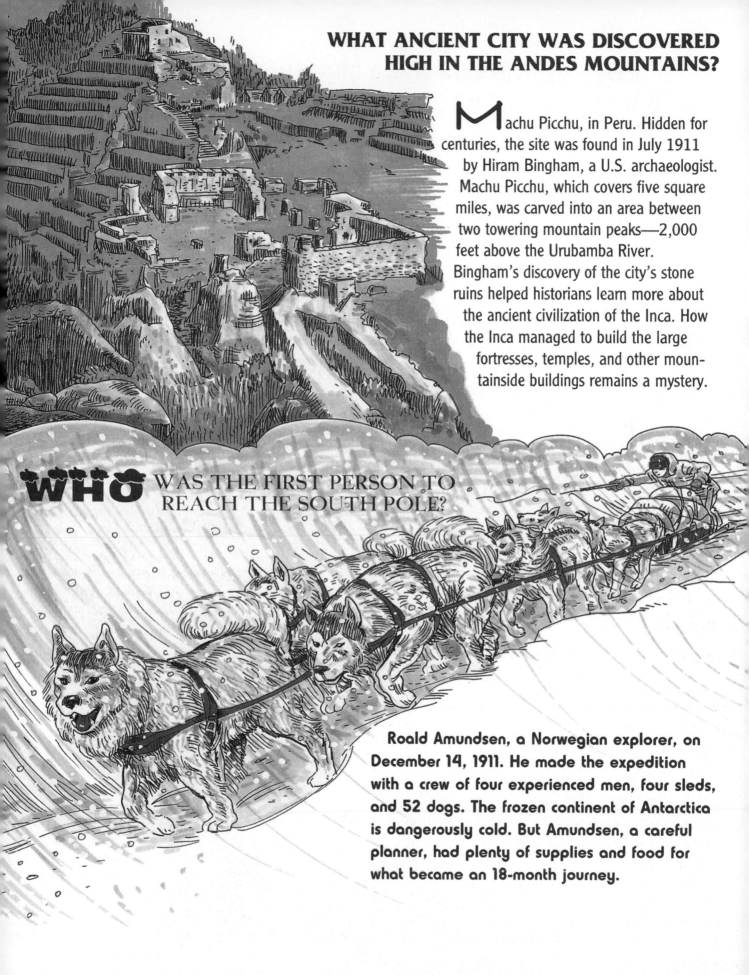

WHAT ANCIENT CITY WAS DISCOVERED HIGH IN THE ANDES MOUNTAINS?

Machu Picchu, in Peru. Hidden for centuries, the site was found in July 1911 by Hiram Bingham, a U.S. archaeologist. Machu Picchu, which covers five square miles, was carved into an area between two towering mountain peaks—2,000 feet above the Urubamba River. Bingham's discovery of the city's stone ruins helped historians learn more about the ancient civilization of the Inca. How the Inca managed to build the large fortresses, temples, and other mountainside buildings remains a mystery.

WHO WAS THE FIRST PERSON TO REACH THE SOUTH POLE?

Roald Amundsen, a Norwegian explorer, on December 14, 1911. He made the expedition with a crew of four experienced men, four sleds, and 52 dogs. The frozen continent of Antarctica is dangerously cold. But Amundsen, a careful planner, had plenty of supplies and food for what became an 18-month journey.

WHERE DID THE WORD *VITAMIN* COME FROM?

In 1912, Polish biochemist Casimir Funk coined the term *vitamine*, meaning *essential to life*. Frank (who moved to the U.S. in 1915) used the word to describe essential factors contained in foods that were vital to the human body. (The *e* was later dropped.)

WHO WAS CALLED "THE GREATEST ATHLETE IN THE WORLD"?

Jim Thorpe, a Native American, was an outstanding college and professional football and baseball player. But it was at the 1912 Olympic Games in Stockholm, Sweden, where he earned this title. Thorpe became the first athlete to win both the pentathlon and the decathlon (track-and-field events). Sweden's king told Thorpe, "Sir, you are the greatest athlete in the world."

WHAT TWO OCEANS WERE LINKED IN 1913?

HOW DO YOU DO!

IT'S A PLEASURE TO MEET YOU!

The Atlantic and the Pacific. They were joined on October 9, 1913, when a dynamite explosion demolished the last barrier, allowing water to flow through the new Panama Canal. The first boat traveled through on January 7, 1914. A decade in the making, the canal eliminated the need for ships to travel around South America. The waterway shortened the sea voyage between New York City and San Francisco from more than 13,000 miles to fewer than 5,200.

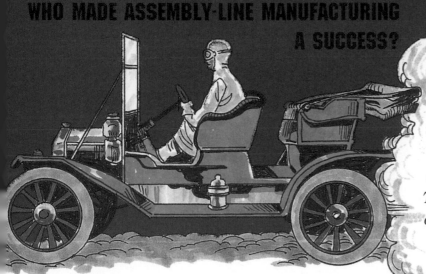

WHO MADE ASSEMBLY-LINE MANUFACTURING A SUCCESS?

Henry Ford. His company used a system by which conveyor belts carried automobile parts to teams of workers. Each team performed a single task, such as adding or tightening a part. When that team finished, the auto was moved on to the next team. This resulted in much greater output and a big drop in price for consumers. Ford's method of assembly forever changed the way products are made.

IT WASN'T MY UNCLE HARRY!

WHO WAS CALLED "THE FUNNIEST MAN IN THE WORLD"?

Silent-film star Charlie Chaplin. His stardom began in 1914, when he first appeared as "The Little Tramp." This comical character wore a derby hat, a jacket that was much too small, and pants that were much too large. Movie audiences adored him. Chaplin was the director, producer, writer, and star of his hilarious films. He composed the music for his later movies, which had sound.

HOW DID HOLLYWOOD BECOME THE FILM CENTER OF THE WORLD?

The first motion-picture companies were based in New York City and Fort Lee, New Jersey. But the weather limited when and where they could film. Lured westward by California's year-round sun, filmmakers started shooting near a little town outside Los Angeles. The first Hollywood studio opened in 1911—and that once-sleepy town soon became "Tinsel Town," film capital of the world.

WORLD WAR I

WHAT SET OFF WORLD WAR I?

On June 28, 1914, the heir to the Austrian throne, Archduke Francis Ferdinand, and his wife, Sophie, were being driven through the Bosnian capital of Sarajevo. A Bosnian Serb ran out from the crowd and fired three shots, killing them. Many people believed that this incident had been carefully planned by the Serbs. Austria-Hungary used the murders as an excuse to declare war on Serbia. Soon, the Central Powers (Germany, Austria-Hungary, and Turkey) and the Allies (France, Britain, Russia, the U.S., and Italy) were engaged in a bloody struggle that lasted until November 1918.

WHAT WAS "TRENCH WARFARE"?

New weapons, such as machine guns and heavy artillery, came into use during World War I. The best defense against them were lines of trenches—pits dug by soldiers. Dugouts made in the sides of the trenches protected men during enemy fire. Soldiers could store weapons and supplies in the dugouts, even live in them. Many troops spent the entire war in the cramped, cold trenches, which often were filled with mud.

WAS THERE REALLY A RED BARON?
Yes. Manfred von Richthofen was the most famous German fighter pilot of his day. The nickname came from his red plane. He supposedly destroyed 80 Allied aircraft in less than two years. He died in 1918, when he was shot down over the battlefields of France.

WHAT WEAPONS CHANGED THE WAY WARS WOULD BE FOUGHT IN THE FUTURE?

The machine gun, whose rapid fire could easily wipe out attacking soldiers, was one. Another was the tank, a British invention that ripped through barbed wire and crossed over trenches. The airplane was also first used in combat during World War I. New technology enabled submarines to torpedo enemy ships from beneath the sea.

WHO WERE CALLED "DOUGHBOYS"?

U.S. soldiers who fought in World War I. The nickname may have referred to the round brass buttons on the infantry uniforms, which looked like pastry. Or perhaps it came from all the doughnuts, supplied by the Salvation Army, that the soldiers ate.

WHO WAS THE FIRST WOMAN EVER ELECTED TO THE U.S. CONGRESS?

Jeannette Rankin. She first served as a member of Congress from 1917 to 1919, representing her home state of Montana. In 1940, she was reelected to the House of Representatives. A statue of Rankin in the U.S. Capitol in Washington, D.C., evokes her home state of Montana.

MUSIC BOX REVUE

WHO WAS IRVING BERLIN?

A popular songwriter. Berlin wrote his first successful song, "Alexander's Ragtime Band," in 1911. Until the early 1930s, he wrote songs for many Broadway musicals. He later moved to Hollywood, where he wrote for motion-picture musicals. Many of his songs are still popular, including "Easter Parade," "God Bless America," and "White Christmas."

WHAT WAS THE RUSSIAN REVOLUTION?

For many years, Russian peasants and workers had been treated unfairly by their government. During World War I, Russians suffered severe shortages of food, fuel, and housing, yet their leader, Czar Nicholas II, lived in luxury. In March 1917, peasants and soldiers protested. After violent riots, the czar was overthrown. Vladimir Lenin set up a new system, the world's first Communist government. The country later became known as the Union of Soviet Socialist Republics, or the Soviet Union.

Czar Nicholas and his family

WHO WAS LAWRENCE OF ARABIA?

Thomas Edward Lawrence was a British soldier, scholar, and writer. He took part in a 1916 British mission to aid the Arabs in their revolt against the Turkish Ottoman Empire. His success in driving the Turks from western Arabia made him a world-famous hero. He wrote a book about his adventure in Arabia, titled *The Seven Pillars of Wisdom*. *Lawrence of Arabia*, the still-popular film released in 1962, spread his fame even further.

WHO WAS THREATENED BY THE INFLUENZA EPIDEMIC OF 1918?

Millions of people worldwide. In October 1918, public-health officials estimated that the influenza epidemic raging across the world could cause 20 million deaths. They were correct. During World War I, it quickly spread through the European and American armies. The U.S. claimed that more servicemen died of influenza than of battle wounds! Then, as quickly and mysteriously as it had come, the epidemic disappeared!

WHAT WAS THE BLACK SOX SCANDAL?

In 1919, the Cincinnati Reds defeated the Chicago White Sox in the World Series. However, eight White Sox players were charged with conspiring with gamblers to lose on purpose. This became known as the Black Sox scandal. It shocked fans and hurt baseball's reputation. Although the players were acquitted by a jury, their careers were shattered. Baseball appointed its first commissioner, who banned the players from major-league baseball.

WHAT TRENDS WERE SET BY THE U.S. BETWEEN 1920 AND 1929?

The U.S. set trends in movies, nightclubs, and music. After the misery of the First World War, people wanted to enjoy life. Women wore makeup and shorter skirts—and smoked cigarettes in public for the first time. Higher wages enabled Americans to buy costly items, such as their first automobile or refrigerator. During the "Roaring Twenties," as this decade is known, the U.S. began to grow into the modern society it is today.

WHO WAS RUDOLPH VALENTINO?

IT'S A SILENT MOVIE!

WHAT WAS PROHIBITION?

On January 16, 1920, the Eighteenth Amendment—known as Prohibition—took effect. It outlawed the making, selling, and transporting of liquor. Illegal bars called speakeasies sprang up, and many Americans secretly brewed liquor at home. The illegal supply of alcohol, called bootlegging, and the competition to control this business led to gang wars.

Rudolph Valentino was the most popular romantic star of the silent movies. Born Rodolfo D'Antonguolla in Italy in 1895, he moved to New York in 1913. He toured the U.S. as a dancer until 1917, when he arrived in Hollywood. In 1921, Valentino's films *The Four Horsemen of the Apocalypse* and *The Sheik* catapulted him into superstardom. Female moviegoers everywhere adored him—some even fainted at the sight of him on the big screen!

WHY WERE THE 1920s KNOWN AS "THE JAZZ AGE"?

At first, jazz was little known, except among mostly black musicians in the southern U.S. But in the 1920s, radio stations began to feature such musicians as Louis Armstrong and Bessie Smith, and jazz won new fans all over the country. Clubs and dance halls sprang up in big cities—Chicago, New York, Paris, and London. "The Jazz Age," also known as "the Golden Age of Jazz," was a time when this style of music first became popular all over the U.S. and in Europe.

What was the COTTON CLUB?

A popular nightclub in Harlem (part of New York City). It featured black music stars, such as Duke Ellington and Count Basie and their bands, performing for white audiences. (The Cotton Club admitted African Americans only as performers, not as patrons.) The club was part of the "Harlem Renaissance" of the 1920s, a time of great creativity among African-American musicians, writers, painters, and other artists living and working in Harlem.

WILL HE MAKE IT?

WAS CHARLES LINDBERGH THE FIRST PERSON TO FLY ACROSS THE ATLANTIC?

No, he was the 67th—but the first to do it alone! On May 20, 1927, Lindbergh took off from Roosevelt Field on Long Island, New York. He arrived, 33 1/2 hours later, at Le Bourget Airport near Paris, France, where he was met by more than 100,000 joyous spectators. Lindbergh's single-engine plane, the *Spirit of St. Louis*, made the dangerous, 3,600-mile, nonstop flight through wind and rain.

Where did the first BLOODY SUNDAY take place?

Dublin, Ireland, in 1920. That year, the British Parliament divided Ireland into two states. Northern Ireland accepted the division, but the southern state began fighting for independence. On Sunday, November 21, the Irish Republican Army (IRA) killed 14 British officials in a raid. British troops retaliated by firing into a crowd of Dubliners, killing 12 and injuring 60. In 1921, the Catholic, southern part of Ireland became the Irish Free State, while the mostly Protestant north remained part of the United Kingdom. (The second Bloody Sunday was a clash in Londonderry, Northern Ireland, on January 30, 1972.)

Where was King Tut's tomb found?

In Egypt's Valley of the Kings. Howard Carter, a British archaeologist, had been searching long and hard for an ancient tomb he believed to be hidden there. In 1922, he finally found it. On November 26, 1922, he and Lord Carnarvon, the man who had funded his search, broke open the sealed doorway to the centuries-old tomb. Inside, they found treasure-filled chambers—and the mummy of Tutankhamen, a pharaoh (king) who was only 17 when he died in 1323 B.C.

HOW DID LON CHANEY PUT A SCARE INTO MOVIEGOERS?

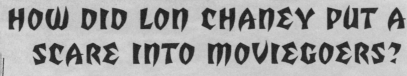

Known as Hollywood's "man of a thousand faces," Lon Chaney was an actor who specialized in horror movies. His use of makeup both terrified and delighted film audiences. In 1923, he starred in *The Hunchback of Notre Dame* as Quasimodo, a fearsome, hunchbacked creature with a bulging eye. For that role, Chaney wore a heavy rubber outfit that changed the shape of his body.

WHAT FEAT DID *"THE FLYING FINN"* ACCOMPLISH?

He won five gold medals at the 1924 Olympic Games in Paris, France. Paavo Nurmi of Finland—known as "the Flying Finn"—took first place in the 1,500-meter, 3,000-meter, and 5,000-meter races; in the cross-country individual race; and as a member of the cross-country team. Nurmi, who had won gold and silver medals in the 1920 Olympics, went on to earn more medals at the 1928 Games.

Who was Mohandas K. Gandhi?

A spiritual and political leader who played a major role in India's struggle for independence from Great Britain. The people of India called him the Mahatma, which means "Great Soul." Gandhi's moral strength and nonviolent methods earned him worldwide admiration. Beginning in 1920, he called for Indians to stop cooperating with Britain's government. He led peaceful protest marches that gave the poor and weak more power than an armed force. After India won independence in 1947, he went on hunger strikes to protest fighting between India's Hindus and Muslims. Though a nonviolent man, Gandhi died by violence. He was shot to death by a Hindu fanatic in 1948.

WHO DISCOVERED ANIMAL FILM STAR RIN TIN TIN?

U.S. Army corporal Lee Duncan found the German shepherd in a bunker during World War I. Back in Los Angeles, the smart canine learned to perform stunts and was a natural in front of a camera. Rin Tin Tin's movies were a mix of drama, comedy, and adventure. For several years, "Rinty" was the Warner Brothers studio's biggest money-earning star!

217

WHAT GROUP MARCHED ON WASHINGTON IN 1925?

The Ku Klux Klan. The KKK first formed in the South after the Civil War. Its goal was to keep newly freed blacks from voting and exercising other rights, by harassing, terrorizing, or even murdering them. On August 8, 1925, members of this racist group marched in the nation's capital, wearing white robes and waving flags. As the 40,000 marchers reached the Washington Monument, a heavy rain began to fall, washing out the KKK's plans to hold a ceremony and burn an 80-foot cross.

WHAT WAS THE TELEVISOR?

SOMEDAY WE'LL SHOW CARTOONS.

A system for sending moving images over airwaves . . . or, simply put, television. John Baird, a Scottish engineer, gave the first public demonstration of his system in London on January 27, 1926. The quality of the images was not as good as that achieved by film, but the demonstration proved that moving pictures could be sent electronically through the air. A few people even thought that the televisor might one day be as popular as radio!

WHO IS CALLED THE "FATHER OF MODERN ROCKETRY"?

Dr. Robert H. Goddard, an American physicist. His experiments led to the development of modern missiles and spacecraft. In March 1926, Goddard launched the world's first liquid-fueled rocket. Critics mocked Goddard's predictions of space travel. Only after his death in 1945 was he recognized for his contributions to space exploration. NASA's Goddard Space Flight Center (its first) was named in his honor.

Where did Babe Ruth play before joining the New York Yankees?

Boston. The famous slugger started out as a pitcher for the Red Sox. In January 1920, the Yankees paid the Red Sox $125,000 for his contract. Ruth's home-run hitting and colorful personality made him a favorite with baseball fans. In 1920, he hit 54 homers. (Only one entire *team* hit more that year!)

What character did writer A. A. Milne introduce to readers in 1926?

Winnie-the-Pooh. Milne, an English author, wrote a book by that name, describing the adventures of a boy named Christopher Robin, a bear named Pooh, and their friends in a forest. (He wrote them for his son, Christopher.) In 1928, Milne came out with more Pooh stories in *The House at Pooh Corner*. The Pooh books have been translated into many languages, making Pooh a beloved character around the world.

WHEN DID THE HARLEM GLOBETROTTERS BOUNCE INTO EXISTENCE?

The all African-American basketball team played their first game in 1927. In the beginning, the Globetrotters played regular basketball, usually beating their opponents. But then the team began to clown around, using trick passes to entertain crowds. The team's reputation for family entertainment continues to draw fans worldwide.

I DON'T PLAY BASEBALL....

...OR BASKETBALL.

219

What was special about Walt Disney's 1928 cartoon, STEAMBOAT WILLIE?

HONK-HONK!

TWEET!

TOOT-TOOT!

It was the first cartoon to feature synchronized sound: characters that could speak, dance to music, and come to life with sound effects. The film starred a character named Mickey Mouse. Mickey's high-pitched voice was performed by one of his creators, Walt Disney. The cartoon was a success, and Disney's company went on to produce some of the most-loved animated films in history.

Whose 1927 film debut was called *Putting Pants on Philip*?

Stan Laurel and Oliver Hardy—considered the most popular comedy duo in U.S. film history. They teamed up in 1926 after meeting in Hollywood. Audiences loved the duo's bumbling and bickering, and their sense of physical comedy. They starred in more than 60 short films and 27 feature films.

What were the LINDY HOP and the CHARLESTON?

Popular dances of the 1920s. The lindy hop began in New York City. Its name came from a dance fan who said, while watching a couple on the dance floor, "Look at those kids hoppin' over there. I guess they're doing the lindy hop!" "Lindy" was Charles Lindbergh, the pilot who had just made a historic transatlantic plane flight. The Charleston—developed in Charleston, South Carolina—was done with turned-in knees and turned-out toes and elbows at a frantic pace. It could be done alone, with a partner, or in a group.

WHO WERE THE MARX BROTHERS?

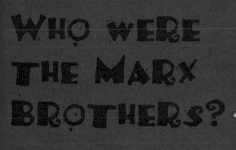

Chico Marx

A famous comedy team from New York City. Originally vaudeville stage performers, Chico, Harpo, Groucho, and Zeppo Marx released their first film, *The Cocoanuts*, in 1929. The brothers shot the film during the day, then performed their Broadway hit, *Animal Crackers*, on the stage at night! Their zany antics, wisecracks, and puns made them hugely popular (and fans still enjoy their films today). The Marx Brothers continued to make movies well into the 1940s.

Groucho Marx

Harpo Marx

Why is October 24, 1929, called Black Thursday?

During the 1920s, the U.S. economy grew rapidly. Many Americans invested money in the stock market, hoping to make a quick profit. But as the decade came to a close, the economy fell into serious trouble. On Saturday, October 19, share prices began to fall—and investors panicked. They sold their stocks at any price, and prices plummeted. On "Black Thursday," a record-high number of shares were traded. By the end of the week, people all over the world were facing financial ruin. The 1929 stock-market crash marked the beginning of the Great Depression of the 1930s.

How was PENICILLIN discovered?

By accident. Alexander Fleming, a Scottish bacteriologist, was trying to find a substance that would kill bacteria without harming humans. In 1928, he noticed that a bit of green mold growing in a culture plate had destroyed the bacteria around it! He isolated the active chemical in the mold, and named it *penicillin*. This nontoxic substance proved to be very effective against many bacteria harmful to people, such as those that cause pneumonia. Penicillin has saved untold millions of lives.

Search & Find®
for these fun
items in the

Roaring
Twenties

- Basketball
- Cactus
- Cane
- Cat
- Coffeepot
- Crown
- Drumsticks
- Envelope
- Fish
- Hearts (6)
- Igloo
- Lost shoe
- Mouse
- Pearl necklaces (2)
- Pyramid
- Red balloons (2)
- Saxophone
- Tepee
- Top hat
- Turtle
- Umbrella
- Unicorn
- Witch

Answers on page 315

What caused the entire world to fall into a period of decline known as the Great Depression?

The stock market crash of 1929, when huge fortunes were lost. Many banks closed. Factory production slowed down. Jobs disappeared. Businesses suffered. Families lost their homes. Hungry people stood in long lines for free soup and bread. Professionals who once had high-paying jobs sold apples on street corners for nickels and dimes. The carefree life of the Roaring Twenties had become just a fading memory.

Who said, "The only thing we have to fear is fear itself"?

Franklin D. Roosevelt, on March 4, 1933, the day he was sworn in as president. As he spoke, 13 million Americans were jobless. "Our greatest primary task," he also said that day, "is to put people to work." Roosevelt held regular "fireside chats" on the radio to speak directly to the American people, explaining what the government was doing to help end the Depression.

How did the unemployed in the U.S. survive?

Some people got food from private charities or religious missions. (Unlike today, there were few public-welfare programs.) Others were reduced to begging. Homeless people crowded into the homes of relatives or friends, or built shacks out of crates and flattened tin cans. Groups of these shacks were often referred to as "Hoovervilles," an insulting reference to Herbert Hoover, who was president when the Depression began. Many homeless men, known as hobos, went from place to place seeking work, walking, hitchhiking, or hopping into railroad freight cars.

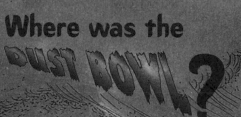

Where was the DUST BOWL?

During a mid-1930s drought, a chain of dust storms swept over a large section of the American Midwest. Clouds of dust destroyed crops and killed herds of cattle, wiping out farmers' livelihoods. People had to wear masks to protect themselves from breathing the harmful, dust-filled air. Thousands of farmers were forced to abandon their land and search for better lives elsewhere.

How did the New Deal help Americans?

After being elected in 1932, President Franklin D. Roosevelt enacted a reform program called the New Deal to help rescue people from the Depression. By raising taxes and borrowing money through the sale of government bonds, FDR's plan put Americans to work building streets, bridges, and public buildings. The New Deal also helped farmers, and provided job training and work for the unemployed.

WHEN DID THE DEPRESSION END?

The Great Depression ended when the U.S. and other nations increased their production of war materials during the buildup for World War II (1939-1945). This created many jobs and pumped large amounts of money into the economy. Factories sprang back to life to manufacture airplanes, weapons, and other military goods. The war, though terrible, helped put an end to worldwide unemployment and poverty.

MAMA MARY!

What Mary Shelley novel became a horror film?

Frankenstein. Shelley, an English author, wrote her now-famous novel in 1818. In 1931, Universal Pictures released a movie based on the book, featuring a little-known actor named Boris Karloff. He played the role of Dr. Frankenstein's monster, a creature made from dead bodies. The film, which made Karloff a star, is now considered an American classic.

Who was Al Capone?

One of the most powerful gangsters in U.S. history, Capone (1899-1947) controlled Chicago's liquor and gambling rackets and built a criminal empire that netted an estimated $100 million a year. Though he was believed to be responsible for more than 400 gang-war killings, law-enforcement officials had trouble proving those charges against him. He was finally convicted and jailed in 1931—for income-tax fraud. After serving eight years in federal prisons, he was released due to illness. Capone died in Florida in 1947.

WHAT KIND OF MUSIC DID PEOPLE "SWING" TO DURING THE THIRTIES?

A new style of jazz, called swing. Big bands—led by such musicians as Woody Herman, Glenn Miller, Count Basie, and Harry James—dominated this era. Benny Goodman was the first white bandleader to feature black musicians and white musicians playing together in public. A big band usually consisted of horns (saxophone, trumpet, and trombone), a rhythm section (bass, drums, piano, and guitar), and a singer. People flocked to theaters and dance halls to hear their favorite big bands.

HOW DID THE MUSICAL
Porgy & Bess
DIFFER FROM PREVIOUS MUSICALS AND OPERAS?

This "folk opera" combined the serious drama and musical treatment of opera with jazz and folk music. It also was the first Broadway musical with an all-African-American cast. *Porgy and Bess* has been called the most popular opera ever written by an American. (George Gershwin wrote the music; his brother, Ira, wrote the lyrics with Du Bose Howard.) *Porgy and Bess* opened on Broadway on October 10, 1935. It was made into a film in 1959.

HOME SWEET HOME!

SKULL ISLAND

WHO WAS CAPTURED ON SKULL ISLAND?

That famous ape of the silver screen, King Kong. The film *King Kong* (released in 1933) is about a gigantic ape that is seized from his home on Skull Island and taken to New York City. Kong breaks free and searches for the fair-haired beauty (played by Fay Wray) he loves. In the film's most famous scene, Kong is gunned down off the top of the Empire State Building by airplanes. Trick photography and stop-action animation (frame-by-frame shooting of an 18-inch-tall toy ape) were used to create a realistic-looking 50-foot ape on big movie screens.

WHERE DID THE "LONG MARCH" TAKE PLACE?

China. In October 1934, Mao Zedong, founder of China's Communist Party, led his army on a 6,000-mile journey across southwestern China. They were being pursued by Chinese Nationalist troops. When the trek and fighting ended 12 months later, only half of Mao's original 90,000 followers had survived. Mao later became ruler of China and one of the world's most powerful people.

How many CURLS did child star Shirley Temple wear in her hair?

Fifty-six! Her mother, Gertrude, who made sure of the exact number, set them. At the 1935 Academy Awards ceremony, Shirley Temple, age 6, was awarded a miniature Oscar for her "outstanding contribution to screen entertainment" in 1934. That same year, she sang and danced in the films *The Little Colonel* and *The Littlest Rebel*. By the time Shirley was 10, she was the biggest box-office attraction in the nation.

Why did Britain's King Edward VIII give up his throne?

To marry Wallis Simpson, a divorced American. The king was under heavy pressure from the British government and church not to marry her. On December 11, 1936, in a radio broadcast that shocked his nation, Edward said that he was unable to bear the burden of being king without her. He gave the throne to his younger brother, George VI.

What did *Guernica*, Pablo Picasso's 1937 painting, depict?

Human terror and suffering when the town of Guernica, Spain, was bombed during the Spanish Civil War (1936-1939). It was the first time in history that a town or city was struck by an aerial bombing raid (1,700 people were killed). The painting was Picasso's protest against the destruction of the town by German bomber planes. The war in Spain was between army rebels (supported by Germany) and the elected government (supported by the Soviet Union). By the time resistance to the army collapsed, Spain was a devastated country.

What was the first recorded radio report to be broadcasted coast to coast?

A report describing the explosion of the German dirigible *Hindenburg*, at Lakehurst, New Jersey, on May 6, 1937. An electrical storm approached as the ground crew struggled to moor the 804-foot, hydrogen-filled aircraft. There was a boom and a flash, then the *Hindenburg* exploded into flames. Thirty-five of the 97 people aboard were killed. A recording of broadcaster Herbert Morrison's description of the historic event was flown to New York, then broadcast nationwide.

WHO WAS JESSE OWENS?

An American track-and-field star of the 1936 Olympic Games. He won four gold medals at the Summer Games in Berlin, Germany. The excellence shown by Owens, an African American, embarrassed Germany's racist leader, Adolf Hitler. Hitler had expected his athletes to prove that Germans were the superior race. When this did not happen, he stormed out of the stadium, refusing to congratulate Owens.

What happened to Amelia Earhart?

She disappeared! Earhart and Fred Noonan, her navigator, were flying over the Pacific Ocean on the hardest leg of a round-the-world flight when their plane vanished near tiny Howland Island. On July 2, 1937, Earhart radioed the island, saying: "We are listening but cannot hear you." Earhart's last message, broadcast 45 minutes later, was unclear. The plane vanished, and she and Noonan were never seen again. Among the many achievements of the "first lady of the air" was becoming the first woman to fly solo across the Atlantic Ocean, in 1932.

What was the major source of home entertainment in the 1930s?

Radio. In the evenings, families gathered in their living rooms to listen to comedies and dramas. Popular programs, such as *The Shadow*, *Dick Tracy*, and *The Lone Ranger*, kept people glued to their radios. Concerts and other music programs were also popular—so popular that the term *disc jockey* was coined to describe radio announcers who played records. In the late 1930s, as another major war seemed likely, radio stations developed news departments to report on the latest events in Europe.

What pre-Halloween radio program made Americans panic?

TRICK OR TREAT?

On October 30, 1938, actor-producer Orson Welles broadcast a science-fiction thriller entitled "Invasion from Mars." The sound effects were so good that millions of radio listeners thought it was the real thing! Welles's radio play (based on the book *War of the Worlds* by H. G. Wells) sounded like a news broadcast about Martians invading New Jersey. It sounded so real that hundreds of people ran out of their homes with handkerchiefs over their mouths to guard against "Martian gas"!

Where did "CRYSTAL NIGHT" take place?

In Germany and Austria. On the night of November 9, 1938, Adolf Hitler's Nazi troops broke into and wrecked thousands of stores run by Jewish merchants. Jews were attacked and beaten, and hundreds of Jewish homes and places of worship were set on fire. That outburst of violence became known as *Kristallnacht*—"the night of broken glass"—because of the piles of broken glass from smashed store windows left in the streets.

Who was the first U.S. president to appear on TV?

Franklin D. Roosevelt. On April 30, 1939, television cameras filmed the speech he gave at opening-day ceremonies for the World's Fair held in Queens, a borough of New York City. The crude TV pictures were fuzzy but recognizable. Development of this new medium was temporarily halted when World War II broke out in Europe four months later.

What comic book character was created by 18-year-old artist Bob Kane?

Batman. Kane originally called his superhero Birdman, but by the time the Caped Crusader appeared in the May 1939 issue of *Detective Comics*, his name had been changed. Kane was one of the first illustrators to use movie-style angles in comics, creating an eerie, shadowy atmosphere. Since 1939, Kane's character has appeared in radio programs, television series, and many movies.

WHAT $3,000,000 MUSICAL FILM FANTASY PREMIERED ON AUGUST 15, 1939?

The Wizard of Oz. Based on a 1900 novel by L. Frank Baum, this classic story had already been made into movies, short cartoons, a stage show, and a radio program. But the 1939 film version, starring Judy Garland as Dorothy, is the most famous. The MGM studio spent an extra $250,000 to promote what it called "the greatest picture in the history of entertainment."

231

What war broke out by 1939?

World War II (1939-1945) broke out in Europe and Asia. It dominated the first half of the century's fifth decade. By the time it was over, some 45 million people worldwide, civilians as well as soldiers, had been killed. When the fighting ended, people turned to building a new future.

Where were paintings by cavemen first discovered?

In Dordogne, France. In September 1940, four schoolboys were hunting rabbits when their dog disappeared down a hole. The boys followed—and discovered a prehistoric cave with walls covered by paintings and engravings of animals! Many of the animals, such as bison and a rhinoceros, were recognizable. But some were unknown creatures that resembled unicorns. Archaeologists estimated that the ancient paintings dated back to 15,000-13,000 B.C.

Who was Alfred Hitchcock?

OUR FAVORITE FILM IS THE BIRDS!

A British movie director and producer who specialized in thrillers. In 1929, he made *Blackmail*, the first British feature film with sound. Ten years later, he moved to the U.S. and won fame with *Rebecca*, which won the 1940 Best Picture Academy Award. Hitchcock made many classic movies, such as *Rear Window*, *Notorious*, and *Psycho*, that blended drama, action, and suspense with comic irony.

DID MOST AMERICAN FAMILIES OWN A TV SET IN THE EARLY 1940s?

No. Up until 1945, there were fewer than 10,000 TV sets in the U.S., and broadcasting was limited to only a few cities. Radio was king. But when World War II ended, a television boom began. New and improved TV sets were introduced, their prices came down to what more people could afford, and TV stations came on the air at a rapid pace. By the end of the 1940s, more than 6 million U.S. households had television sets.

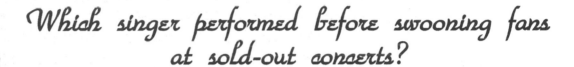

Which singer performed before swooning fans at sold-out concerts?

Frank Sinatra. He first gained popularity while touring as a singer with the Tommy Dorsey Band. But he catapulted to fame in 1942, when he began singing solo—and broke all attendance records at New York's Paramount Theater. His fans—mostly young women, at first—were known as bobby-soxers (for their socks and saddle shoes). Through his countless recordings, concert and television appearances, and starring roles in hit movies, Francis Albert Sinatra (1915-1998) became one of the most popular entertainers in the world.

WHAT WAS BEBOP?

A new style of music that small groups of jazz musicians began playing in the early 1940s. Bebop, or bop, was usually played by a five- or six-piece combo. These jazz bands played complicated melodies with improvised solos. Saxophonist Charlie Parker, trumpeters Dizzy Gillespie and Miles Davis, and pianist Thelonious Monk were a few of the extraordinary musicians who created this style of music.

WHAT WAS THE BATTLE OF BRITAIN?

Germany's attempt to conquer Great Britain. German leader Adolf Hitler set off World War II by invading Poland in September 1939. In August 1940, the German air force began sending an average of 400 planes a day to bomb British airfields and towns. But the tiny Royal Air Force (RAF)—aided by radar, a new invention—valiantly defended the British Isles. That dashed Germany's hopes for a quick surrender, and Hitler had to abandon the idea of invading Britain.

How did the United States enter the war?

On December 7, 1941, Japan attacked and destroyed much of the U.S. Pacific fleet anchored at Pearl Harbor, Hawaii. The next day, the U.S. declared war on Japan. A few days later, Germany and Italy declared war on the U.S. The Allies (Great Britain, Canada, Australia, New Zealand, France, China, the Soviet Union, and the U.S.) were then at war with the Axis Powers (Germany, Japan, and Italy). In all, World War II involved 40 countries and almost 70 million soldiers.

Who was "Rosie the Riveter"?

"Rosie" was not a real person, but a symbolic name for all the U.S. women who went to work—many for the first time—while the men were at war. Women became expert welders, truck drivers, and crane operators and did many other jobs once done only by men. Female factory and shipyard workers helped the country through a difficult time.

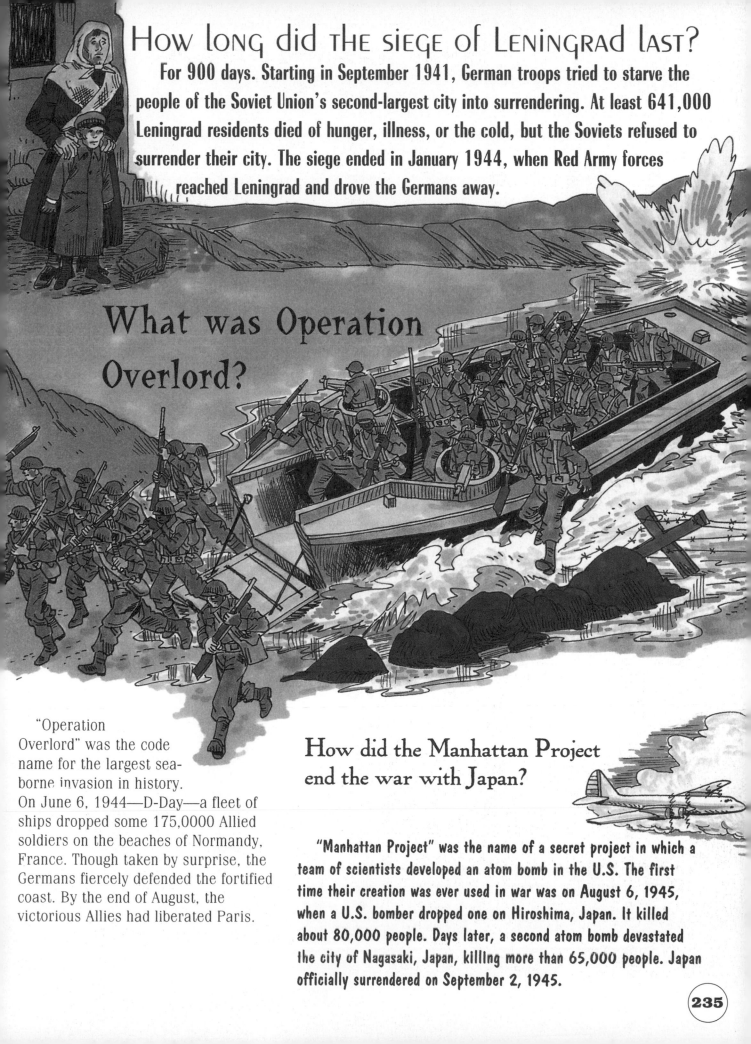

How long did the siege of Leningrad last?

For 900 days. Starting in September 1941, German troops tried to starve the people of the Soviet Union's second-largest city into surrendering. At least 641,000 Leningrad residents died of hunger, illness, or the cold, but the Soviets refused to surrender their city. The siege ended in January 1944, when Red Army forces reached Leningrad and drove the Germans away.

What was Operation Overlord?

"Operation Overlord" was the code name for the largest sea-borne invasion in history. On June 6, 1944—D-Day—a fleet of ships dropped some 175,0000 Allied soldiers on the beaches of Normandy, France. Though taken by surprise, the Germans fiercely defended the fortified coast. By the end of August, the victorious Allies had liberated Paris.

How did the Manhattan Project end the war with Japan?

"Manhattan Project" was the name of a secret project in which a team of scientists developed an atom bomb in the U.S. The first time their creation was ever used in war was on August 6, 1945, when a U.S. bomber dropped one on Hiroshima, Japan. It killed about 80,000 people. Days later, a second atom bomb devastated the city of Nagasaki, Japan, killing more than 65,000 people. Japan officially surrendered on September 2, 1945.

WHAT WAS THE JITTERBUG?

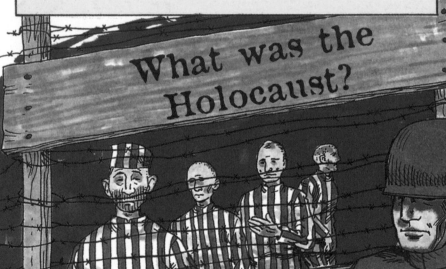

Which U.S. President was elected to office four times?

Franklin D. Roosevelt. He was the only U.S. president elected four times. FDR was first elected in 1932 during the Great Depression, and was reelected in 1936, 1940, and 1944. He died in office in 1945. In 1951, the states approved Amendment XXII to the Constitution, which limits the presidency to two terms.

What was the Holocaust?

The mass murder of European Jews by German Nazis during World War II. Nazi dictator Adolf Hitler planned to wipe out the entire Jewish population as part of his attempt to conquer the world. (The word *holocaust* has come to mean "widespread destruction.") Concentration and work camps were established to imprison Jews of all ages. Millions of Jews were killed in the camps and elsewhere. The Germans tried to keep their destructive actions a secret. But as the war came to an end, Allied forces began to discover the camps—and the horrors of Hitler's plan.

It was a very popular dance. The jitterbug was first seen in the U.S. during the 1930s, but American soldiers stationed in Europe started a jitterbug craze in the 1940s. Female dancers wore swirling skirts, turned-down socks, and saddle shoes. The jitterbug was danced to swing music. Both partners had to be athletic to perform the "underarm swing."

When did the United Nations hold its first session?

On January 11, 1946, in London, England. Delegates from 51 countries discussed where the permanent headquarters should be located. (It was later agreed that it would be in New York City.) They also solved their first real problem—a conflict between Iran and the Soviet Union—by getting the two countries to settle their differences through negotiation, rather than war. The UN has worked toward world peace ever since.

WHAT WAS THE IRON CURTAIN?

"Iron curtain" was a phrase used by Britain's Sir Winston Churchill, in a 1946 speech, to describe the threat of communism. Churchill said that Europe was being divided by an "iron curtain": a split between democratic countries (such as Britain and France) and communist countries (led by the Soviet Union). He urged the U.S. and Britain to join efforts to discourage the spread of communism.

What piece of clothing caused a shock in 1946?

The bikini. It caused a sensation when it was first revealed in Paris, France, on July 5, 1946. The daring, tiny, two-piece swimsuit was created by a French designer, who named it after Bikini Atoll, a tiny island in the Pacific. (Four days earlier, an atom bomb had been tested on the island.) The name fit the swimsuit's "explosive" impact on the fashion world.

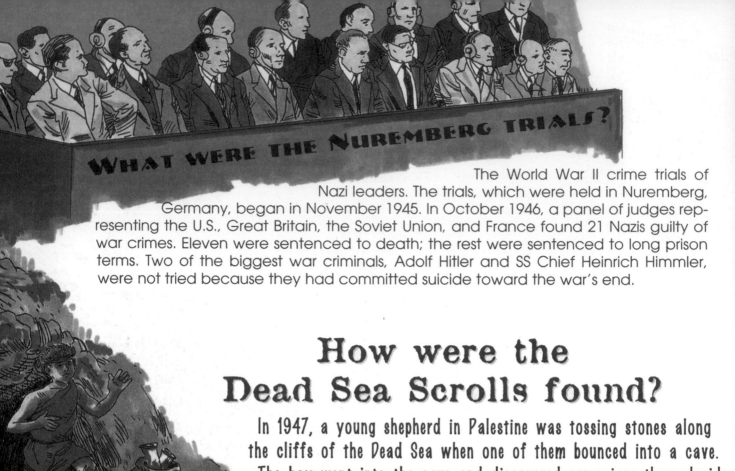

WHAT WERE THE NUREMBERG TRIALS?

The World War II crime trials of Nazi leaders. The trials, which were held in Nuremberg, Germany, began in November 1945. In October 1946, a panel of judges representing the U.S., Great Britain, the Soviet Union, and France found 21 Nazis guilty of war crimes. Eleven were sentenced to death; the rest were sentenced to long prison terms. Two of the biggest war criminals, Adolf Hitler and SS Chief Heinrich Himmler, were not tried because they had committed suicide toward the war's end.

How were the Dead Sea Scrolls found?

In 1947, a young shepherd in Palestine was tossing stones along the cliffs of the Dead Sea when one of them bounced into a cave. The boy went into the cave and discovered some jars there. Inside the jars were fragile parchment scrolls, later found to date back to the first century B.C.! They were copies of stories from the Old Testament. This was one of the great archaeological finds of the 20th century.

How did Jackie Robinson become major-league baseball's first African-American player?

Branch Rickey, general manager of the Brooklyn Dodgers, knew that it would take a special man to be the first black player in the all-white major leagues. Rickey chose Jackie Robinson to be that man.

In April 1947, Robinson made his first appearance at Brooklyn's Ebbets Field. Despite racial slurs and threats of violence from some players and fans, he excelled on and off the field, and had an outstanding 10-year career with the Dodgers. Robinson was inducted into the Baseball Hall of Fame in 1962, the first year he was eligible.

Why was Anne Frank's diary published?

Anne Frank was a German-Jewish girl who kept a diary while hiding from the Nazis with her family and other Jews during World War II. They hid in secret rooms behind her father's office in Amsterdam. Anne wrote about life in hiding, as well as her private hopes and dreams. The Nazis found the hiders and sent them to concentration camps. Only Anne's father, Otto Frank—and her diary—survived. He had *Anne Frank: The Diary of a Young Girl* published in 1947, to give people a sense of what it was like to live through the Holocaust.

What two Asian nations became independent in 1947?

PAKISTAN

WQPEI

INDIA

PAKISTAN

ARABIAN SEA

BANGLADESH (NOW)

BAY OF BENGAL

India and Pakistan. That year, after 163 years as a colony of Great Britain, India finally achieved independence. But violence continued between India's Hindus and Muslims until that country's leaders divided the country, creating East and West Pakistan. Many Muslims fled from India to Pakistan, and many Hindus from Pakistan to India. East Pakistan later became the independent country of Bangladesh.

6062

WHAT AMAZING FEAT DID PILOT CHUCK YEAGER PERFORM?

Yeager was the first person to fly faster than the speed of sound. On October 14, 1947, he boarded the *Glamorous Glennis*, a Bell X-1 rocket plane, and made aviation history. Yeager flew at an altitude of 43,000 feet at up to 700 mph, breaking the sound barrier. (The speed of sound is about 741 mph at sea level; less at higher altitudes.) When the sound barrier is broken, people on the ground hear a loud, thunder-like sound called a sonic boom.

Who developed the first instant camera?

Edwin Land, founder and president of the Polaroid Corporation. In 1947, he demonstrated the first instant camera. It took black-and-white pictures that developed into prints in only 60 seconds! By the 1970s, Land had improved the Polaroid camera to take and develop color pictures within 50 seconds.

What did scientist Percy Spencer discover by accident?

Microwave cooking. While working in a lab, Spencer noticed that a candy bar in his pocket had melted. He figured out that the microwave signals he had been using in the lab had caused the candy bar's molecules to vibrate rapidly. This caused friction among the molecules, which created heat, which melted the candy bar. The first microwave oven was patented in 1945.

WHEN WERE LONG-PLAYING RECORDS INTRODUCED?

In 1948. Before then, most records were made of a shellac-and-clay mixture and were played on a phonograph at 78 rpm (revolutions per minute). They broke easily, and could hold only four minutes of music per side. In 1948, Columbia Records developed a 33 1/3-rpm, long-playing (LP) record made of vinyl. LPs held nearly 25 minutes of music per side, provided better sound quality, and were more durable. The vinyl LP was the standard for decades—until the arrival of cassette tapes (1963) and compact discs (1982).

Who was the first baseball player to earn $100,000 a year?

Centerfielder Joe DiMaggio, in 1949. Many people criticized his big contract request, but DiMaggio was invaluable to his team, the New York Yankees. He was voted the American League's MVP (Most Valuable Player) in 1939, 1941, and 1947. In 1941, he set the hitting-streak record by hitting safely in 56 consecutive games! DiMaggio, who played his entire career (1936-1951) with New York, was nicknamed "the Yankee Clipper" for the classy, determined, and graceful way he played the game.

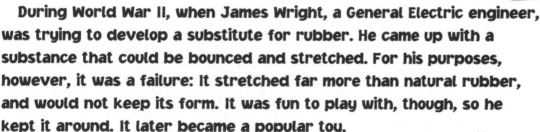

When was Silly Putty™ invented?

During World War II, when James Wright, a General Electric engineer, was trying to develop a substitute for rubber. He came up with a substance that could be bounced and stretched. For his purposes, however, it was a failure: It stretched far more than natural rubber, and would not keep its form. It was fun to play with, though, so he kept it around. It later became a popular toy.

WHO FOUNDED THE PEOPLE'S REPUBLIC OF CHINA?

Mao Zedong. He led the long struggle against Chiang Kai-shek for control of China. Mao proclaimed the People's Republic in October 1949. As chairman of China's Communist Party, he controlled the nation's artistic, military, industrial, and agricultural policies. Mao gave up his title in 1959, but kept control of the country until his death in 1976.

What was the Cold War?

Though peace after World War II ended brought economic security, political troubles brewed and the Cold War broke out—not actual fighting, but an intense rivalry between the world's two new superpowers, the U.S. and what was then known as the Soviet Union (today, a group of countries dominated by Russia). A deep distrust arose between the two nations because both had the technology to produce nuclear weapons and both sought to influence or control developing Third World nations.

Who was called Mr. Television?

Milton Berle, a comedian who was early television's first star. He hosted a live, phenomenally popular musical-comedy program that aired every Tuesday at 8 p.m. Berle helped establish television as a form of home entertainment. Millions of Americans bought their first TV sets in order to watch "Uncle Milty."

DID THE U.S. TAKE PART IN THE KOREAN WAR?

Yes. The war began on June 25, 1950, when troops from Communist-ruled North Korea invaded South Korea. To aid South Korea, 41 member-countries of the United Nations sent soldiers and/or military supplies. To aid North Korea, China sent troops and the Soviet Union sent military aid. By the time a cease-fire ended the fighting in July 1953, the Korean War had taken the lives of more than three million civilians and soldiers—including 36,916 Americans.

THAT WAS MY GREAT-GRANDFATHER.

What was the world's first commercial computer?

The Universal Automatic Computer, or UNIVAC. Invented by two American engineers, UNIVAC was the first machine able to handle both numeric and alphabetical characters. The enormous computer was installed in Philadelphia, Pennsylvania, in 1951. The U.S. Census Bureau used it to process huge amounts of data.

What was tested over Eniwetok Atoll in the South Pacific?

A hydrogen bomb. In November 1952, the U.S. set off an H-bomb with a force 500 times greater than the atom bomb dropped on Hiroshima in 1945. The test blast totally destroyed a small island off Eniwetok Atoll, and produced a radioactive mushroom cloud 25 miles high and 100 miles wide. Not long after the U.S. test, the Soviet Union produced and tested its own H-bomb. The two countries' new weaponry heated up the Cold War.

Who discovered DNA's double helix?

Biologists James Watson of the U.S. and Francis Crick of Britain, in 1953. Watson and Crick showed that molecules of DNA (deoxyribonucleic acid) have two intertwined strands, resembling a twisted rope. That double twist is called a double helix. The DNA molecule carries the genetic information that shapes all living things. Watson and Crick's work enabled scientists who followed them to figure out how living things reproduce.

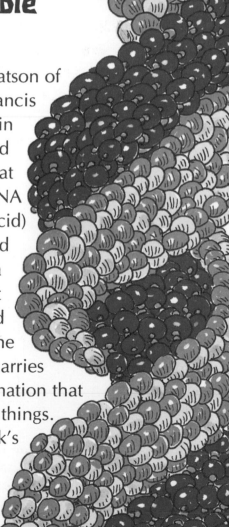

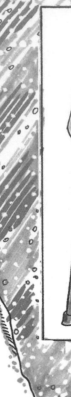

What new vaccine was first used in 1954?

A vaccine that protects against polio, a disease that can leave people paralyzed for life. In 1952, Dr. Jonas Salk developed a new vaccine that he hoped would prevent polio. The following year, the vaccine was tested on 1,830,000 schoolchildren. Salk's vaccine was found to be safe and effective. Since then, polio has all but been eliminated worldwide.

Who were the first men to reach the summit of Mt. Everest?

Edmund Hillary of New Zealand and Tenzing Norgay of Nepal. At 11:30 a.m. on May 29, 1953, they reached the top of the tallest mountain in the world, having climbed to a height of 29,028 feet above sea level. Hillary and Norgay stayed "on top of the world" for 15 minutes, taking photographs and planting the flags of the United Kingdom, the United Nations, and Nepal, before making their descent.

What was *Brown v. the Board of Education?*

One of the most influential legal cases in U.S. history. Oliver Brown sued the Board of Education of Topeka, Kansas, for not allowing his seven-year-old daughter, Linda, to attend the public school near the family's home. Linda was black, and the school was attended by "whites only." In 1954, the U.S. Supreme Court heard the case. It ruled that racial segregation in public schools was unconstitutional. The Court's historic decision triggered a powerful civil-rights movement that began to break down all racial barriers in U.S. society.

SUMNER ELEMENTARY SCHOOL

WHAT WAS THE RED SCARE?

Americans' fear of communism, which peaked during the Cold War of the 1950s. As Americans watched the Soviet Union's push to spread communism in Eastern Europe, they worried that it could reach the U.S. In Congress, the House Un-American Activities Committee (HUAC) investigated charges that people in key positions—in government, business, even the movie and TV industries—might be communists. At the Red Scare's height, some Americans were suspicious of everyone—even their neighbors.

Who was Senator Joseph McCarthy?

A U.S. senator from Wisconsin. In 1950, McCarthy claimed to have a list of communists working at the U.S. State Department. Using rumors, fake photos, and imaginary lists, McCarthy set off a wave of panic among the American people. McCarthy widened his attacks until, in 1954, he took on the U.S. Army. His downfall came during Senate hearings that were televised live that spring. Americans were shocked to see him bully witnesses—without any evidence—and he lost his influence almost overnight. Shortly afterward, the Senate condemned McCarthy for misconduct.

How did the movie industry compete against television?

In the 1950s, more and more people stayed home to watch TV. To lure them back to movie theaters, Hollywood introduced Cinerama, a wide screen with brilliant color and stereophonic sound. Another gimmick was 3-D movies, at which audiences wore special eyeglasses that made action seem to leap off the screen. Other attractions: big-budget epics, such as *Ben Hur*, and monster movies, such as *Godzilla*.

What new kind of popular music emerged in the mid-1950s?

Rock 'n' roll—a mixture of rhythm-and-blues (R&B) and country music. This upbeat music—and such performers as Bill Haley and the Comets, Chuck Berry, and the hugely popular Elvis Presley—appealed to teenagers. When disc jockeys began playing rock 'n' roll records on radio, those tunes outsold all other kinds of music. Popular music was never the same again!

Why did African Americans boycott buses in Alabama?

On December 1, 1955, a black woman named Rosa Parks took a seat on a public bus in Montgomery, Alabama. In the American South at that time, race determined where a person could sit in public places. When Parks refused to give up her seat to a white man, she was arrested, fined, and jailed. African Americans boycotted buses in protest. The bus companies refused to change their policy until the Supreme Court ruled against segregated public transportation in November 1956.

What was Ray Kroc responsible for starting?

BECAUSE OF HIM, I'VE BEEN EATEN BILLIONS AND BILLIONS OF TIMES!

McDonald's franchise restaurants, in 1955. Kroc, a milk-shake-mixer salesman, was impressed by a busy drive-in restaurant owned by the McDonald brothers in San Bernardino, California. They were selling 15-cent hamburgers, 10-cent fries, and 25-cent milk shakes. The brothers agreed to Kroc's idea of creating a franchise chain, if they could keep the original McDonald's. Within five years, Kroc had 228 successful restaurants—and kept growing!

What U.S. movie star became a real-life princess?

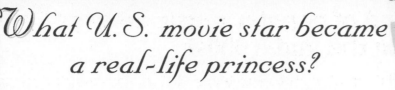

Grace Kelly. On April 19, 1956, she married Prince Rainier of Monaco, becoming Princess Grace. Kelly, an award-winning actress, appeared in 11 films, including three Alfred Hitchcock hits, before giving up her career. She met the prince at the Cannes Film Festival in 1955. Their wedding on the French Riviera was attended by more than 1,200 guests and dignitaries from 25 nations.

How did Althea Gibson achieve greatness?

On July 6, 1957, she became the first African-American tennis player to win a singles title at the Wimbledon tournament in England. As a young girl, Gibson was so good at paddleball that a tennis club sponsored her tennis lessons. She became one of the leading players of the decade. Gibson later wrote a book about her life called *I Always Wanted to Be Somebody*.

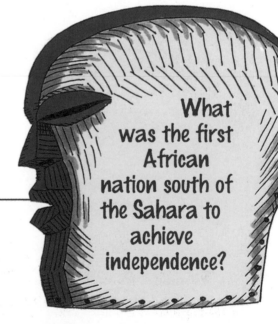

What was the first African nation south of the Sahara to achieve independence?

Ghana. Portuguese explorers who landed there in 1470 found so much gold that they called it the Gold Coast. It became a British colony in 1901. When the Gold Coast gained its independence on March 6, 1957, it took the name *Ghana* from a kingdom of ancient Africa.

WHO LAUNCHED THE FIRST ARTIFICIAL SATELLITE?

WHERE DID THAT COME FROM?

The Soviet Union astonished the world when it launched *Sputnik I* on October 4, 1957. At 184 pounds, it was many times heavier than the satellite the U.S. launched the following year. *Sputnik I* circled Earth once every 96 minutes for 92 days, sending back radio signals. Today, many weather, military, communications, and scientific satellites orbit Earth.

WHAT WERE TWO OF THE MOST POPULAR TOYS DURING THE 1950s?

The Frisbee and the hula hoop. In 1957, an executive from the Wham-O toy company noticed college students twirling pie tins through the air— tins that were made by the Frisbie Pie Company. (Wham-O adapted the name.) The popular Frisbee is still being tossed around today. The following year, Wham-O introduced the plastic hula hoop. Twenty million were sold in less than a year!!

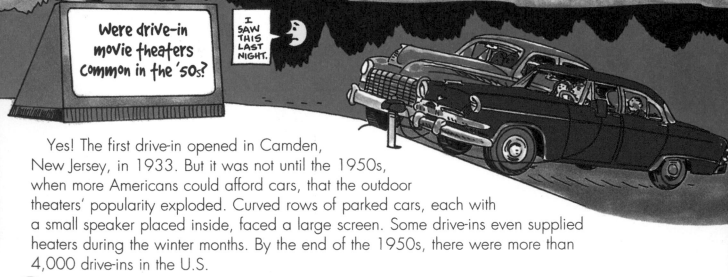

Were drive-in movie theaters common in the '50s?

I SAW THIS LAST NIGHT.

Yes! The first drive-in opened in Camden, New Jersey, in 1933. But it was not until the 1950s, when more Americans could afford cars, that the outdoor theaters' popularity exploded. Curved rows of parked cars, each with a small speaker placed inside, faced a large screen. Some drive-ins even supplied heaters during the winter months. By the end of the 1950s, there were more than 4,000 drive-ins in the U.S.

Who were the first seven astronauts chosen by NASA?

Scott Carpenter, Gordon Cooper, John Glenn, Gus Grissom, Walter Schirra, Alan Shepard Jr., and Deke Slayton. They were chosen out of more than 500 candidates as the first American astronauts. This group, selected in April 1959, was made up of Air Force, Navy, and Marine Corps test pilots. The National Aeronautics and Space Administration (NASA) had great plans for them in the approaching decade.

What does the phrase "the day the music died" refer to?

February 3, 1959. On that day, a plane crash took the lives of three popular rock 'n' roll performers. Buddy Holly *(right)*, Ritchie Valens, and J. P. "Big Bopper" Richardson had played a sold-out show in Mason City, Iowa. Instead of taking a bus to the next stop on their tour, they took a single-engine aircraft, which crashed in a snowstorm.

WHAT WAS THE QUIZ SHOW SCANDAL?

In November 1959, TV's most popular quiz show, *Twenty-One*, was revealed as a fake! A contestant named Charles Van Doren, who had won $129,000, admitted that he had been given the answers to difficult questions in advance. *Twenty-One*'s producer testified before Congress that the goal of the deception was to create excitement and to boost ratings. Soon other quiz and game shows were accused of cheating. The scandal led to the FCC (Federal Communications Commission) setting new standards for TV broadcasters.

GLENN COOPER CARPENTER SHEPARD SCHIRRA GRISSOM SLAYTON

What protests and demonstrations did young people take part in during the 1960s?

Young people, both African-American and white, took part in protests and demonstrations against racial segregation and later, against America's role in the Vietnam War. The decade's tone was set on February 1, 1960, when a group of African-American students staged a "sit-in" in Greensboro, North Carolina. They took seats at a whites-only lunch counter and refused to move until they were served.

Who were the candidates in the first televised presidential debate?

It featured Vice President Richard M. Nixon, the Republican candidate, and Senator John F. Kennedy, the Democratic candidate. Newscasters from the TV networks questioned them on the evening of September 26, 1960, to give voters a firsthand look at both candidates and their positions. Although neither "won" the debate, Kennedy's relaxed manner and good looks impressed many viewers. Kennedy was elected president that November.

What structure, built in 1961, divided BERLIN?

Since the end of World War II in 1945, almost three million people had moved from communist East Germany to democratic West Germany. In August 1961, the East German government built a wall of concrete blocks and electrical fences that split the city of Berlin in two. It was guarded by armed soldiers. The government hoped that the Berlin Wall would prevent East German citizens from fleeing to the politically freer and more prosperous West.

Why was the Telstar communications satellite important to TV viewers?

On July 10, 1962, *Telstar I* went into operation, enabling TV viewers in North America to see live TV broadcasts from Europe for the first time. Communications satellites serve as relay stations—they receive messages from one location and send them to another. Stations on the ground are equipped with large antennae for transmitting and receiving the broadcasts.

WHAT DANCE CRAZE DID CHUBBY CHECKER START?

The twist, a dance craze shared by both teens and adults. Checker re-recorded a little-known song called "The Twist," which became a huge rock 'n' roll hit. He danced it on TV—and soon everyone was doing it. The tune was #1 in September 1960 and stayed on the charts for four months. In 1961, it hit #1 a second time! The market was flooded with such products as Twist socks, Twister shoes, and even a type of spaghetti called the Twist.

WHAT WAS THE BOOK SILENT SPRING ABOUT?

Silent Spring, published in 1962, was written by Rachel Carson, an American marine biologist. It describes the dangerous side effects of chemical pesticides commonly used on farms and in homes. Carson warned that strict controls were needed to protect our environment. Her book started a nationwide environmental movement, and led to tighter governmental restrictions on the use of pesticides.

What was the Cuban Missile Crisis?

For one week in October 1962, it seemed as if the Cold War between the Soviet Union and the United States was going to get very hot. U.S. spy planes had spotted Soviet nuclear-missile bases on communist-controlled Cuba, just 90 miles from Florida. President John F. Kennedy ordered a naval blockade of Cuba and put U.S. troops on alert. People everywhere were terrified, thinking that nuclear war could start at any moment. Finally, on October 28, the Soviets agreed to remove the nuclear weapons. The world breathed a sigh of relief.

What was unique about the Motown record label?

Motown was the first major label owned and operated by African Americans. It was started in 1959 by Berry Gordy Jr., a songwriter. Motown tunes topped hit charts through most of the 1960s. Unlike other "black music," Motown records were bought by both blacks and whites. Gordy ran his label like a film studio: The songs were written, arranged, and recorded all under the same roof. Motown's roster included the Four Tops, Smokey Robinson and the Miracles, Mary Wells, the Supremes, the Temptations, Stevie Wonder, and the Jackson Five.

What famous African-American leader told the world, "I have a dream"?

Dr. Martin Luther King Jr., noted civil-rights leader. On August 28, 1963, he led more than 200,000 peaceful demonstrators for equal rights on a march through Washington, D.C. It was the largest protest of its kind in the history of our nation's capital. King inspired the crowd—and people around the world—when he said, "I have a dream that one day this nation will rise up and live out the true meaning of its creed, 'We hold these truths to be self-evident, that all men are created equal.'"

When was U.S. President Kennedy assassinated?

On November 22, 1963. President John F. Kennedy and his wife, Jacqueline, were in Dallas, Texas, on a speaking tour. At 12:30 p.m., as they were riding in an open convertible in a motorcade, shots rang out. Kennedy slumped in the car's back seat as his horrified wife looked on. The 46-year-old president died 25 minutes later at Parkland Memorial Hospital. Vice President Lyndon B. Johnson was sworn in as president shortly thereafter.

Who were the Fab Four?

The Beatles, a hugely popular British rock 'n' roll group. When they first arrived in the U.S. on February 7, 1964, 25,000 fans greeted them at New York's Kennedy Airport. The pandemonium that followed John Lennon, Paul McCartney, George Harrison, and Ringo Starr wherever they went was known as Beatlemania. Sold-out concerts, huge record sales, and hit movies confirmed the Beatles' stardom. The band broke up in 1970, but its impact on popular music is still being felt today.

In what movie was the expression "SUPERCALIFRAGILISTICEXPIALIDOCIOUS" sung?

Mary Poppins. This Disney musical comedy (1964) was adapted from P. L. Travers's children's stories about a nanny named Mary Poppins who has magical powers. It starred Julie Andrews as Mary and Dick Van Dyke as Bert, her chimney-sweep friend. *Mary Poppins* featured "Supercalifragilisticexpialidocious" and other memorable songs. The film, which combined live action with animation, won five Academy Awards.

When did the U.S. enter the conflict in Vietnam?

In March 1965, 3,500 U.S. Marines were sent to protect an air base at Da Nang, in South Vietnam. The base was being attacked by communist guerrilla troops known as the Vietcong. A year earlier, U.S. warplanes had begun bombing North Vietnam. By the end of 1965, a total of 250,000 U.S. troops had been sent to Vietnam. That year marked the beginning of U.S. involvement in a long and bloody war that continued until the U.S. withdrew in 1973. (U.S. involvement peaked in 1969, with 543,400 troops in Vietnam.)

Who was Indira Gandhi?

The first female prime minister of India. Her father, Jawaharlal Nehru, was India's first prime minister (1947-1964), after the country won independence from Great Britain. Indira Gandhi was elected its third prime minister in 1966, and held the office until 1977. In 1980, she was reelected to Parliament, and became prime minister for the second time. Gandhi's term was cut short in 1984, when she was assassinated by two of her security guards. Her son, Rajiv Gandhi, was elected prime minister in her place.

WAS *STAR TREK* AN INSTANT HIT WHEN IT PREMIERED ON TELEVISION?

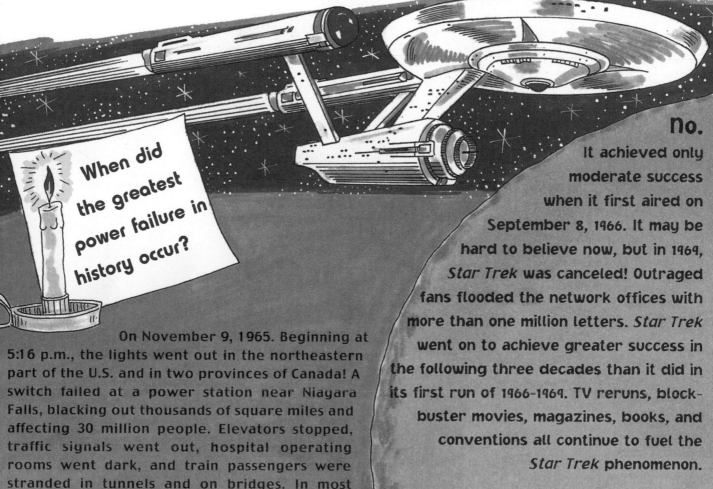

When did the greatest power failure in history occur?

On November 9, 1965. Beginning at 5:16 p.m., the lights went out in the northeastern part of the U.S. and in two provinces of Canada! A switch failed at a power station near Niagara Falls, blacking out thousands of square miles and affecting 30 million people. Elevators stopped, traffic signals went out, hospital operating rooms went dark, and train passengers were stranded in tunnels and on bridges. In most areas, power was restored by the next morning.

no. It achieved only moderate success when it first aired on September 8, 1966. It may be hard to believe now, but in 1969, *Star Trek* was canceled! Outraged fans flooded the network offices with more than one million letters. *Star Trek* went on to achieve greater success in the following three decades than it did in its first run of 1966-1969. TV reruns, blockbuster movies, magazines, books, and conventions all continue to fuel the *Star Trek* phenomenon.

THE SPACE AGE

Who was Yuri A. Gagarin?

The first man in space. Cosmonaut Yuri A. Gagarin of the Soviet Union rocketed into orbit on April 12, 1961. He made one orbit of Earth in his *Vostok 1* spacecraft during a flight that lasted 1 hour, 48 minutes. The 27-year-old Air Force major was universally praised as a hero. He died in a plane crash seven years later.

WHAT DID AMERICAN ASTRONAUTS ALAN SHEPARD JR. AND JOHN GLENN ACHIEVE?

On May 5, 1961, 23 days after Yuri Gagarin's flight, Alan Shepard Jr. became the first American in space. His 15-minute flight took him 115 miles above Earth. Following Shepard's trip, President John F. Kennedy asked Congress to approve a program to send men to the moon by the end of the decade. On February 20, 1962, John Glenn became the first American to orbit Earth.

Which American astronaut took the first "walk" in space?

Edward White.

On June 3, 1965, White opened the hatch of his space capsule, floated out into space, and took a "stroll" 100 miles above Earth. The mission plan called for a 12-minute space walk, but White was enjoying himself so much that he was nine minutes late getting back to his capsule! White was not the first person to leave an orbiting spacecraft (Soviet Cosmonaut Aleksei Leonov was, in 1965), but he did set a time record by walking through space for 36 minutes.

What happened to the Apollo 1 launch?

Apollo 1 never launched. On January 27, 1967, astronauts Gus Grissom (the second American in space), Edward White, and Roger Chaffee were killed when a flash fire engulfed their spacecraft. The three were in the midst of a full-scale simulation on the ground when an electric spark ignited the pure oxygen inside the cabin of *Apollo 1*. The tragedy resulted in important safety changes to all future missions.

How many people have walked on the moon?

What was historic about the Apollo 8 flight?

The astronauts on the *Apollo 8* flight were the first people ever to orbit the moon and see it up close. James Lovell, William Anders, and Frank Borman blasted off on December 21, 1968, and reached the moon by Christmas Eve. The crew made 10 orbits around the moon. People all over the world watched parts of their mission via TV.

The grand total is 12. The first people to set foot on the moon were *Apollo 11* astronauts Neil Armstrong and Edwin Aldrin, on July 20, 1969. After that mission, five more *Apollo* missions went to the moon, with two astronauts walking on the lunar surface on each mission. No one has set foot on the moon since 1972. Here is a full list of the privileged few:

Armstrong & Aldrin, 1969 • Charles Conrad Jr. & Alan L. Bean, 1969 • Alan B. Shepard Jr. & Edgar D. Mitchell, 1971 • David R. Scott & James B. Irwin, 1971 • John W. Young & Charles M. Duke Jr., 1972 • Eugene A. Cernan & Harrison H. Schmitt, 1972

NEIL ARMSTRONG

LEARN ABOUT NEIL ARMSTRONG AS YOU LOOK FOR THESE FUN ITEMS:

- Balloon
- Banana peel
- Bird
- Cactus
- Can
- Cloud
- Firecracker
- Fire hydrant
- Fish (3)
- Flashlight
- Flying saucer
- Heart
- Hot-air balloon
- Hot dog
- Ice-cream cone
- Key
- Kite
- Lamp
- Mouse
- Paper airplane
- Pencil
- Police officer
- School bus
- Sock
- Superhero
- Top hat
- Umbrella
- Wagon wheel

Answers on page 316

Which teams played in the first Super Bowl?

The Green Bay Packers of the National Football League and the Kansas City Chiefs of the American Football League. The Packers won the January 15, 1967, game by a score of 35-10. The Los Angeles stadium where the much-publicized game was played was only two-thirds full! Today, the annual Super Bowl is the single most-watched sports event in the U.S.

What was the Tet Offensive?

A military campaign by North Vietnamese and Vietcong (communist) troops during the Vietnam War. It began on January 30, 1968, at the start of Tet, which is the Vietnamese New Year celebration. Major cities in South Vietnam were heavily attacked. The plan failed in the end, but it made many Americans begin to question whether the U.S. should keep fighting the war.

Where did a giant rock concert take place in 1969?

On a 600-acre farm near Bethel, New York. The three-day concert, known as Woodstock, began on August 15. Almost 500,000 people were entertained by some of the biggest names in rock 'n' roll, including Jimi Hendrix, The Who, Janis Joplin, and Crosby, Stills, Nash and Young. Heavy rains turned the concert grounds into a muddy swamp, but the young audience stayed on to enjoy the Woodstock experience.

Which "bird" became a popular TV character in 1969?

Big Bird! This seven-foot-tall yellow creature starred in the children's TV series *Sesame Street*, which debuted in November 1969. On this popular program, Big Bird and his human and Muppet friends use fun songs, stories, and skits to teach preschoolers the basic concepts of reading and arithmetic.

Whose work was called "pop art"?

Artists who, in the 1960s, started using everyday images as the basis for their work. The most famous were painters Roy Lichtenstein and Andy Warhol, and sculptor Claes Oldenburg. In his 1963 work titled *Whaam!*, Lichtenstein used tiny dots of color to create a comic-book like painting of one jet fighter blowing up another. Warhol, in one of his most famous works, painted exact copies of Campbell Soup cans, repeating the image over and over again in the same painting.

Which articles of clothing caused a 1960s fashion revolution?

In 1961, First Lady Jacqueline Kennedy popularized the short, tailored two-piece suit and the pillbox hat. Other 1960s styles were the miniskirt, made popular by Twiggy, an English model; high-heeled boots made of plastic or leather; and collarless jackets for men. In 1965, the "flower child" image included bell-bottomed blue jeans, tie-dyed T-shirts, and sandals. By 1968, fashion trends included cashmere turtlenecks, French-cut jeans, silk shirts, and flamboyant wide ties for men—something for everyone!

Why was the World Wildlife Fund formed?

To protect and help the world's wildlife, to educate people about the environment, and to raise money for conservation. The World Wildlife Fund (WWF) is dedicated to keeping wildlife from becoming extinct. The charitable organization, which was formed on September 11, 1961, has a panda in its logo.

WE PROTEST!

Why did Americans turn to disco music, dancing and club hopping in the late 1970s?

By the end of the 1970s, Americans turned to dancing and music as a way escape from the troubles of the early part of the decade. The early 1970s was a time of protest—against the Vietnam War, and for greater rights for women and minorities. Scandal forced U.S. president Richard Nixon to resign, and civil wars broke out abroad. By the end of the decade, Americans were ready to seek out fun.

Who uttered the words, "Houston, we have a problem"?

U.S. astronaut Jim Lovell. On April 11, 1970, he and crewmates Jack Swigert and Fred Haise were launched toward the moon on *Apollo 13*. But two days into the flight, there was an explosion that crippled the spacecraft and threatened the crew. NASA and the astronauts stayed calm and averted catastrophe. On April 17, after 90 tense hours, *Apollo 13* made a safe splashdown in the Pacific.

When was the first Earth Day celebrated?

April 22, 1970. On this first nationwide celebration, Americans peacefully marched and demonstrated with the slogan "Give Earth a Chance." The day helped to raise awareness of pollution, ecology, and conservation. Discussions were held in schools about pesticides, population growth, endangered animals, and nuclear power. Although Earth Day is not a legal holiday, it is observed each year by people who care about our planet.

What happened at Kent State?

During the early 1970s, many protests against the Vietnam War were held on college campuses. On May 4, 1970, National Guard soldiers fired on students demonstrating against the war at Kent State University in Ohio. Four students were killed; eight were wounded. Most Americans were stunned by the violence. The incident made more Americans call for peace in Vietnam—and at home.

WHAT ADVERTISEMENTS WERE BANNED FROM TV AND RADIO IN THE 1970s?

Ads for tobacco products were banned from TV and radio as of January 1, 1971, by a new U.S. law. The law also required that, six months later, this message be printed on all cigarette packets: "Warning: The Surgeon General has determined that cigarette smoking is dangerous to your health."

How did the women's liberation movement emerge?

It was inspired by the civil-rights campaigns of the 1950s and 1960s. Until the 1970s, only a tiny percentage of doctors, lawyers, business leaders, and elected politicians were women. But then women began demanding equal job opportunities with equal pay. New rights organizations, as well as media attention, helped women achieve greater equality then and in the following decades.

WHEN DID THE U.S. STOP FIGHTING IN VIETNAM?

By August 1972, U.S. ground combat troops had left Vietnam, but American warplanes continued to bomb the North Vietnamese. U.S. involvement ended when a peace treaty was signed in Paris, France, on January 27, 1973. Within a few months, American prisoners and troops began to leave Vietnam. (The last U.S. troops left in March 1973.) However, the conflict between North Vietnam and South Vietnam did not end until 1975.

Where did the Battle of Wounded Knee take place?

● WOUNDED KNEE

The last major battle between the U.S. cavalry and Native Americans took place in 1890 at Wounded Knee, South Dakota. But on February 27, 1973, members of the American Indian Movement (AIM) held a protest at the Pine Ridge Sioux Reservation in Wounded Knee. They took over a trading post and church, and demanded that the U.S. Senate investigate the government's unfair treatment of Indians. The "new" Battle at Wounded Knee—a 70-day standoff with FBI agents—resulted in two deaths, many injuries, and more than 300 arrests.

How did people deal with the mid-1970s gasoline shortage?

NO GAS TODAY

PUSH!

In 1973, an embargo (ban) on oil shipments to the U.S. forced many gas stations to close for lack of gas. Open stations had lines miles long! In some places, sales were limited to $2 or $3 per car. In others, people with odd-numbered license plates could buy gas on odd-numbered days, while people with even-numbered plates did so on even-numbered days. Things got easier in April 1974, when the embargo was lifted.

Who broke Babe Ruth's career home-run record?

OUCH! THAT'S 715!

I GOT IT!

Henry (Hank) Aaron. He made baseball history on April 8, 1974. Aaron entered that day's game tied with Babe Ruth's 39-year-old record of 714 career home runs. At his second at-bat, "Hammerin' Hank" slammed a fastball over the outfield fence! Fireworks went off and the hometown crowd in Atlanta, Georgia, went wild. By the time Aaron retired in 1976, he had set a new career-homers record: 755.

Who was the first U.S. president to resign?

Richard M. Nixon. He announced his resignation on August 8, 1974, because Congress was about to impeach him (charge him with wrongdoing) for his part in a scandal known as Watergate. Nixon's troubles began in 1972, when five men were caught bugging the Democratic Party's election-campaign headquarters. The investigation that followed exposed President Nixon as being involved in covering up illegal acts by his aides.

In what country were the "killing fields"?

In 1975, Cambodia, a country in southeast Asia, was taken over by a communist group called the Khmer Rouge. This regime, led by a man named Pol Pot, terrorized the Cambodian people. Educated or professional people were murdered. City dwellers were taken into the countryside and forced to work as farmers; many starved to death while laboring in the fields. At least one million Cambodians lost their lives in what came to be known as "the killing fields."

HOW DID ARTHUR ASHE ACHIEVE GREATNESS?

On July 5, 1975, Ashe beat tennis star Jimmy Connors in an exciting four-set final to win the Wimbledon singles championship in England. He was the first African-American male player to win at Wimbledon. Ashe was no stranger to success. In 1968, he had won the U.S. Open and played on the U.S. Davis Cup team. In 1970, he won the Australian Open. Ashe retired in 1980 and became a writer and an activist for racial and social justice.

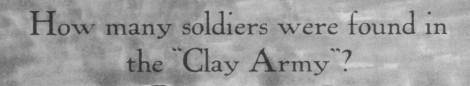

How many soldiers were found in the "Clay Army"?

Six thousand! The lifelike clay statues, lined up in battle formation, were discovered in July 1975. They were found under a three-acre burial mound in northwestern China. Experts believe that the figures were built during the reign of Emperor Shi Huangdi, from whom the name China is taken. His tomb and the clay warriors date from 210 to 206 B.C.!

Which Olympic athlete scored the first perfect "10"?

Nadia Comaneci. This tiny 14-year-old gymnast from Romania scored the first perfect "10" in gymnastic history. She scored 10 an amazing seven times at the 1976 Summer Games in Montreal, Canada. She won three individual gold medals: in the uneven parallel bars, balance beam, and all-around competitions. Barely 5 feet tall and only 83 pounds, Comaneci was the biggest star of the Montreal Olympics.

What is Legionnaires' disease?

A baffling and deadly virus. After an American Legion convention held in Philadelphia over the 1976 July 4th weekend, 221 Legionnaires became mysteriously ill. By the end of August, 29 were dead. Not until 1977 were scientists able to link the virus to the presence of bacteria in the drinking water. Today, Legionnaires' disease can be treated and prevented.

What two robots starred in a science-fiction movie?

R2D2 and C-3PO, in the 1977 blockbuster film *Star Wars*. This sci-fi movie, directed by George Lucas, used state-of-the-art technology to tell its classic story of good versus evil. Although there were exciting and dramatic moments among Luke Skywalker, Princess Leia, Han Solo, and Darth Vader, the funniest and most peculiar situations involved the robots.

Where was the world's first "test-tube baby" born?

The first baby conceived outside the human body was born in Manchester, England, on July 25, 1978. The healthy five-pound, twelve-ounce girl, named Louise, was born to Lesley and John Brown. Two British researchers, Dr. Robert Edwards and Patrick Steptoe, pioneered the "test-tube baby" technique, called in vitro fertilization. (*In vitro* is Latin for *in glass*.) One of Lesley Brown's eggs was fertilized in a test tube, then implanted in her womb to grow normally.

What special TV series drew 80 million viewers in 1977?

An eight-part drama called *Roots*. Its final two-hour episode, which aired on January 30, 1977, was seen by about 80 million viewers. Based on the book by Alex Haley, *Roots* traced the Haley family's history through the generations they lived as slaves in the American South, all the way back to an 18th-century ancestor abducted from West Africa.

WHAT DAREDEVIL BECAME A 1970s ICON?

Evel Knievel, who became the best-known daredevil in America for his dangerous and thrilling motorcycle stunts. Knievel would zoom his motorcycle up a ramp and into the air, leaping over parked cars. In February 1973, he jumped his motorcycle over a row of 50 cars at a demolition derby in Los Angeles. Not all of Knievel's stunts were successful, however. He nearly lost his life in September 1974, while trying to leap across a canyon in Idaho.

What nuclear accident threatened the people of Pennsylvania?

The worst nuclear accident in U.S. history began on March 28, 1979, at the Three Mile Island power plant near Harrisburg, Pennsylvania. Due to equipment failure and human error, small amounts of dangerous radiation began to leak from the plant. Experts feared that a bubble of radioactive hydrogen might explode or that a full meltdown might occur. The problems at Three Mile Island were brought under control and disaster was averted, but the accident heightened Americans' concerns about the risks of nuclear power.

Computers, games, calculators, and many other electronic devices became smaller, more powerful, and cheaper. A microchip is a tiny piece of material—usually silicon—that contains a complex and powerful electronic circuit. The microchip, developed in 1971, made desktop calculators possible. The mighty microchip, which is smaller than a thumbnail, has since given us lightweight video cameras, video games, and computers small enough to hold in your hand.

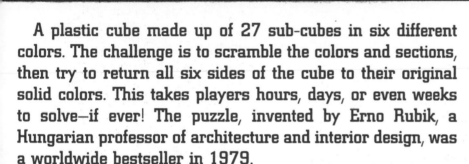

What is Rubik's cube?

A plastic cube made up of 27 sub-cubes in six different colors. The challenge is to scramble the colors and sections, then try to return all six sides of the cube to their original solid colors. This takes players hours, days, or even weeks to solve—if ever! The puzzle, invented by Erno Rubik, a Hungarian professor of architecture and interior design, was a worldwide bestseller in 1979.

WHAT WAS THE DANCE CRAZE OF THE DECADE?

Disco! Performers such as Donna Summer and the Bee Gees, who recorded hit songs that were danced to in discotheques, helped make this dance style popular. Disco reached new heights in 1977, when John Travolta danced it in the film *Saturday Night Fever*. The disco craze fizzled out by the 1980s, but its music and dance steps make a nostalgic comeback from time to time.

What was a major focus for many Americans during the 1980s?

Business and the economy were a major focus for people, as well as for Ronald Reagan, who was the U.S. president for most of the decade. A boom in computer technology was part of the focus, as new inventions made many tasks easier and faster. On the dark side, terrorism and other violence plagued the decade, but as the 1980s went on, old tensions between the U.S. and what was then known as the Soviet Union began to relax.

What natural disaster hit Washington state?

The eruption of the Mount St. Helens volcano. After lying dormant for more than 120 years, Mount St. Helens erupted on May 18, 1980, with the force of a hydrogen bomb. The eruption triggered mudslides that snapped bridges and swept away homes. More than 100 people were killed or reported missing, and damage to property and wildlife was as high as $2.7 billion. U.S. President Jimmy Carter called the destruction "the worst thing I've ever seen."

Who was Gordie Howe?

One of the greatest players in ice-hockey history. He played pro hockey for 32 years (26 in the National Hockey League). When Howe hung up his skates in 1980, he was 52 years old—and playing on the same pro team as his sons! Howe's career mark of 1,850 points (goals plus assists) was an NHL record that stood until 1989.

WHAT KIND OF SKATING BECAME POPULAR IN THE 1980S?

In-line skating. In-line skates, developed by U.S. ice-hockey players Scott and Brennan Olson, first appeared in 1980. Soon, an in-line skating craze was sweeping the country. In-line skate wheels are arranged one behind the other—more like ice-skate blades than regular roller skates. Their smooth wheels and lightweight design enable skaters to travel quite fast. (That's why it's a good idea to wear protective gear!)

What actor was elected president of the U.S.?

Ronald Reagan. After graduating from college in 1932, he worked as a radio sports announcer. A screen test led to his 1937 film debut in *Love Is on the Air*. (He played a radio announcer!) He became a star in TV as well as movies. By the 1960s, Reagan was more involved in politics than movies. He was elected governor of California in 1966. In 1980, he was elected the nation's 40th president and was reelected in 1984.

What was unique about the space shuttle *Columbia*?

It was the world's first reusable spacecraft. On April 14, 1981, it landed at Edwards Air Force Base in California, after completing its first orbital flight. Astronauts John Young and Robert Crippen orbited Earth 36 times during their 54-hour, 21-minute mission. A space shuttle is launched into space like a rocket, but lands on Earth like an airplane. This design enabled space flights to become less expensive and more routine.

Who was the first woman nominated to the U.S. Supreme Court?

Sandra Day O'Connor. Born in El Paso, Texas, in 1930, she received a law degree from Stanford University in 1952. O'Connor was elected judge in 1974, and later served on the Arizona Court of Appeals. When Justice Potter Stewart retired in 1981, President Ronald Reagan nominated O'Connor to take his place. She was sworn in as a justice on the Supreme Court—the highest court in the nation—on September 25, 1981.

When did MTV begin broadcasting?

August 1981. At first, this cable-TV station showed only music videos—it was like a 24-hour radio station for your eyes as well as ears. VJs (video jockeys) talked about and showed the latest videos. Exposure on MTV helped launch many new recording artists, such as Duran Duran and Billy Idol, to superstardom. As the 1980s came to a close, MTV changed its all-video format, adding game shows, gossip programs, and culture-related documentaries.

Whose wedding was watched by 700 million people?

The wedding of Prince Charles (son of Great Britain's Queen Elizabeth II) and Lady Diana Spencer. The ceremony took place at St. Paul's Cathedral in London on July 29, 1981. Outside the cathedral, cheering crowds lined the streets, hoping to catch a glimpse of the royal couple. The one-hour service was attended by 2,500 guests, but worldwide broadcasts of the ceremony expanded the "guest list" to 700 million people!

What Nobel Peace Prize winner was assassinated in 1981?

President Anwar Sadat of Egypt. On October 6, while he was watching a military parade, several men broke out of the procession and opened fire. Sadat and five bystanders were killed, and thousands of frightened guests ran for cover. One assassin died in the gun battle that followed; the rest were arrested later. They were angry at Sadat for signing a peace treaty with Israel (for which he won the Nobel Prize) and cracking down on Muslim radicals.

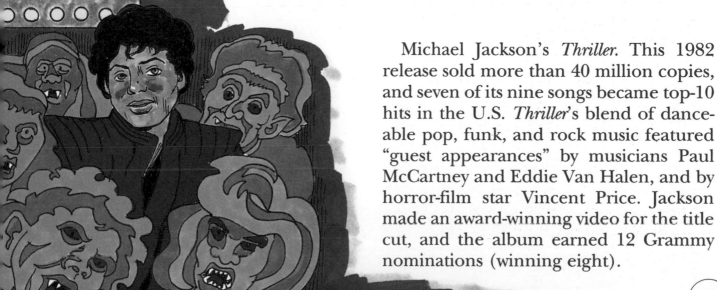

WHAT POPULAR BRAINTEASER GAME WAS INTRODUCED IN 1982?

Trivial Pursuit. This brainteaser board game for adults was a top-seller during the 1980s. It was created in 1979 by Chris Haney, a Canadian photo editor; his brother, John; and Scott Abbott, a sportswriter. Players advance on a game board by answering trivia questions about sports, movies, history, science, literature, and nature. Later, specialty versions were added—including a young players' edition.

What is widely recognized as the most successful music album ever?

Michael Jackson's *Thriller.* This 1982 release sold more than 40 million copies, and seven of its nine songs became top-10 hits in the U.S. *Thriller's* blend of danceable pop, funk, and rock music featured "guest appearances" by musicians Paul McCartney and Eddie Van Halen, and by horror-film star Vincent Price. Jackson made an award-winning video for the title cut, and the album earned 12 Grammy nominations (winning eight).

How were Vietnam War veterans honored on November 13, 1982?

On that day, the Vietnam Veterans Memorial was dedicated in Washington, D.C. The memorial is a *V*-shaped wall made of dark-gray granite inscribed with the names of more than 58,000 Americans who were killed or classified as missing in action in Vietnam. About two million people a year visit the site to remember or honor those lost in the war. The memorial was designed by a college student, Maya Ying Lin.

WHEN WAS THE FIRST ARTIFICIAL HEART IMPLANTED?

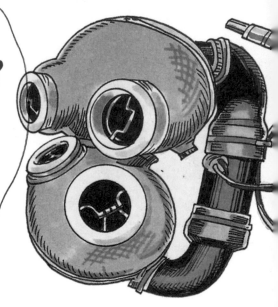

On December 2, 1982. The recipient was Barney Clark, a 61–year–old retired dentist. A surgical team headed by Dr. William C. DeVries performed the seven–and–a–half hour operation at the University of Utah Medical Center. The plastic–and–metal device (called the Jarvik–7, after its inventor, Dr. Robert Jarvik) replaced the two ventricles of the human heart, which pump blood to the lungs and the rest of the body.

How old was the Brooklyn Bridge in 1983?

One hundred years old! The world's first steel-wire suspension bridge was hailed as the "eighth wonder of the world" when it opened on May 24, 1883. At that time, it was the tallest structure in New York City's skyline. The Brooklyn Bridge crosses the East River, connecting the boroughs of Brooklyn and Manhattan. Birthday celebrations on May 24, 1983, included a parade across the bridge, then music, tributes, and festivities capped off by a spectacular fireworks display.

Who was Lech Walesa?

The leader of Solidarity, a workers' union that helped end communist control in Poland. Walesa, a shipyard worker, founded Solidarity in 1980. By 1981, it had 9.5 million members! Walesa organized huge strikes that shut down the country. He and other Solidarity leaders were arrested, and the government declared martial (military) law. But by 1989, the government was forced to make huge changes, including allowing free elections. Walesa's work won him the 1983 Nobel Peace Prize. He was elected president of Poland in 1990.

WHAT NEW KILLER ILLNESS WAS IDENTIFIED DURING THIS DECADE?

Acquired Immunodeficiency Syndrome, or AIDS, which severely damages the body's disease-fighting immune system. The illness was first identified by physicians in the late 1970s; the name AIDS was adopted in 1982. The virus that causes AIDS—called HIV (human immunodeficiency virus)—was not discovered until 1983. By 1998, 33.4 million people worldwide were living with AIDS, and 13.9 million had died of it.

What did the U.S. Surgeon General warn the public about in May of 1984?

That nonsmokers can suffer lung damage from being exposed to other people's cigarette smoke. For two decades, cancer and other lung diseases had been connected with cigarette smoking. In 1984, a government report on the health risks of smoking warned nonsmokers as well. In time, that report led to many changes: Today, for instance, smoking is banned in many public places throughout the U.S.

Why did scientists warn of a global warming?

They said that it could cause many environmental problems, including melting the polar ice caps. That would make the sea level rise one to six feet in the next century. Even a small rise would flood the world's coastal areas—permanently! Thousands of square miles would be under water in the U.S. alone. More than one-third of the world's population now lives within 40 miles of a seacoast. Scientists said that Earth's atmosphere is warming faster than ever before, but reducing air pollution could slow that rate.

WHAT WAS LIVE AID?

A rock concert held to raise relief funds for the drought-starved people of Ethiopia. Live Aid was staged in two cities simultaneously! David Bowie, Paul McCartney, George Michael, and other stars performed at London's Wembley Stadium, while Madonna, Prince, Tina Turner, and others performed at Philadelphia's JFK Stadium. Phil Collins performed at both locations—thanks to the *Concorde* supersonic jet. The July 13, 1985, event—televised worldwide—had 1.5 billion viewers and raised more than $70 million.

WHAT DID THE CREW OF AN UNDERWATER EXPEDITION FIND IN 1985?

The remains of the luxury liner *Titanic*. Ever since this ship sank in 1912, there had been many plans and attempts to find it. Improvements in deep-ocean technology finally made that possible. In September 1985, a team of French and U.S. researchers found the wreck 400 miles southeast of Newfoundland, in water 12,500 feet deep. A robot craft equipped with TV cameras recorded the first images of the sunken *Titanic*. The exact location was kept secret, to prevent fortune hunters from looting the famous sunken ship.

WHO MADE DRAMATIC POLICY CHANGES IN THE SOVIET UNION?

Soviet leader Mikhail Gorbachev, who became General Secretary of the Soviet Communist Party in 1985. Gorbachev began a program of economic and political reforms called *perestroika* (Russian for *restructuring*), and announced a new policy called *glasnost* (meaning *openness*). He also proposed drastic reductions in nuclear arms and restored friendly relations with the U.S. and other Western countries. In many ways, this was the beginning of the end of the Cold War.

What happened to the space shuttle *Challenger*?

On January 28, 1986, the *Challenger* lifted off from Cape Canaveral, Florida. Just 73 seconds after liftoff, 46,000 feet above Earth, it exploded. Millions of stunned TV viewers watched as two huge smoke streams spewed from the fireball, then debris fell into the sea. Among the seven astronauts killed was Christa McAuliffe, a schoolteacher chosen to be the first private citizen in space. Experts found that a solid-rocket joint had failed, causing the blast.

What happened at Chernobyl?

A major nuclear accident. On April 26, 1986, fires and explosions ripped through the reactors at the Chernobyl nuclear-power plant in Ukraine (then part of the Soviet Union), releasing huge amounts of radiation into the air. A reported 31 people died from radiation burns or sickness; more than 200 others were seriously injured. Winds carried radioactive substances over large parts of the Soviet Union and into northern and central Europe. Poor safety controls and human error were blamed for the accident—the worst in the history of nuclear power.

How did millions of gallons of oil pollute Alaska's shoreline?

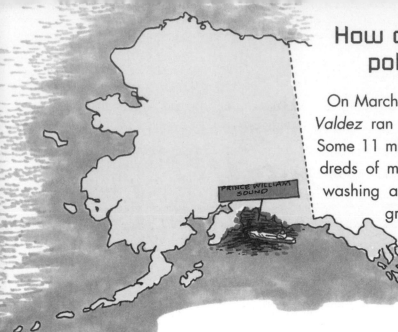

On March 24, 1989, a large oil tanker called the *Exxon Valdez* ran aground in Alaska's Prince William Sound. Some 11 million gallons of oil spilled out, blackening hundreds of miles of coastline. Dead birds and fish began washing ashore, and Alaska's fishing industry suffered great losses. Exxon promised to clean up the area, but Alaska sued, charging the company with failing to adequately staff the tanker and supervise its crew.

How did nature delay the 1989 World Series?

At 5:04 p.m. on October 17, 1989, an earthquake struck San Francisco, where the San Francisco Giants and the Oakland Athletics were about to start the third game of the World Series. None of the 58,000 fans at Candlestick Park was seriously hurt, but city-wide about 90 people were killed and 3,000 were injured. The Bay Area suffered billions of dollars' worth of damage. The tremor, which measured 6.9 on the Richter scale, lasted 15 seconds. The Series resumed 10 days later at Candlestick Park. (Oakland won the Series in a four-game sweep.)

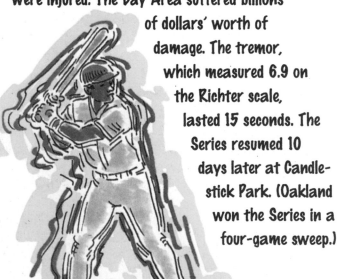

Who was the first woman inducted into The Rock and Roll Hall of Fame?

Aretha Franklin. Known as the "Queen of Soul," she was born on March 25, 1942, in Memphis, Tennessee. She made her first recordings at the age of 14 and released her first full album five years later. She has released many hit songs, including "Respect" and "(You Make Me Feel Like) A Natural Woman," and recorded over 40 albums. On January 3, 1987, she was inducted into the Rock and Roll Hall of Fame—an honor awarded to the most influential members of the music industry.

What famous "lady" celebrated her 100th birthday in 1986?

The Statue of Liberty—a gift from France that was dedicated on October 28, 1886. Americans celebrated Lady Liberty's 100th birthday on July 4, 1986. That day, despite temperatures in the 90s, long lines of people visited the newly restored Statue. Celebratory festivities included a parade of tall ships through New York Harbor and a huge fireworks display.

What was sold for the record-setting price of $53.9 million in 1987?

Irises, a painting by Vincent van Gogh (1853-1890). The art world was astounded when Alan Bond, an Australian businessman, paid that huge amount for a single painting. Van Gogh would have been, too: During his lifetime, he sold only one painting. But his popularity grew after his death. By the 1980s, museum exhibits of his vibrant, brightly colored paintings were drawing record-breaking crowds.

What symbolic divider was torn down in 1989?

The Berlin Wall *(below)*. That symbolic—and actual—barrier between East and West Berlin, in East Germany, came down in November 1989, as joyous crowds celebrated. Two years before, U.S. President Ronald Reagan and Soviet leader Mikhail Gorbachev had agreed to reduce the number of nuclear weapons aimed at one another's country, relaxing tensions between the Eastern and Western blocs. East and West Germany were reunited in 1990—after 41 years as two separate countries.

What use of technology expanded from businesses to American homes in the 1990s?

The use of computers expanded from mostly business use into more and more American homes. In the 1990s, the technological revolution of the 1980s kept going—and growing. As the 1990s drew to a close, people everywhere began looking ahead to a new century—and a new millennium.

What Nobel Peace Prize winner announced her retirement in 1990?

Mother Teresa, who received the 1979 Nobel Peace Prize for her dedicated work with the poor. The Roman Catholic nun planned to retire as head of the Missionaries of Charity, which she founded in Calcutta, India, in 1950. It provides food for the needy and operates hospitals, schools, orphanages, and youth centers in India and about 30 other countries. However, the sisters of the order reelected her, so Mother Teresa continue to serve. She died in 1997.

What two countries were united by the Channel Tunnel?

Britain and France. At 11:15 a.m. on December 1, 1990, a worker's jackhammer broke through the last inch of rock separating the two countries. The 30.7-mile-long "chunnel," which runs under the English Channel, opened to the public in 1994. Its trains can travel between Folkestone, England, and Coquelles, France, in just 30 minutes. (Automobiles can be carried across on special train cars.)

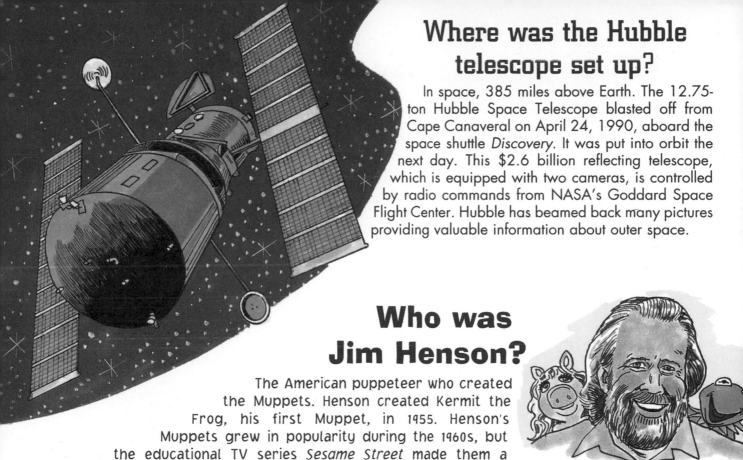

Where was the Hubble telescope set up?

In space, 385 miles above Earth. The 12.75-ton Hubble Space Telescope blasted off from Cape Canaveral on April 24, 1990, aboard the space shuttle *Discovery*. It was put into orbit the next day. This $2.6 billion reflecting telescope, which is equipped with two cameras, is controlled by radio commands from NASA's Goddard Space Flight Center. Hubble has beamed back many pictures providing valuable information about outer space.

Who was Jim Henson?

The American puppeteer who created the Muppets. Henson created Kermit the Frog, his first Muppet, in 1955. Henson's Muppets grew in popularity during the 1960s, but the educational TV series *Sesame Street* made them a household name. *The Muppet Show* was hugely successful: It had an estimated 235 million viewers in more than 100 countries! The Muppets also starred in hit films. Henson died on May 16, 1990, but his Muppets live on—to the delight of children and adults the world over.

The breakup of the Soviet Union resulted in how many independent countries?

Fifteen: Armenia, Azerbaijan, Belarus, Georgia, Estonia, Kazakstan, Kyrgyzstan, Latvia, Lithuania, Moldova, Russia, Tajikistan, Turkmenistan, Ukraine, and Uzbekistan. All had been Soviet republics. Russia declared itself successor to the Soviet Union in 1991. The others declared their independence in 1990 and 1991. Twelve of the fifteen new countries formed an alliance called the Commonwealth of Independent States (CIS) to help support one another through economic growth and political changes.

HIGH-TECH TIMES

WHAT IS THE WORLD WIDE WEB?

A key feature of the Internet—a vast network of computers that connects businesses, institutions, and individuals. Anyone with a computer and modem can connect to the Web. The World Wide Web provides information on a vast array of topics, along with sound, pictures, and video. Users can also communicate with one another by e-mail.

What was unique about the movie *Toy Story*?

It was the first movie created entirely on computer. Pixar Animation Studios used the latest, most sophisticated technology available to create dazzling effects and realistic detail for the 1996 Disney hit. The only thing "human" in the movie were the characters' voices, supplied by an all-star cast of actors including Tom Hanks, Tim Allen, and Don Rickles.

How is virtual reality used?

Virtual reality (VR) technology was first developed in the 1960s as flight simulators, to help train pilots. NASA and the U.S. military developed it further, improving computer imagery. By the 1990s, VR was being used to train U.S. troops and astronauts, as well as medical students studying surgery and other medical techniques. VR also became popular in computer and video games and other fields of entertainment. Engineers, architects, advertisers, and workers in many other fields have found it useful, too.

What is the International Space Station?

The International Space Station is a large spacecraft that orbits around the earth. The U.S., Canada, Russia, Japan, Brazil, and 11 European countries worked together to build it. It provides a "home" to astronauts traveling to space, and is also a science lab that's used to help NASA learn about living and working in space.

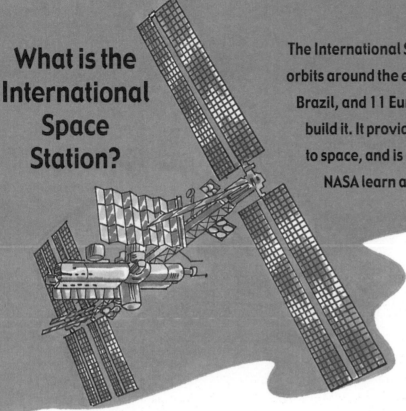

How did technological advances change communications in the 1990s?

New technologies enabled people to communicate over great distances faster and more easily than ever. Telephones went wireless, then got smaller, lighter, and more powerful. So did computers. Satellites linked vast communications networks together, so that any one communications device (phone, computer, fax machine) could "talk" and send pictures to another, anywhere in the world. This created a whole new way of working: telecommuting. Telecommunication enables workers to take part in meetings, treat patients, supply clients, and provide other types of services to people hundreds or thousands of miles away.

What was the first animal ever cloned?

THAT'S US!!

A female sheep named Dolly. A clone is a genetically identical copy of a living organism. Dolly, born in July 1996, was the first mammal ever created from the nonreproductive tissue of an adult animal. Dr. Ian Wilmut and a team of scientists in Edinburgh, Scotland, took a normal embryo (egg) cell from an adult sheep and removed its nucleus (which contains the genetic material). Then they took a cell from another sheep's mammary gland and fused it to the emptied cell. In other words, they grew an animal from scratch!

What was Operation Desert Storm?

The U.S. military's part in the Persian Gulf War of 1991. The fighting occurred between the Middle Eastern country of Iraq and a force of international allies, including the U.S. On August 2, 1990, Iraq invaded Kuwait, its tiny, oil-rich neighbor. When Iraq's President Saddam Hussein refused to remove his troops, Operation Desert Storm was launched. Air attacks began on January 17, 1991; ground fighting started on February 24. U.S. President George Bush ordered a cease-fire on February 27, after Iraqi troops retreated.

Which New York City skycraper was bombed in 1993?

The 110-floor twin towers of the World Trade Center. On February 26, 1993, a bomb exploded in a parking garage below the towers. Six people were killed and more than 1,000 were injured. Rescuers helped some 55,000 workers escape and firefighters struggled for two hours to control the fire. FBI investigators found that the bomb had been planted by terrorists angry about U.S. policy in the Middle East.

Which two long-time adversaries shook hands at the White House in 1993?

Yitzhak Rabin, prime minister of Israel, and Yasser Arafat, chairman of the Palestine Liberation Organization (PLO), on September 13, 1993—as U.S. President Bill Clinton looked on. At meetings arranged by the U.S., Rabin and Arafat agreed that limited self-rule would be granted to Palestinians living in the Gaza Strip, Jericho, and parts of the West Bank. (Those areas are part of a Middle East region that Israelis and Arabs both claim as their own.)

WHICH U.S. CITY WAS SHAKEN BY A MAJOR EARTHQUAKE IN 1994?

Los Angeles. At 4:36 a.m. on January 17, an earthquake measuring 6.8 on the Richter scale struck L.A. It was the strongest quake to hit the city in this century. Building walls cracked, freeways crumbled, broken gas pipes shot flames skyward, and water mains burst; 61 people were killed. The next day, aftershocks measuring 4.7 added more damage. Property damage was estimated at $7.2 billion.

How were the four Beatles able to release new songs in 1995 and 1996?

John Lennon was killed in 1980, but a brand-new song featuring all four Beatles was released in 1995! Producers used the tape of a half-completed song called "Free As a Bird," which Lennon recorded in 1980. They expanded it into a 48-track recording by adding vocals, guitars, and drums from Paul McCartney, George Harrison, and Ringo Starr to Lennon's voice and piano. "Real Love," another Lennon song produced the same way, was released in 1996.

285

What was apartheid?

An official policy of South Africa that divided people by race. (*Apartheid* means *apartness*.) The people were divided into four groups: white, black, Asian, and Coloured (mixed race). The law limited where each group could live, work, and attend school, and blacks were not allowed to vote. In 1990, after years of worldwide protest, Nelson Mandela—a black leader who had been in jail 27 years for opposing apartheid—was released. Other apartheid rules crumbled. In 1994, Mandela was elected president, and all laws that classified people by race were abolished.

How long did the 1994 major-league baseball strike last?

For 232 days. It began on August 12, 1994, when players and team owners could not settle their financial disagreements. When there was no settlement by September, the rest of the season—including the World Series—was canceled. (It was the first time since 1904 that a World Series did not take place!) The strike ended on April 2, 1995. By then, many fans had lost interest in the game and respect for players and owners alike.

What disaster struck Oklahoma City in 1995?

A huge car bomb exploded outside that city's Alfred P. Murrah Federal Building on April 19. The blast killed 168 people, including 19 children, and tore a gaping hole in the side of the structure. The Drug Enforcement Administration; the Bureau of Alcohol, Tobacco, and Firearms; and other federal agencies were housed in the Murrah building, as was a child-care center. Two days later, FBI agents arrested Timothy McVeigh, 27, a former U.S. soldier. He was convicted of his part in the blast in 1997. Later that year, another man, Terry Nichols, was convicted of helping him.

When did Diana, Princess of Wales, die?

On August 31, 1997, in Paris, France. She was killed in a car crash that also took the lives of her friend Emad "Dodi" Fayed and their driver, Henri Paul. The crash was a result of a high-speed chase, as the car was being followed by photographers on motorcycles. The driver, who had been drinking, lost control. An ambulance arrived within 10 minutes, but rescue workers could not revive the princess. A memorial service for Diana, held in London's Westminster Abbey on September 6, was broadcast live all over the world.

Which 15-year-old became the youngest person ever to win an Olympic gold medal in skating?

Tara Lipinski, at the 1998 Winter Games in Nagano, Japan. The Philadelphia-born champ began skating at age six. In 1997, she became the youngest female skater to be crowned number one in the world. Though not favored to win at the 1998 Olympics, Lipinski skated brilliantly, and captured the gold as well as the hearts of fans worldwide.

What was the largest package ever sent?

An orca (killer whale) named Keiko, in September 1998. Keiko—the whale that starred in the *Free Willy* movies—was sent from the Oregon Coast Aquarium in Portland to his home in Iceland. The 4.5-ton orca had to be lifted by crane into a United Parcel Service truck, then driven to a U.S. Air Force cargo plane to be flown home.

I WONDER HOW MUCH POSTAGE IT TOOK?

WHAT WAS THE Y2K BUG?

The Y2K bug, also called the Year 2000 Bug or the Millennium Bug, was a problem in the coding of computer systems. It was expected that the change from the numerals 1999 to 2000 would cause major disruptions in computerized systems across the world. For more than a year people worked to prevent the anticipated computer disaster, but nothing major happened when the century changed.

Why was the state of Florida important in the 2000 presidential election?

The presidential election of 2000 was a contest between then Vice President Al Gore and then governor of Texas George W. Bush, and after most of the votes were counted, the winner depended on the votes of the state of Florida. First the television networks said Al Gore had won Florida, then the state was considered "too close to call," and then George W. Bush seemed to take the lead. It took about five weeks to decide the winner, and in the end, George W. Bush, with a higher count in Florida of 537 votes, became the 43rd president of the United States.

WHAT WAS THE USS COLE AND WHAT HAPPENED TO IT IN 2001?

The USS Cole was a U.S. Navy destroyer. It was getting fuel in the harbor of the city of Aden in Yemen, a country on the Arabian Peninsula, when it was struck by suicide bombers driving a small boat. Seventeen sailors were killed. The extreme terrorist group al-Qaeda took responsibility for the attack.

WHO WAS OSAMA BIN LADEN?

Osama bin Laden was the militant leader of al-Qaeda. This terrorist group claimed responsibility for many devastating terrorist attacks, including the September 11, 2001, attacks on New York City and the Pentagon in Washington, D.C. Bin Laden was killed by U.S. military forces in 2011.

WHAT HAPPENED ON SEPTEMBER 11, 2001?

On September 11, 2001, 19 terrorists associated with the extremist group al-Qaeda hijacked four U.S. airliners and used them to attack targets in the United States. Two of the planes were flown into the World Trade Center towers in New York City; the third plane hit the Pentagon just outside Washington, D.C. The fourth plane, which may have been headed for the White House, crashed in a field in Pennsylvania, possibly when passengers attempted to take control from the hijackers. About 3,000 people were killed in the U.S. attacks that day, including more than 400 police officers and firefighters.

What was Operation Enduring Freedom?

Operation Enduring Freedom was the military effort to remove the Taliban from power in Afghanistan and destroy Osama bin Laden's al-Qaeda terrorist network in that country. This military campaign was led by the United States and began on October 7, 2001.

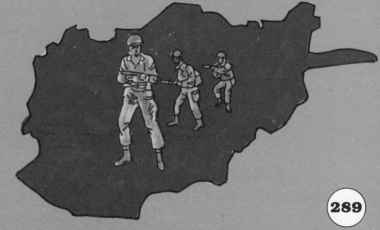

What is the Taliban?

The Taliban is an Islamic militant political movement based in Afghanistan that in some regions took over as a kind of government.

WHAT WAS AMERITHRAX?

Amerithrax was the name the Federal Bureau of Investigation (FBI) gave to a series of anthrax attacks that happened in the fall of 2001, following the September 11 terrorist attacks on New York City and Washington, D.C. Anthrax is a disease that can be deadly to humans. Letters containing anthrax bacteria spores were mailed to several news media offices and two U.S. senators, killing five people and infecting seventeen more.

TO U.S. NEWS MEDIA

WHAT IS THE USA PATRIOT ACT?

Signed by President George W. Bush on October 26, 2001, the USA Patriot Act (officially called the Uniting and Strengthening America by Providing Appropriate Tools Required to Intercept and Obstruct Terrorism Act of 2001) is a law designed to help the U.S. government hear about, prevent, and punish terrorist acts in the United States and throughout the world.

What is the "axis of evil"?

It is a term President George W. Bush used in his State of the Union address on January 29, 2002. He used the term to describe the governments of Iran, Iraq, and North Korea—all of which he accused of furthering terrorism around the world.

Who was Saddam Hussein?

Saddam Hussein was president of Iraq for more than 20 years. During his rule, Saddam was seen as a brutal dictator to his people and caused military conflicts with Iran, the United States, and other countries. After conflicts with military forces led by the United States in 2003, Saddam was captured and killed.

What was Operation Iraqi Freedom?

In a live, national address on March 19, 2003, President George W. Bush announced the beginning of Operation Iraqi Freedom. The goal of this mission was to remove Saddam Hussein from power in Iraq, along with his suspected ability to develop weapons of mass destruction. These are kinds of weapons that can kill large numbers of people and include nuclear, biological, and chemical weapons.

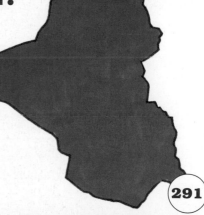

WHAT HAPPENED TO THE SPACE SHUTTLE COLUMBIA?

On February 1, 2003, the space shuttle Columbia broke apart on its reentry into the atmosphere. The explosion happened over Texas, just before the space shuttle was supposed to land at Kennedy Space Center in Florida. All seven crew members were killed. Investigators later discovered that the problem probably occurred when a piece of foam insulation broke off from the shuttle's propellant tank, damaging the edge of the shuttle's left wing.

When did the deadliest tsunami on record happen?

On December 26, 2004, when an earthquake of magnitude 9.1 in the Indian Ocean caused a tsunami (a series of massive, deadly waves). It is the most destructive tsunami on record. The disaster left more than 225,000 people dead and nearly 50,000 missing, and millions of people in a dozen countries from Africa to Thailand were left homeless.

WHO WAS JOHN PAUL II?

He was the first non-Italian pope in 445 years. He died on April 2, 2005 and the Roman Catholic church declared him a saint less than 10 years after his death.

WHO IS BENEDICT XVI?

German cardinal Joseph Ratzinger was elected after John Paul II's death, becoming Pope Benedict XVI. In February 2013, at the age of 85, Benedict XVI announced his retirement, becoming the first pope in six centuries to step down.

Who was Steve Jobs?

Steve Jobs was the cofounder of Apple Computer in 1976. In the twenty-first century, while Steve Jobs ran the company, Apple launched a series of technologies that changed the way people live and work, including the iPhone and the iPad.

WHAT WAS HURRICANE KATRINA?

Hurricane Katrina was a catastrophic storm that struck the Gulf Coast of the United States and made landfall in the early morning hours of August 29, 2005. The storm brought sustained winds of 100 to 175 miles per hour, and was about 400 miles wide. While the storm itself created a lot of damage, the majority of the devastation came from massive flooding caused by the breaching of levees, or dams, as occurred in the city of New Orleans.

Search & Find®
for these fun
items in the

Digital
Age

- Apple core
- Birdcage
- Bone
- Drum
- Earmuffs
- Envelope
- Feather
- Football
- Graduation cap
- Hammer
- Hourglass
- Kangaroo
- Mouse
- Musical note
- Owl
- Paper airplane
- Pizza
- Propeller
- Rabbit
- Turtle
- TV

Who is Mark Zuckerberg?

Mark Zuckerberg is cofounder and CEO of the social-networking website Facebook. He started the site while in college, but he left Harvard University after his sophomore year so he could work on developing it. Facebook's user base has grown to more than one billion people, and Zuckerberg is one of the world's youngest billionaires.

Why was the election of Barack Obama as the 44th president of the United States so significant?

Barack Obama, the 44th president of the United States, was the first African American to be elected U.S. president. He first became president in 2008, and he won a second term in 2012 when he ran against Republican candidate Mitt Romney.

How many people died in the massive earthquake that struck Haiti in 2010?

Death estimates vary, but anywhere from 100,000 to 316,000 people were killed when an earthquake struck the island nation of Haiti on January 12, 2010. The earthquake measured 7.0 on the Richter scale and also injured 300,000 people.

What was the largest marine oil spill in history?

The Deepwater Horizon oil spill, which began on April 20, 2010. It happened in the Gulf of Mexico, and was caused by an explosion on the Deepwater Horizon oil rig. The oil rig sank on April 22. Still, oil flowed from the well for 87 days, pouring 4.9 million barrels, or 210 million gallons, of oil into the Gulf. Because of the length of time the oil continued to leak, there was major damage to marine and wildlife habitats, fishing, and tourism along the Gulf Coast.

What happened in Fukushima, Japan in March 2011?

A 9.0-magnitude earthquake occurred off the coast of Japan on March 11, 2011, causing a tsunami that generated waves possibly up to 32 feet high. The tsunami killed more than 12,000 people, and in the Fukushima region north of Tokyo, it also caused the partial meltdown of the Fukushima nuclear reactor. It is expected to take decades to fully clean up this devastating nuclear accident.

Which hurricane hit the East Coast of the United States in 2012?

Hurricane Sandy, also known as "Superstorm Sandy," became the deadliest and most destructive hurricane of the 2012 Atlantic hurricane season when it struck the East Coast of the United States on October 29, 2012. It was also the largest Atlantic hurricane on record, measuring 900 miles across. The storm caused about 125 deaths in the United States and 80 deaths in Canada and the Caribbean.

TONY TALLARICO

Which music legend died unexpectedly in 2009?

Also known as the "King of Pop," singer-songwriter Michael Jackson died unexpectedly in 2009. While he began his career as the lead singer of the sibling group Jackson 5, at the time of his death he was one of the most internationally famous music legends of all time. His death was ultimately ruled a homicide, and the doctor who had been caring for him at the time of his death was sentenced to jail for his role in Jackson's death.

Who is Catherine, Duchess of Cambridge?

Catherine, Her Royal Highness the Duchess of Cambridge, is married to Prince William, the future king of England. She also is known by her "common" name, Kate Middleton. The couple was married in 2011 at Westminster Abbey in London, England.

Who is Prince George?

Prince George of Cambridge is the son of the Duke and Duchess of Cambridge (also known as Prince William and Kate Middleton). He is third in line to the throne after his father, Prince William, and his grandfather, Prince Charles.

Which internationally known civil rights activist died in 2013?

Nelson Mandela, former president of South Africa and global human-rights activist, died in 2013 after a life lived advocating for human rights and an end to apartheid, which is a rigid system of segregation. His beliefs and actions landed him in jail for nearly 30 years. A few years after he was released, he became the first black president of South Africa.

What genre of television exploded in popularity in the twenty-first century?

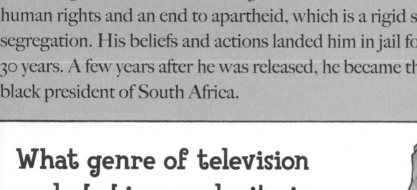

Reality television, which features ordinary people in unscripted situations, gained great popularity in the twenty-first century.

Which queen celebrated a milestone anniversary in 2012?

Queen Elizabeth II celebrated her 60th anniversary as queen of England in 2012. This was known as her Diamond Jubilee, and it was marked with a multinational, multiday celebration.

TEST YOUR KNOWLEDGE!

What do you know about dinosaurs and prehistoric times?
Test your knowledge with this True or False quiz and
then read more about it in the following pages.

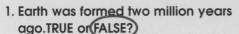

1. Earth was formed two million years ago. TRUE or FALSE?

False. Earth was formed between 4.5 and 4.6 billion years ago.

2. Insects were the first living organisms. TRUE or FALSE?

False. Microscopic bacteria were the earliest living organisms.

3. The Mesozoic era was divided into three periods: the Triassic, the Jurassic, and the Cretaceous. TRUE or FALSE?

True. During the Triassic period, dinosaurs and early forms of mammals emerged.

4. It is believed that most dinosaurs roamed the earth during the Cretaceous period. TRUE or FALSE?

True. The Cretaceous period ended with the extinction of the dinosaurs.

5. Dinosaurs and people lived on Earth together at the same time. TRUE or FALSE?

False. People did not appear on Earth until about sixty-five million years after the dinosaurs had disappeared.

6. All dinosaurs were carnivores. TRUE or FALSE?

False. There were carnivorous (meat-eating) dinosaurs and herbivorous (plant-eating) dinosaurs.

7. The Iguanodon was among the first dinosaurs identified by scientists. TRUE or FALSE?

True. The Iguanodon was identified about 190 years ago.

8. A Stegosaurus would use its spiked tail as a weapon. TRUE or FALSE?

True. Although the Stegosauruses were herbivores, they may have used their spiky tails for protection.

9. The Tyrannosaurus rex was an herbivore, meaning it did not eat meat. TRUE or FALSE?

False. The Tyrannosaurus rex was a carnivore, and is believed to have been able to eat 500 pounds of meat in one bite!

10. The smallest dinosaurs were only as big as today's birds. TRUE or FALSE?

True. One of the small dinosaurs known, the Compsognathus, was similar in size to a chicken.

11. The largest dinosaur known stood as tall as a four-story building. TRUE or FALSE?

True. This dinosaur was the Brachiosaurus and was about forty feet in height and eighty-five feet long.

12. The largest dinosaur was also an herbivore. TRUE or FALSE?

True. A Brachiosaurus would have used its long neck to reach into the tops of tall trees.

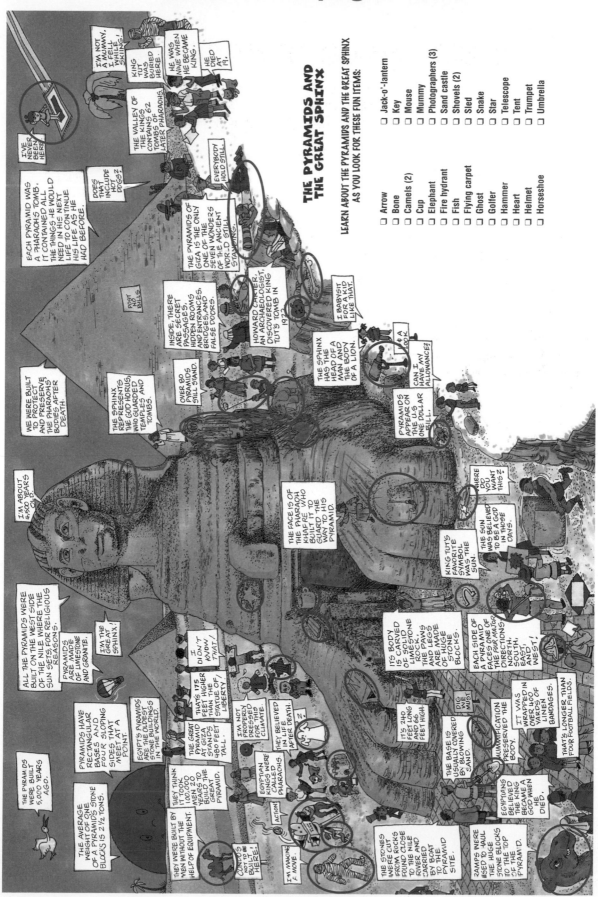

Answers for page 43

Ancient History Word Search

Search for the ancient history words listed below. Circle horizontally, vertically, backwards, or diagonally as you find each word.

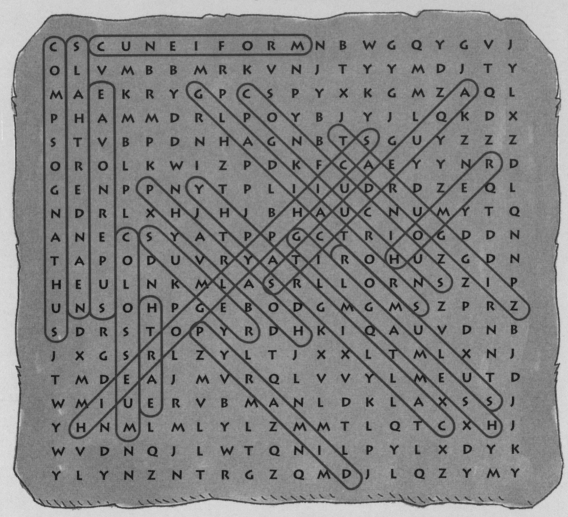

SUPERNOVAE	ROMULUS	PYRAMID
COMPSOGNATHUS	REMUS	CONFUCIUS
EARTH	GLADIATORS	CALLIGRAPHY
NEANDERTHALS	AQUEDUCTS	ZIGGURAT
COLOSSEUM	SPHINX	GILGAMESH
HOMER	HIEROGLYPHICS	CUNEIFORM
	PHARAOH	

Lead the Knight to the Castle

Help the knight find his way back to the castle by following the maze from start to finish.

START

FINISH

MIDDLE AGES

Search for the middle ages words listed below. Circle horizontally, vertically, backwards, or diagonally as you find each word.

```
S R O M A N E S Q U E G V B P M A X H F
Q J D O L A A F F V J J O N A X Z H B E
E K W N H C U G M D H N O L Y R C N T U
H D G A U T J T A G Z E O S U R O U C D
E L A S T K D G H W H E E S H A O N G A
R N V T C T Q P A C A D L W C R O X D L
A I Z E N N M E T R A X D U N G E O N S
L T T R D X X U T S D P G U K P W S G D
D I E Y S D C U U R V E C Q B J M H U K
E U Z S X S J R E L R I R G K D D V I C
S N G M E B C I X I H N Y O J O E R L O
W M W C J O R B U T G R L W B V X P D M
M P M G Y T B Q O Y L I B P D E T E J Q
F J N E S M S G C A Y Y V G J C J A M K
Z Y B E L Q E Y V Q K F W A X O T S N Y
J D D S E I A I A T H Z I R U T F A A X
M A N O R N H Q L P S C Q M P E L N Y C
Z K B U G C H F Z Z Y N E O G S M T N Z
Z J O U S T I N G D Y X L R L J Q S H G
F R M E K K F R B J K N I G H T N Y D G
```

ARMOR	BARON	CHIVALRY
CRUSADES	DESTRIER	DOVECOTE
DUNGEON	ESCUTCHEON	FEUDAL
GARDEROBE	GOTHIC	GUILD
HERALD	JOUSTING	KNIGHT
MANOR	MONASTERY	PEASANTS
ROMANESQUE	SQUIRE	

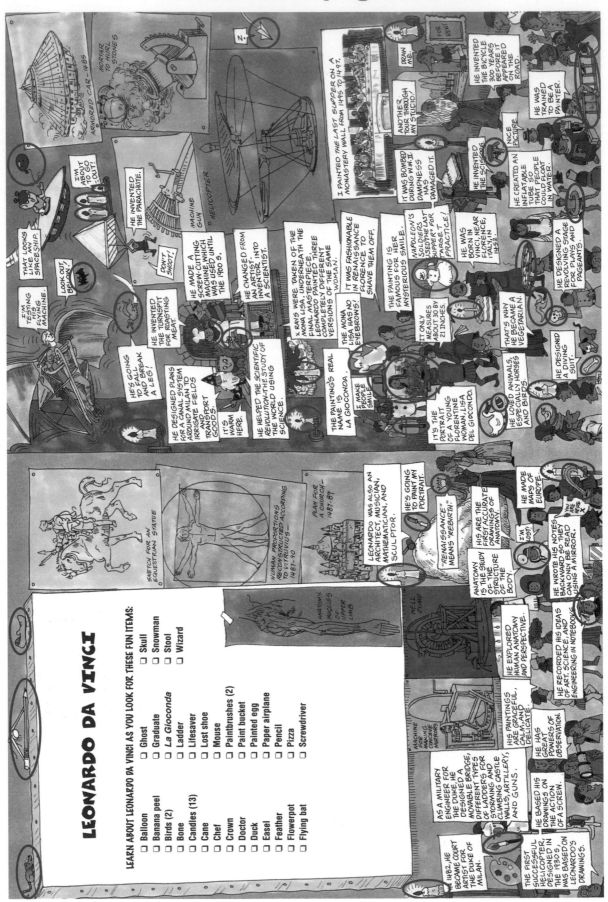

HELP THE MAYFLOWER SAIL FROM ENGLAND TO PLYMOUTH HARBOR.

← Start

WELCOME TO PLYMOUTH HARBOR

← Finish

Answers for page 135

SEVENTEENTH CENTURY
WORD SEARCH

Search for the seventeenth century words listed below.
Cirlcle horizontally, vertically, backwards, or diagonally
as you find each word.

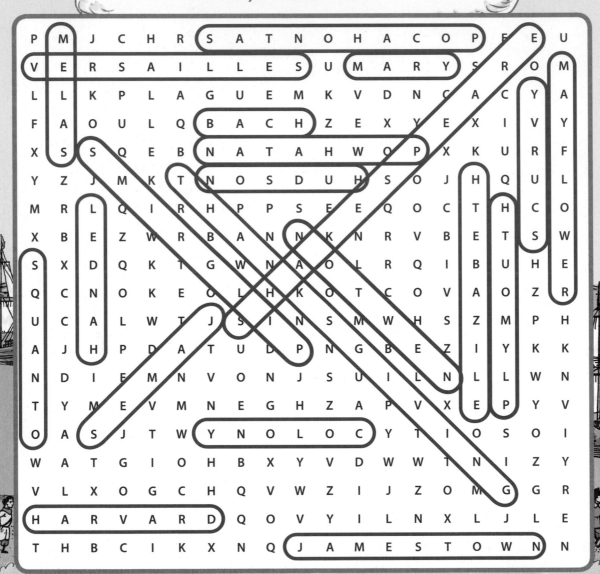

P M J C H R S A T N O H A C O P F E U
V E R S A I L L E S U M A R Y S R O M
L L K P L A G U E M K V D N C A C Y A
F A O U L Q B A C H Z E X Y E X I V Y
X S S Q E B N A T A H W O P X K U R F
Y Z J M K T N O S D U H S O J H Q U L
M R L Q I R H P P S E E Q O C T H C O
X B E Z W R B A N N K N R V B E T S W
S X D Q K T G W N A O L R Q I B U H E
Q C N O K E O L H K O T C O V A Z Z R
U C A L W T J S I N S M W H S Z M P H
A J H P D A T U D P N G B E Z I Y K K
N D I E M N V O N J S U I L N L L W N
T Y M E V M N E G H Z A P V X E P Y V
O A S J T W Y N O L O C Y T I O S O I
W A T G I O H B X Y V D W W T N I Z Y
V L X O G C H Q V W Z I J Z O M G G R
H A R V A R D Q O V Y I L N X L J L E
T H B C I K X N Q J A M E S T O W N N

BACH	HUDSON	NEWTON	SCURVY
COLONY	JAMES	PILGRIMS	SHAKESPEARE
ELIZABETH	JAMESTOWN	PLYMOUTH	SQUANTO
HANDEL	LONDON	POCAHONTAS	THANKSGIVING
HARVARD	MARY	POWHATAN	VERSAILLES
	MAYFLOWER	SALEM	

Answers for page 196

Nineteenth Century Word Search

Look for these nineteenth century words listed below. Circle horizontally, vertically, backwards, or diagonally as you find each word.

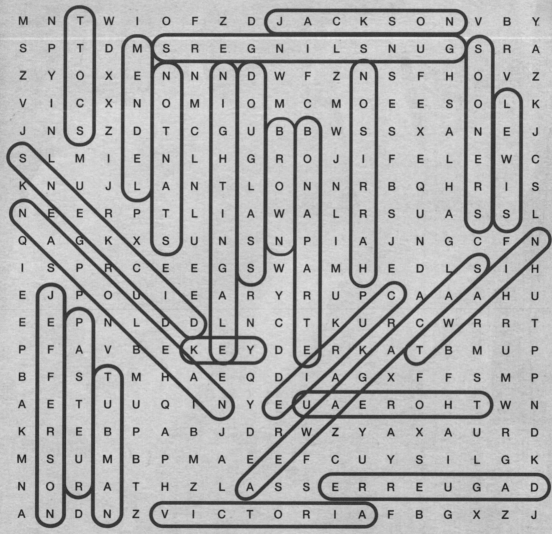

M	N	T	W	I	O	F	Z	D	J	A	C	K	S	O	N	V	B	Y
S	P	T	D	M	S	R	E	G	N	I	L	S	N	U	G	S	R	A
Z	Y	O	X	E	N	N	N	D	W	F	Z	N	S	F	H	O	V	Z
V	I	C	X	N	O	M	I	O	M	C	M	O	E	E	S	O	L	K
J	N	S	Z	D	T	C	G	U	B	B	W	S	S	X	A	N	E	J
S	L	M	I	E	N	L	H	G	R	O	J	I	F	E	L	E	W	C
K	N	U	J	L	A	N	T	L	O	N	N	R	B	Q	H	R	I	S
N	E	E	R	P	T	L	I	A	W	A	L	R	S	U	A	S	S	L
Q	A	G	K	X	S	U	N	S	N	P	I	A	J	N	G	C	F	N
I	S	P	R	C	E	E	G	S	W	A	M	H	E	D	L	S	I	H
E	J	P	O	U	I	E	A	R	Y	R	U	P	C	A	A	A	H	U
E	E	P	N	L	D	D	L	N	C	T	K	U	R	C	W	R	R	T
P	F	A	V	B	E	K	E	Y	D	E	R	K	A	T	B	M	U	P
B	F	S	T	M	H	A	E	Q	D	I	A	G	X	F	F	S	M	P
A	E	T	U	U	Q	I	N	Y	E	U	A	E	R	O	H	T	W	N
K	R	E	B	P	A	B	J	D	R	W	Z	Y	A	X	A	U	R	D
M	S	U	M	B	P	M	A	E	E	F	C	U	Y	S	I	L	G	K
N	O	R	A	T	H	Z	L	A	S	S	E	R	R	E	U	G	A	D
A	N	D	N	Z	V	I	C	T	O	R	I	A	F	B	G	X	Z	J

Bonaparte	Douglass	Mendel	Stanton
Brown	Gunslingers	Napolean	Thoreau
Clark	Harrison	Nightingale	Tubman
Curie	Jackson	Pasteur	Twain
Daguerre	Jefferson	Sacagawea	Victoria
Dickens	Key	Scott	
	Lewis	Sooners	

Name Matching

Match the nineteenth-century person with his or her description:

F Ulysses S. Grant

D Robert E. Lee

I Thomas Jefferson

C Samuel L. Clemens

E Napoleon

H Andrew Jackson

G Marie Curie

A Jesse James

J Harriet Tubman

K Dred Scott

L Susan B. Anthony

B Florence Nightingale

A. One of the famous gunslingers of the Wild West.

B. Pioneered modern medical practices during the Crimean War and helped establish nursing as a profession.

C. Went by the pen name Mark Twain; authored several famous novels including The Adventures of Tom Sawyer and Adventures of Huckleberry Finn.

D. Leader of Confederate forces during the Civil War.

E. Military general and the first emperor of France.

F. Leader of the Union forces during the Civil War.

G. Nobel prize winner in physics and chemistry.

H. Seventh president of the United States; general during the War of 1812.

I. Third president of the United States; had his presidency decided by the House of Representatives because of a tie.

J. A former slave who helped other slaves escape using the Underground Railroad.

K. A slave who made history by waging a legal battle to gain his freedom; his case went all the way to the U.S. Supreme Court.

L. One of the leaders of the women's voting-rights movement, along with Elizabeth Cady Stanton.

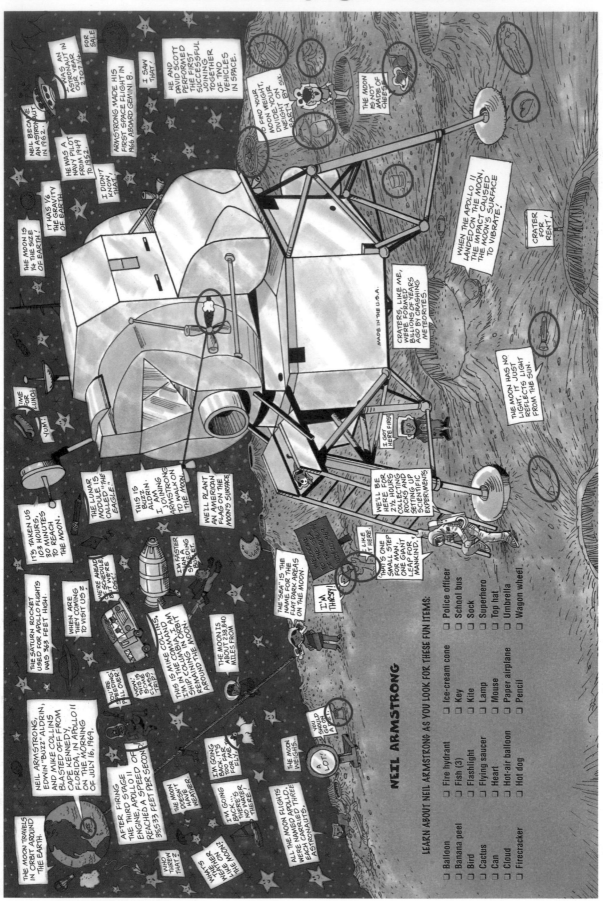

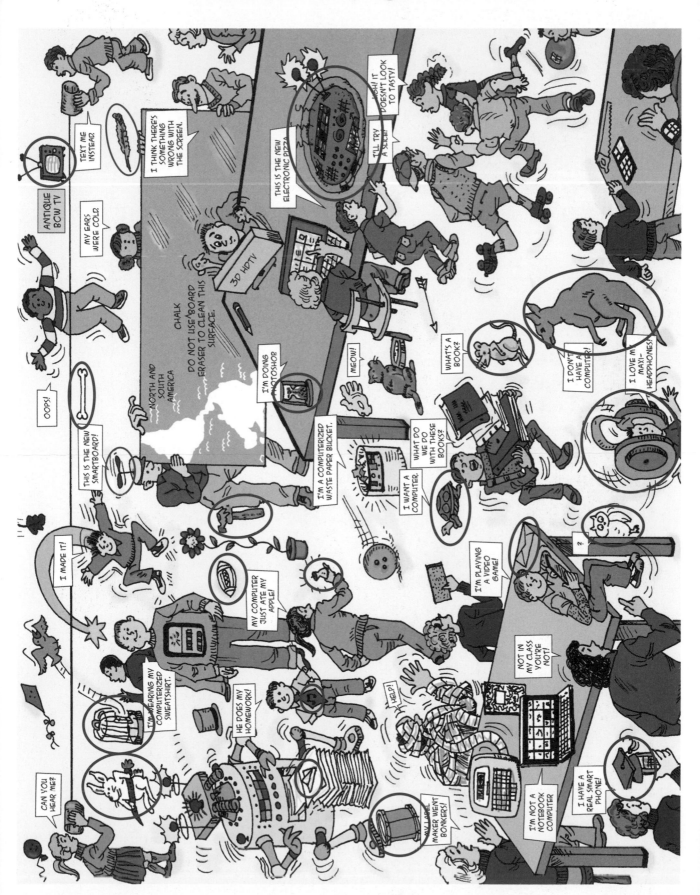